Chronicles of Dissent

Chronicles
of
Dissent

Noam Chomsky

Interviews with
David Barsamian

Common Courage Press
Monroe, Maine

AK Press
Stirling, Scotland

Library of Congress Cataloging-in-Publication Data
Chomsky, Noam
Chronicles of dissent / Noam Chomsky; interviews with David
Barsamian.
p. cm.
Includes bibliographical references.
ISBN 0-9628838-9-1 (cloth). -- ISBN 0-9628838-8-3 (paper)
1. Chomsky, Noam--Political and social views. 2. Chomsky,
Noam--Interviews. I. Barsamian, David. II. Title.
P85.C47C46 1992
410'.92--dc20
92-19429

Common Courage Press
Box 702
Monroe, ME 04951 U.S.A.
207-525-0900

British Library Cataloging in Publication Data
Chomsky, Noam
Chronicles of Dissent
I. Title
081
1-873176-85-6 paper; 1-873176-90-2, cloth

AK Press
3 Balmoral Place
Stirling, Scotland FK8 2RD

Second Printing

For Mama,
Araxie Giragosian Barsamian

Acknowledgements

This series has its origin in a casual letter I wrote to Noam Chomsky in the early 1980s. The detail of his response flabbergasted me, and our ongoing correspondence led me to do our first interview ("Language in the Service of Propaganda").

Some of the following interviews were broadcast on KGNU public radio in Boulder, Colorado. Others have been broadcast nationally and internationally through Alternative Radio.

Sandy Adler is a superb transcriber whose contribution to my work is immense. Jack Logan came up with the title while we were cross country skiing near Brainard Lake in the Colorado Rockies. Working with Noam Chomsky is among my richest experiences. I am very much grateful to him.

David Barsamian
August 1992

Contents

Introduction

Excavating the Truth

Chomsky went to the dentist, who made his inspection and observed that the patient was grinding his teeth. Consultation with Mrs. Chomsky disclosed that teeth-grinding was not taking place during the hours of sleep. When else? They narrowed it down quickly enough to the period each morning when Chomsky was reading the *New York Times,* unconsciously gnashing his molars at every page.

I asked Chomsky why, with the evidence and experience of a lifetime, he kept hoping against hope that the corporate press, particularly the *New York Times,* was going to get it right. Reality should long since have conditioned him to keep his jaw muscles relaxed. Chomsky sighed, as if in anticipation of all the stupid perversions of truth he was condemned to keep reading for the rest of his life, jolted each morning into furious bouts of bruxism.

Chomsky knows the score; he is not under the illusion that one day he will write a critique so compelling that the owner of the *New York Times* will suddenly perceive the error of his ways and order his minions to tilt towards truth. But he also believes in the power of reason, of compelling evidence carefully marshalled. Hence the grinding of the teeth. "I don't know why they aren't drowning in their own hypocrisy," he remarked to me on the phone the other day, speaking with a kind of violent astonishment as we discussed the furor over "ethnic cleansing" in Bosnia-Herzegovina, in which were raised voices of American Jews who had spent a lifetime keeping quiet about the ethnic cleansing that commenced in Israel in 1948.

Chomsky feels the abuses, cruelty and hypocrisies of power more intensely than anyone I know. It's a state of continual alertness. Often, after I've glanced at a story in the paper and skipped rapidly over the familiar rubble of falsification, a week or two later will drop into my mailbox a photocopy of that same story marked up by Chomsky, with sentences underlined and a phrase or two in the margin etched deep into the paper by an angry pen.

People sometimes spot a reference in some column of mine to an off-beat paper or some foreign language publication and ask me how I manage to keep up with such a tide of newsprint. They imagine that I subscribe on a daily basis to *El Pais,* or the *Jerusalem Post,* or the *Anchorage Times* and hundreds more.

This apparent omnivorousness is mostly an illusion. Readers send things that have caught their eye. A fair-sized chunk of the weekly trawl is stuff sent on by Chomsky.

The times I've stayed the night at Noam and Carol Chomsky's house in Lexington I've watched him at eventide working his way through a capacious box of the day's intake of tripe—newspapers, weeklies, monthlies, learned journals, flimsy mimeo-ed mailers—while Carol Chomsky does the same thing on the other side of the room.

Add to this a voluminous correspondence—Chomsky once told me he spends 20 hours a week answering letters—plus telephone conversations, encounters with visitors to his office at MIT and we end up with a formidable intelligence system. The first duty of an intellectual is to know what's going on and it's very hard work.

Fred Gardner, writing a story for the *Anderson Valley Advertiser* about a visit by Chomsky to the Bay Area in the spring of 1991, remarked that "It's true that Chomsky has a fine understanding of history and contemporary politics; that he speaks to the point; that he has unrelenting courage...but he doesn't have any special inside sources; there's nothing in what he does or how he does it that's beyond the ability of any radical professor. There should be a Chomsky or two on every campus. The fact that it's a wasteland from Cambridge to Berkeley— that people have to wait for this linguist from MIT to come to town and critique U.S. foreign policy—says a lot about our intellectually bankrupt academies."

This is true up to a point. Most of the time you don't need "special sources," merely the ability and stamina to read intelligently what material there is in the public domain. (One of the most successful efforts at information collection in the Second World War was run by a U.S. Army intelligence officer who simply had roomsfull of people reading the Japanese and German press. At one point—the result of a political row and consequent leak— the *Chicago Tribune* published the entire U.S. Navy order of battle in the Pacific, a useful item apparently missed by the Japanese.)

There are in fact many campuses across America which have a radical faculty member or two doing their best to excavate the truth and bring it to light. Chomsky's most frequent observation about his innumerable speaking forays across the country concerns precisely the illusion that there is a wasteland between Cambridge and Berkeley, as against the reality—one that I've noted often enough myself—that the enquiring and even radical spirit flourishes widely, often in supposedly stony soil, such as at Texas A&M at College Station.

What Chomsky offers is a coherent "big picture," buttressed by the data of a thousand smaller pictures and discrete theaters of conflict, struggle and oppression. People will go to a talk by Chomsky partly just to reassure themselves that they haven't gone mad; that they are right when they disbelieve what they read in the papers or watch on TV. For hundreds of thousands of people— over the years, he must have spoken to more American students than any other person alive—Chomsky has offered the assurance, the intellectual and moral authority, that there is another way of looking at things. In this vital function he stands in the same relationship to his audience as did a philosopher he admires greatly, Bertrand Russell.

There is the view, not unsympathetic to Chomsky, that he has been marginalised by the dominant culture. Until quite recently the man regarded internationally as among the U.S.'s most outstanding and influential intellectuals had never been interviewed on American network television, was the subject of slander and abuse in the corporate press.

Such vilification is entirely predictable. Much of Chomsky's work involves memory, the memory of everything that vested power prefers to forget. Essays such as the one in honor of A.J. Muste where Chomsky evokes U.S. policy toward Japan in the 1930s are, for the ruling elites, definitively out of bounds. To accept them is to acknowledge culpabilities of intolerable dimension.

One prominent member of the British intellectual elite, warning a colleague against getting into a dispute with Chomsky, described him as "a terrible and relentless opponent," by which he meant that Chomsky never surrenders ground, never cedes a position as part of some more elaborate maneuver. This is why, surely, abuse of the foulest and most childish kind descends upon him. His opponents shirk the real argument they fear they will lose, and substitute insult and distortion.

But beyond this, has Chomsky truly been marginalised? There have long been fierce attempts to exclude him from any orthodox venue of intellectual debate, most intense at moments when supposedly dissident intellectuals are beating a retreat towards the permitted terrain of official discussion—on Vietnam, the Middle East, Central America, and so forth. But to say that in consequence he is "marginalised" is absurd, given his actual weight in the culture at large.

"But it's all so depressing," cried JoAnn Wypijewski, managing editor of *The Nation,* when Chomsky had finished outlining to her his analysis of some supposed break-through in Palestinian-Israeli peace talks. "It's not my job to cheer you up," Chomsky replied.

I've heard people lament, after listening to a talk by Chomsky, that he doesn't always offer, in the time allotted, the requisite dose of uplift and a simple route map to a benign future. One person I met, I think it was in Boulder, told me that he had written to the professor, reproaching him for just such omissions and had duly received a three-page, single-space letter setting forth the elements of a positive strategy and vision. Chomsky is a realist, not a pessimist, though the two, these days as almost always, tend to run in symbiotic harness. Chomsky believes deeply in the benign tendencies of human kind. He wouldn't be an anarchist by political conviction if he did not.

(Chomsky does not, I have to admit, evince much interest in the tendencies and behavior of the natural kingdom, excluding humankind. I once chided him for describing Haitian refugees as having to guide their boats through "shark-infested waters." On average, I reminded him, sharks kill about 25 humans around the world each year, in return for which humans kill, each year, about 25 million sharks. It was the sort of contrast between legend and reality Chomsky loves to expose on the human plane, but I could tell that the shark-icide had not really struck home. I mentioned to him not so long ago that I had some horses at my place in Humboldt county, northern California. He was incredulous. "Horses?" he snorted, asking sarcastically whether I played polo. It was the same when I mentioned I had cats.)

Chomsky's greatest virtue is that his fundamental message is a simple one. Here's how he put it in that interview in the *Anderson Valley Advertiser:*

"Any form of authority requires justification; it's not

self justified. And the justification can rarely be given.
Sometimes you can give it. I think you can give an argument that you shouldn't let a three-year old run across the
street. That's a form of authority that's justifiable. But
there aren't many of them, and usually the effort to give
a justification fails. And when we try to face it, we find
that the authority is illegitimate. And any time you find
a form of authority illegitimate, you ought to challenge it.
It's something that conflicts with human rights and liberties. And that goes on forever. You overcome one thing and
discover the next.

"In my view what a popular movement ought to be
is just basically libertarian: concerned with forms of oppression, authority and domination, challenging them.
Sometimes they're justifiable under particular conditions,
sometimes they're not. If they are not, try to overcome
them."

Alexander Cockburn
Petrolia, California,
August 1992

Language in the Service of Propaganda

December 1, 1984

DB: *What is the relationship between politics and language?*

There is a tenuous relationship, in fact several different kinds. I think myself that they're exaggerated in importance. There is in the first place the question discussed, for example, by Orwell and by a number of others of how language is abused, tortured, distorted, in a way, to enforce ideological goals. A classic example would be the switch in the name of the Pentagon from the War Department to the Defense Department in 1947. As soon as that happened, any thoughtful person should have understood that the United States would no longer be engaged in defense. It would only be engaged in aggressive war. That was essentially the case, and it was part of the reason for the change in terminology, to disguise that fact. One can go on to give innumerable examples of that sort. Perhaps the classic discussion of it is Orwell's *Politics and the English Language*.

There's also a more subtle and more interesting but even more tenuous connection: any stance that one takes with regard to social issues, for example, advocacy of some kind of reform or advocacy of a revolutionary change, an institutional change, or advocacy of stability and maintaining structures as they are—any such position, assuming that it has any moral basis at all and is not simply based on personal self-interest, is ultimately based on some conception of human nature. That is, if you suggest things should be reformed in this or that fashion and there's a moral basis for it, you are in effect saying,

1

"Human beings are so constituted that this change is to their benefit. It somehow relates to their essential human needs." The underlying concept of human nature is rarely articulated. It's more or less tacit and implicit and nobody thinks about it very much. But if we were ever to achieve the state—and we're very far from this—if the study of humans were ever to reach the point of a discipline with significant intellectual content, this concept would have to be understood and articulated. If we search our souls we find that we do have a concept and it's probably based on some ideas about the underlying and essential human need for freedom from external arbitrary constraints and controls, a concept of human dignity which would regard it as an infringement on fundamental human rights to be enslaved, owned by others, in my view even to be rented by others, as in capitalist societies, and so on. Those views are not established at the level of science. They're just commitments. They could be issues of scientific investigation, that is, humans are what they are just as birds are what they are. The study of language may have some indirect relation, since it ultimately does investigate some fundamental components of human intelligence and their nature and is at least suggestive of what human cognitive faculties are ultimately like. One might draw some tenuous speculations about other aspects of human nature of a sort that I mentioned with regard to freedom from external constraints, to subordination to external power, etc. But that's a real long distance, a hope for the future more than any present reality.

DB: *Is freedom a linguistic imperative?*

Just a superficial and obvious fact about human language is that it has an essentially creative aspect to it. Every normal human, independently of what we call "intelligence," over a huge range, apart from really severe pathology, quickly and with amazing rapidity, acquires a linguistic system which enables them to express and create new thoughts and to interact with others who are also creating and expressing new thoughts and to do it without bounds, though in a highly constrained fashion in terms of a rule system that's relatively fixed in its character as part of essential human nature, but that does permit and facilitate free creative expression. That's a fundamental aspect about human intelligence. It apparently differentiates humans from any other organism that we know about. How much that extends to other domains is an area of speculation but I think one can make some interesting guesses.

DB: *Could you address the notion that words, language, have inherent power, concepts convey meaning beyond their words? What is happening mechanically when certain phrases are used, such as "the free world" or "strategic interests" or "national interests"?*

That's the usual topic that's discussed when people talk about politics and language, and I think it's worth discussing, but I think it's almost obvious to the point of banality. Terms like "the free world" and "the national interest" and so on are mere terms of propaganda. One shouldn't take them seriously for a moment. They are designed, often very consciously, in order to try to block thought and understanding. For example, about the 1940's there was a decision, probably a conscious decision, made in public-relations circles to introduce terms like "free enterprise" and "free world" and so on instead of the conventional descriptive terms like "capitalism". Part of the reason was to insinuate somehow that the systems of control and domination and aggression to which those with power were committed here were in fact a kind of freedom. That's just vulgar propaganda exercises. We are inundated with this every moment of our lives. Many of us internalize it, one has to defend oneself against it. But once one realizes what's going on it's not very hard to defend against. These are ways in which our intellects are dulled and our capacity for thought is destroyed and our possibility for meaningful political action is undermined by very effective systems of indoctrination and thought control that involve, as all such systems do, abuse of language. One can see this everywhere.

DB: *You have written, "Among the many symbols used to frighten and manipulate the populace of democratic states, few have been more important than terror and terrorism." Could you talk about that?*

For example, for the last several years, something called "international terrorism" has been right at the front of the agenda. There are conferences about it, books, articles, etc. We were told when the Reagan administration came in that the struggle against international terrorism was going to be the centerpiece of their foreign policy, and it's continued that way. People debate as if they were in the real world. They're not in the real world. There is such a thing as international terrorism, and the United States is one of the main sponsors of it. For example, according to the official doctrine, the one that we discuss and the one that [Secretary of State] George Shultz talks about, Cuba is one of the main centers of international terrorism.

The propaganda literature on this topic, meaning authors like Claire Sterling and Walter Laqueur and others—basically commissars—even argues that the proof that the communists are behind it all is that terrorism is in the so-called "free world." The fact of the matter is that Cuba has been subjected to more international terrorism than probably the rest of the world put together. This began in the early 1960's when the Kennedy administration launched a major terrorist war against Cuba. It went on for many years; for all we know it's still going on. There's very little reporting on it. You have to work hard to find out what's going on from memoirs and participants' reports and so on. What has happened is a level of international terrorism that as far as I know has no counterpart, apart from direct aggression. It's included attacking civilian installations, bombing hotels, sinking fishing vessels, destroying petrochemical installations, poisoning crops and livestock, on quite a significant scale, assassination attempts, actual murders, bombing airplanes, bombing of Cuban missions abroad, etc. It's a massive terrorist attack. But this never appears in the discussions of international terrorism. Or, for example, take the Middle East.

The very symbol of terrorism is the PLO. The PLO has certainly been involved in terrorist acts, but Israel, which is our client, has been involved in far greater—incomparably greater—terrorist acts. But we don't call them terrorist acts. For example, in the spring of this year, four young Palestinians in the Gaza Strip, who live under conditions of extreme oppression, hijacked a bus and tried to drive it out of the Gaza Strip. They apparently didn't have weapons; the bus was stopped by Israeli soldiers and in the fire they killed an Israeli woman on the bus. The soldiers knew that the bus was hijacked because these Palestinians had allowed a pregnant woman to leave the bus. It was a humanitarian act on their part. The people who hijacked the bus were captured. Two were killed at once and two were taken away and murdered, apparently after torture by Israeli soldiers. That's all described as an act of Palestinian terrorism. There was an investigation of the murder of the two Palestinians by the Israeli army but nothing ever came of it; there's been no prosecution. About the same time, Israel bombed an area in Baalbek in Lebanon. According to the press reports, including American press reports, there were about 400 casualties, including approximately 150 children who were killed or wounded in an attack which destroyed a schoolhouse. That wasn't regarded as terrorism. Nobody ever referred to that as a terrorist act paid for by the United States, even though they used American jets. That's just called an "unwise retaliatory strike" or something of that kind.

This goes all the way back to the early 1970's, which was the high point of Palestinian terror attacks, and they were terror attacks, as in Maalot, etc. At that point, Israel was carrying out extensive bombardment of civilian targets in southern Lebanon to the extent that they actually drove out several hundred thousand people. That was never called terrorism. To use the term "double standard" for our approach is to really abuse the term; it goes beyond anything that you could call a double standard. It's almost a kind of fanaticism. It's a reflection of the extreme success of indoctrination in American society. You don't have any other society where the educated classes, at least, are so effectively indoctrinated and controlled by a propaganda system.

DB: *Let's talk about that propaganda system. You've referred many times to the "state propaganda apparatus." What role do the media play in promoting and serving state interests?*

One should be clear that in referring to the "state propaganda apparatus" here I do not mean that it comes from the state. Our system differs strikingly from, say, the Soviet Union, where the propaganda system literally is directed and controlled by the state. We're not a society which has a Ministry of Truth which produces doctrine which everyone then must obey at a severe cost if you don't. Our system works much differently and much more effectively. It's a privatized system of propaganda, including the media, the journals of opinion and in general including the broad participation of the articulate intelligentsia, the educated part of the population. The more articulate elements of those groups, the ones who have access to the media, including intellectual journals, and who essentially control the educational apparatus, they should properly be referred to as a class of "commissars." That's their essential function: to design, propagate and create a system of doctrines and beliefs which will undermine independent thought and prevent understanding and analysis of institutional structures and their functions. That's their social role. I don't mean to say they're conscious of it. In fact, they're not. In a really effective system of indoctrination the commissars are quite unaware of it and believe that they themselves are independent, critical minds. If you investigate the actual productions of the media, the journals of opinion, etc., you find exactly that. It's a very narrow, very tightly constrained and grotesquely inaccurate account of the world in which we live.

The cases I mentioned in point are examples. There has never been more lively and extended debate in the United States, to my knowledge, than occurred over the war in Vietnam. Nevertheless, except for the very margins at the outside, the debate was entirely between those who were called "doves" and "hawks." Both the doves and the hawks began by accepting a lie so astonishing that Orwell couldn't have imagined it. Namely the lie that we were defending South Vietnam when we were in fact attacking South Vietnam. Once you begin with that premise, everything else follows.

Pretty much the same is true right now. Let's take the recent flap about the MIG's in Nicaragua. What was happening? The United States is sending advanced aircraft to El Salvador so that we are able to step up our attack on the population of El Salvador. The army that's carrying out this attack is really an occupying army, just like the Polish army is an occupying army of Poland, supported by a foreign power, except that the one in El Salvador is far more brutal and carrying out vastly more atrocities. We are trying to step up this attack by sending advanced aircraft and American pilots are now directly participating in controlling air strikes, etc. It's perfectly natural, and any student of Orwell would expect that we would accuse the other side of bringing in advanced aircraft. We're also conducting a real war against Nicaragua through a mercenary army. They're called "guerrillas" in the press, but they're nothing like any guerrilla army that's ever existed. They're armed at the level of a Central American army. They often outgun the Nicaraguan army. They're completely supplied and controlled by a foreign power. They have very limited indigenous support, as far as anybody knows. It's a foreign mercenary army attacking Nicaragua, using Nicaraguan soldiers, as is often the case in imperial wars.

In this context, the big discussion is whether the Nicaraguans did or did not bring in aircraft which they could use to defend themselves. The doves say they probably didn't bring them in and therefore it was exaggerated. The doves also say, and here you can quote them—Paul Tsongas, for example, or Christopher Dodd, the most dovish Senators in Congress—that if indeed the Nicaraguans did bring in jets, then we should bomb them, because they would be a threat to us.

When one looks at this, one sees something almost indescribable. Fifty years ago we heard Hitler talking about Czechoslovakia as a dagger pointed at the heart of Germany and people were appalled. But Czechoslovakia was a real threat to Germany as compared with the threat that Nicaragua poses to the United States. If we heard a discussion like this in the Soviet Union, where people were asking whether, let's say, Denmark should be bombed because it has jets which could reach the Soviet Union, we would be appalled. In fact, that's an analogy that's unfair to the Russians. They're not attacking Denmark as we're attacking Nicaragua and El Salvador. But here we accept it all. We accept it because the educated classes, the ones who are in a position, through prestige, privilege, education, etc., to present an intelligible understanding of the world, are so subordinated to the doctrinal system that they can't even see that two plus two equals four. They cannot see what's right in front of their eyes:

that we are attacking Nicaragua and El Salvador and that of course the Nicaraguans have every right to defend themselves against our attack. If the Soviet Union had a mercenary army attacking Denmark, carrying out terrorist acts and trying to destroy the country, Denmark would have a right to defend itself. We would agree with that. When a comparable thing happens in our domains, the only thing we ask is, are they or are they not bringing in planes to defend themselves? If they are then we have a right to attack them even more.

That assumption is essentially across the board. There's virtually no voice in the press which questions our right to take even more violent action against Nicaragua if they're doing something serious to defend themselves. That's an indication of a highly brainwashed society. By our standards Hitler looked rather sane in the 1930's.

DB: *Let's talk a bit further about language and politics, specifically in the case of Nicaragua. The United States' Ambassador to Costa Rica was quoted in the New York Times as saying that "The Nicaraguan government has an extreme left network working for them in Washington. This is the same network that worked against American interests in Vietnam. It's sad to say that many Congressmen are prisoners of their own staffs, who rely on a preponderance of information from the left." The Ambassador then likens Nicaragua to Nazi Germany, and he makes this final statement that I'd particularly like you to address: "Nicaragua has become just like an infected piece of meat attracting these insects from all over," the insects being Libyans, Basque separatists, Cubans, the PLO, etc.*

All of this is very reminiscent of Nazi Germany. The Ambassador's remarks are very typical of those produced by the Nazi diplomats at the same point, even in their style, the talk about "insects" and so on. Of course, what he describes is so remote from reality that it's superfluous even to discuss it. The idea of a leftist network in Washington is hilarious. What he would call "leftists" are people like Tsongas and Dodd. Those are precisely the kind of people he's referring to. The people who say that we should bomb Nicaragua if they do something to defend themselves. That's what to the Ambassador is a leftist attempting to undermine our policy. This is like a discussion of true Nazi propaganda, which doesn't even make a pretense of being related to reality and regards any deviation as unacceptable. We have to have total conformity, from his view, to the position that we are permitted and justified in carrying out any act of subversion, aggression, torture, murder, etc. Any deviation from that position is, from his point of view, a leftist conspiracy directed from Moscow. This is the extreme end of the propaganda system, but it's not the important part, in my view. It's so crazy that anybody can see through it.

The important part is the kind that doesn't seem so crazy, the kind that's presented by the doves, who ultimately accept not dissimilar positions. They accept the principle that we do have the right to use force and violence to undermine other societies that threaten our interests, which are the interests of the privileged, not the interests of the population. They accept that position and they discuss everything in those terms. Hence our attack against another country becomes "defense" of that country. Hence an effort by Nicaragua to acquire jets to defend itself becomes an unacceptable act that should evoke further violence on our part. It's that apparently critical position that plays the most significant role in our propaganda system. That's a point that's often not recognized.

The point is clearer if it's something that's a little more remote, so that we're not directly engaged in it now. Let's take the Vietnam War. The major contribution to the doctrinal system during the Vietnam War period, in my view, is certainly the position of the doves. The doves were saying that we were defending South Vietnam, that's just a given, but that it was unwise, that it was costing too much, that it was beyond our capacity and beyond our power. If we're capable of thinking, we'll see that their position is very much like that of Nazi generals after Stalingrad, who said it was a mistake to get into a two-front war, and we probably won't carry it off, and this is probably an effort that should be modified and changed, though it is of course just and right. We don't consider the Nazi generals doves. We recognize what they are. But in a society in which that position is considered to be the dissenting, critical position, the capacity for thought has been destroyed. It means the entire spectrum of thinkable thoughts is now caught within the propaganda system.

It's the critics who make the fundamental contribution to this. They are the ones who foreclose elementary truth, elementary analysis, independent thought by pretending and being regarded as adopting a critical position, whereas in fact they are subordinated to the fundamental principles of the propaganda system. In my view that's a lot more important than the really lunatic comments that you just quoted.

DB: *What can people do to cut through this elaborate and ornamented framework of propaganda and get at what is real, get at the truth?*

I frankly don't think that anything more is required than ordinary common sense. What one has to do is adopt towards one's own institutions, including the media and the journals and the schools and colleges, the same rational, critical stance that we take towards the institutions of any other power.

For example, when we read the productions of the propaganda system in the Soviet Union or Nazi Germany, we have no problem at all in dissociating lies from truth and recognizing the distortions and perversions that are used to protect the institutions from the truth. There's no reason why we shouldn't be able to take the same stance towards ourselves, despite the fact that we have to recognize that we're inundated with this constantly, day after day. A willingness to use one's own native intelligence and common sense to analyze and dissect and compare the facts with the way in which they're presented is really sufficient.

If the schools were doing their job, which of course they aren't, but they could be, they would be providing people with means of intellectual self-defense. They would be devoting themselves with great energy and application to precisely the kinds of things we're talking about so that people growing up in a democratic society would have the means of intellectual self-defense against the system. Today, individuals have to somehow undertake this task themselves. I don't think it's really very hard. Once one perceives what is happening, they have to take the first step of adopting a stance that is simply one of critical intelligence towards everything you read, in this morning's newspaper or tomorrow's newspaper or whatever and discover the assumptions that underlie it. Then analyze those assumptions and restate the account of the facts in terms that really are true to the facts, not simply reflections of the distorting prism of the propaganda system. Once one does that I think the world becomes rather clear. Then one can become a free individual, not merely a slave of some system of indoctrination and control.

DB: *Could you talk about the twentieth century nation-state? You've written extensively about it. What is it in its makeup that permits first genocide, and now what Edward Said called in an article in Harper's the "phenomenon of refugees." Are these phenomena of the twentieth century nation-state? Would you accept those assumptions?*

I don't entirely. I think there's some truth to it, simply because the modern nation-state and the European model, that is, including the United States, happened to be by historical standards enormously powerful. The degree of power in the hands of a modern nation-state is something with no historical parallel. This power is centrally controlled to a very high extent with a very limited degree of popular participation in how that power is exercised. Also, we have an awesome increase in the level of power in the hands of the state, and as a result an enormous amount of violence.

However, it's very misleading to think of, say, genocide as being a twentieth century phenomenon. Let's just take our own history, the history of the conquest of the Western Hemisphere. We celebrate every year, at least in Massachusetts, we have a holiday called "Columbus Day," and very few people are aware that they're celebrating one of the first genocidal monsters of the modern era. That's exactly what Columbus was. It's as if they celebrated "Hitler Day" in Germany. When the colonists from Spain and England and Holland and so on came to the Western Hemisphere, they found flourishing societies. Current anthropological work indicates that the number of native people in the Western Hemisphere may have approached something like 100 million, maybe about 80 million south of the Rio Grande and 12 million or so north of the river. Within about a century, that population had been destroyed. Take just north of the Rio Grande, where once there were maybe 10 or 12 million native Americans. By 1900 there were about 200,000. In the Andean region and Mexico there were very extensive Indian societies, and they're mostly gone. Many of them were just totally murdered or wiped out, others succumbed to European-brought diseases. This is massive genocide, long before the emergence of the twentieth century nation-state. It may be one of the most, if not *the* most extreme example from history, but far from the only one. These are facts that we don't recognize.

The ways in which we protect ourselves from these facts are often quite astonishing. Let me give you a per-

sonal example. This past Thanksgiving, last week, my
family visited. We went for a walk in a nearby national
park. We came across a gravestone which had on it an
inscription, placed by the National Parks as a testimonial,
in fact as a gesture, no doubt conceived as a liberal gesture
toward the Indians in the past: "Here lies an Indian
woman, a Wampanoag, whose family and tribe gave of
themselves and their land that this great nation might be
born and grow." That is so appalling that one doesn't even
know how to discuss it. She and her family didn't "give of
themselves and their land." Rather they were murdered
by our forefathers and driven out of their land. It's as if
200 years from now you came to Auschwitz and found a
gravestone saying, "Here lies a Jewish woman. She and
her family gave of themselves and their possessions so
that this great nation might grow and prosper." These are
reflections of what is regarded here as a liberal, accommo-
dating, forthcoming attitude. All of these aspects of our
historical experience, of the foundations of our own society, we are protected from seeing. Looking at that gravestone, any person of even minimal common sense and just
the most elementary knowledge of history should be able
to see the propaganda. But person after person passes it
by and thinks it's fine, an indication of a frightening level
of indoctrination.

DB: *This raises the question of who controls history in our
society.*

History is owned by the educated classes. These are
the people who are the custodians of history. They are the
ones who are in universities and throughout the whole
system of constructing, shaping and presenting to us the
past as they want it to be seen. These are groups that are
closely associated with power. They themselves have a
high degree of privilege and access to power. They share
class interests with those who control and in fact own the

economic system. They are the cultural commissars of the system of domination and control that's very pervasive. I'm avoiding nuances. There are important exceptions. There are people who write honest history. But the point I'm describing is something that is overwhelmingly dominant, to the extent that only specialists would be likely to know things that fall outside it. For the ordinary citizen, one that doesn't have the resources or the time or the training or the education to really dig into things deeply on their own. The position they're presented with is the one I've described. For example, the gravestone implicitly supports the idea that genocide is a twentieth-century phenomenon, failing to recognize what happened not too far back in our own past.

DB: *Could you talk about what is called "the first genocide of the twentieth century," which occurred in 1915 in Ottoman Turkey to the Armenians. Why is that a virtually unknown event? Why is that relegated to the periphery of our awareness?*

Essentially because people had very little interest in it at the time. What happened is that something between several hundred thousand, maybe over a million people, were massacred in a quite short period. It was in Turkey, remote, no direct interest to Westerners. I think much more dramatic and striking is the suppression of comparable genocidal acts which are much closer to us, and in fact in which we have been directly involved. For example, I would wager that more people are aware of the Armenian genocide during the First World War than are aware of the Indonesian genocide in 1965 when 700,000 people were massacred within a couple of months, with the support of the United States. It was greeted with polite applause in the United States because it "returned Indonesia to the free world," as we described it at the time. Genocide was used, including by American liberals, I should say, as justification for our war in Indochina. It was described as having provided a "shield" behind which these delightful events could take place. That's a much more striking fact than our casual attitude towards a genocidal attack on the Armenians 70 years ago.

DB: *That connects directly with a two-volume set that you co-authored with Edward Herman,* The Washington Connection and Third World Fascism *and* After the Cataclysm. *You talk extensively about the 1965 coup in Indonesia and then the events in 1975, in East Timor...*

Which are still going on, incidentally. There's a case of genocide that's going on right today and is continuing precisely because the United States supports it. That's what blocks any possible termination of that genocidal attack. There's one right in front of our eyes for which we're directly responsible and there's virtually no awareness of it. I doubt if one person in 100 in the United States ever even heard of Timor [East Timor was a former Portuguese colony].

DB: *Why is that? Does it serve some ideological interest that there's no information?*

Sure. It's improper for people in the United States to know that their own government is involved in a genocidal massacre which is quite comparable to Pol Pot. Therefore they better not know about it, and they don't. This is particularly striking because it began, as you say, in 1975, just at the time that the Pol Pot massacres began. They're rather comparable in many ways, except that the Timorese massacre was carried out by an invading army rather than being a peasant revolution taking revenge and controlled by a gang of fanatics who were carrying out huge massacres in their own society. These two are rather comparable in scale. Relative to the population, in fact, the Timorese massacre is maybe two or three times as great, once all the propaganda is filtered away and we look at the actual facts. The treatment of them was quite different. The Pol Pot massacres received enormous attention, tremendous protest, and was compared to the Nazis. The Timorese massacre, that we were responsible for, was suppressed. People went way out of their way to try to find Cambodian refugees on the Thai-Cambodian border so that they could tell horror stories. They didn't go to Lisbon, which is much easier to reach than the Thai-Cambodian border, to talk to Timorese refugees who would tell them what the United States was backing in Timor.

That whole near-genocidal attack, the term is not exaggerated in this case, was almost entirely suppressed for over four years. Even today it's barely discussed, and when it is discussed, the American role is suppressed. For example, the *New York Times* finally began to talk about it and ran editorials. One was called "The Shaming of Indonesia." Sure, it's the shaming of Indonesia, but it's also the shaming of the United States. We're the ones who blocked every diplomatic effort to stop it. The Carter administration, which was supposedly committed to human rights, vastly increased the flow of arms to Indonesia with the certain knowledge that they were going to be used to extend the massacre in East Timor. There was nothing else that they could be used for. None of this is the shaming of the United States, nor is it the shaming of the *New York Times* that they didn't report it for four years, and even today aren't reporting what's going on.

These are again ways of protecting ourselves from understanding the world. The population has to be protected from any understanding of that. That's one of the main purposes of the indoctrination system, to prevent the population from understanding what they are participating in indirectly through the institutions that they support.

DB: *And one sees, for example, in the case of the massacre and ongoing killings in East Timor, a certain sense of bipartisan-*

ship. It started under the Ford administration in 1975, it continued during the Carter years...

It escalated during the Carter years, the worst period was Carter, and it's still continuing now. Last year there was another major Indonesian offensive. Once again the Red Cross has been withdrawn, so there's virtually no international observation. About the only information we're getting is from refugees and the Catholic church. The church has been reporting these atrocities, but that virtually never reaches an American audience. We should ask ourselves, why are our institutions so concerned to prevent us from knowing what we're doing? I think the people in power are simply afraid of the population. If the general population has any awareness and understanding of what the state is up to, they'll protest and they'll stop it. That's why we have these extremely elaborate and very effective systems of thought control. Why don't they just tell us the truth? They don't tell us the truth because they're afraid of us. They're afraid that if we know we're going to stop them. Hence the lies. Hence the educational system. Hence the media. And so on.

DB: *Let's talk about what I reluctantly call "censorship." Perhaps you can find a better word for it here in the United States. Earlier I mentioned the two-volume set that you have co-authored with Edward Herman,* The Washington Connection *and* After the Cataclysm. *Correct me if I'm mistaken, but I believe that neither of those books received any prominent media coverage or book reviews, and now you have a new book with the title* The Fateful Triangle *which has only received two reviews. One can draw two conclusions: Either the books are indeed terrible and not worth writing about, or perhaps a more cynical point of view would be that there's some kind of censorship being exercised here.*

As to whether they're worth writing about, obviously I think so or I wouldn't have written them. We can make a kind of objective test of that. For example, we can ask how the same books are received in other societies similar to ours. Take, say, Canada. Canada is a country very similar to the United States and has essentially the same values, institutions, social organizations, etc. Kind of like an adjunct to the United States. But as soon as we cross the border, we find that the treatment of these books and their authors is radically different than it is here.

For example, *The Fateful Triangle,* which came out about a year ago, is primarily concerned with American policy. It's peripheral to the interests of Canadians, but central to the interests of Americans. It was barely mentioned in the press here, and is very hard to find. You have to really work to dig it out somewhere. It's probably not in the libraries. But in Canada it was reviewed in major journals and most minor journals; even in the *Financial Post,* which is sort of like the *Wall Street Journal.* It was reviewed in the news weeklies, the equivalent of *Time* and *Newsweek.* Every time I go to Canada I'm immediately on radio and television. I was there last week for a day, and I had three interviews on national CBC. In the United States, people with similar views, not just me, are marginalized, excluded, no reviews. You rarely find such books in the libraries; the media are almost totally closed off.

If we look at other countries similar to the United States, the same is true. In England and Australia, again countries very much like us, these books are reviewed, discussed, etc. Not in the United States, however. If the judgment is one of quality, then it's striking that the judgment is so different across the border. Incidentally, many of the reviews are quite critical, but that's fair enough. People say what they think.

DB: *Could you speculate why, for example, you're not on occasionally Dan Rather's CBS Evening News or National Public Radio's All Things Considered? Has Noam Chomsky been marginalized, to use the very term that you've coined?*

That's always been the case. For example, during the Vietnam War, when I was very visible in opposition to the war on the international scene and here too, I live in Boston and I was constantly in the radio and television studios here. But for foreign interviews. I think I was once on public radio in the Boston area during the Vietnam War. I had just returned from a trip to Indochina and I was on for about five minutes.

But I was constantly on Australian, Canadian, British, continental European radio and television. That's consistently the case. Just in the last few weeks I've been on national Italian television, on Canadian television, on Irish radio, all over the place. In another couple of weeks I'm going to England for a day for a big television program discussing politics. In the United States it's virtually unknown.

In fact it's very striking that I'm now talking over a Colorado radio station. When you get out of the main centers in the United States, out of New York, Boston and Washington, then the controls ease. If I go to Denver or Boulder or Des Moines or Minneapolis or San Diego, then it's not at all unlikely that I'll be asked to talk on political topics on radio and sometimes television. But in the main ideological centers it's unimaginable. Again, that's not just me, but also other people who are essentially dissenting critics. This reflects the sophistication of our ideological system.

What happens in areas that are marginal with respect to the exercise of power doesn't matter so much. What happens in the centers of power matters a great deal. Therefore the controls are tighter as you get closer to the center. As soon as you cross the border to Canada nobody really cares much what happens, so therefore it's much freer.

DB: *So essentially if, as you did last year, you come to Boulder and give many public lectures and appear on KGNU and now doing a phone interview on KGNU, that's OK since we're out here in the boondocks, as it were.*

It's not totally OK, but it's better. It could never happen on National Public Radio. [On March 30, 1988 Noam Chomsky was interviewed for the first time on National Public Radio's *All Things Considered.*]

DB: *One final question, about George Orwell. I sense from your writing and from some of the comments you've made in this interview that you feel a certain kinship with Orwell. Have you been influenced by him at all?*

It's a little complicated. I think Orwell wrote one really great book which did influence me a lot. That was *Homage to Catalonia,* the book that he wrote about his experiences during the Spanish Civil War in the late 1930's. The history of that book is itself interesting and revealing. It appeared in 1937 but was not published in the United States. It was published in England, and it sold a couple hundred copies. The reason that the book was suppressed was because it was critical of communists. That was a period when pro communist intellectuals had a great deal of power in the intellectual establishment. It's similar to the kind of control that many people called "pro-Israel," although I think it's a bad term, but people who are called "pro-Israel" have over media and expression today. They're similar in many respects. They succeeded in preventing Orwell's book from appearing.

It did appear about 10 years later, and it appeared as a Cold War tract because it was anti-Russian and fashions had changed. That was a really important book. I think there were things wrong with it, but it was a book of real great significance and importance. It's probably the least known of Orwell's major political books.

His better-known books in my view are not very significant. For example, *1984,* which is very popular here, in fact it's a major bestseller, because it can be easily construed as anti-Russian propaganda. But it's a very shallow book, basically. Orwell was giving a satirical analysis based upon existing Soviet society. Existing Soviet society and its terror have been very well described by factual analyses not very well known here, but they existed. People like Maximov, for example, the anarchist historian, had given excellent detailed analyses of Leninist and Stalinist institutionalized terror going back to the Revolution. You didn't have to go to Orwell and fantasy to find this out. Orwell's fictionalized account was in my view no major contribution and also not very well done. We also tend to suppress some of the aspects of it. He was also talking about England, not just Russia. He was talking about what he expected to happen in the industrial democracies, and as a prediction that was very bad, that hasn't happened.

I also think he missed the main techniques of thought control and indoctrination in the democracies. For example, in England and the United States we do not use the devices for control he described: crude vicious use of highly visible power. That's not the way thought control works here. It works by more subtle and much more effective devices, the kinds we've been talking about. Orwell completely missed this.

On the other hand, he was an honest man. He did try to, and often succeeded, in extricating himself from the systems of thought control, and in that respect he was very unusual and very praiseworthy.

DB: *Bernard Crick, a British biographer of Orwell, seems to corroborate what you say. He suggests that it is in the essays where "the dirty work of imperialism is illuminated," such as "A Hanging" and "Shooting an Elephant," that Orwell would be best remembered and the earlier mentioned "Politics and the English Language."*

I agree with that. The famous works are the least significant.

Israel: The Strategic Asset

March 23, 1985

DB: *One of the most interesting aspects of the relationship between the United States and Israel is that in this country there is virtually unanimous agreement on U.S. support for Israeli policies. To cite one example, in the March 4, 1985 New York Times, Senator Daniel Inouye said he "doesn't understand why administration after administration, Republican and Democrat, puts the squeeze on Israel. I am convinced that it is in our best national interest to make sure a strong, viable Israel continues to exert its influence in that part of the world." He continues, in asking for more aid for Israel, that "we have received more than our money's worth." I'd like you to discuss some of the factual and moral premises inherent in Inouye's comments about Israel and that it is in our "best national interest."*

I'd also like to comment about how we "put the squeeze on Israel." Since 1978 they've gotten something ranging between a third to a half of total American military and economic aid in the world. That's a country of 4 million people, so the concept of the "squeeze" is interesting.

I think it's clear what Inouye means, and there's some logic to it. Israel has served certain kinds of American interests, and the aid to Israel is closely correlated to the American conception of how they can serve American interests. What the United States wants from Israel is that it become a technologically advanced, highly militarized society without any independent or viable economy of its own so that it's totally dependent on the United States and therefore dependable. We maintain it in a position, our policy is designed to create a system of dependence with a capacity for organized violence so that we can use it as what we call a "strategic asset," which means a kind of an attack dog. It's what was called under the Nixon doctrine a "guardian of the Gulf." Namely, a force which can be used either as a base for projection of American military force or its own military force in the case of any conceived threat to quite narrowly perceived American interests in the region. The main interest is to ensure that there's no development of what we call "radical nationalism." Radical nationalism is a technical term meaning nationalist forces that don't obey American orders.

It's counterposed to "moderate nationalism," which means nationalism that does follow American orders. The major American interest in the region is of course not Israel but the energy resources which, it's been known for 40 or 50 years, are the largest and cheapest in the world. We want to make sure that there's no indigenous threat to our domination of that system.

In the early years we assumed that our own power could achieve that result. But increasingly over the years, as the world has become more complex and the American capacity to intervene directly has reduced, the United States has turned to surrogates. This became more or less formalized in the Nixon-Kissinger doctrine, which quite explicitly explained that while the United States would be committed to maintaining what Kissinger called the "overall framework of order," regional powers would pursue particular goals within this system. That meant it was a matter of designating the "local cop on the beat" to control the neighborhood, while police headquarters remains in Washington. That's in effect the Nixon-Kissinger doctrine.

With regard to the extremely crucial Middle East region, primarily the Gulf and the Arabian Peninsula, where most of the oil is, the conception was that Israel and Iran under the Shah would be what was then called "guardians of the Gulf." That's the primary basis for this enormous military support, which has the predictable consequence of turning Israel into a kind of Sparta, essentially eliminating its status as a viable society other than as a military force designed to serve American interests in the region. Correspondingly, Israel is also expected to provide subsidiary services. That's part of the quid pro quo.

This began in the 1960's as Israel began to be framed in the American geopolitical conception as a strategic asset. In the 1960's, under a large CIA subsidy, Israel penetrated black Africa, in the interests of American power. They were, for example, the main force that succeeded in establishing the Mobutu dictatorship in Zaire. They supported Idi Amin in Uganda in the early days, Haile Selasse in Ethiopia, Emperor Bokassa in the Central Africa Republic, and various others who the United States was trying to cultivate and use for its Latin Americanization of Africa. The establishment of dependable client regimes, generally military-based, would be assured to control the local societies.

Increasingly, these secondary services have moved elsewhere, however, primarily Latin America. During the 1970's, under popular pressure, Congress legislated human rights constraints which restricted the American executive in its attempts to support the worst murderers and monsters in Latin America. Therefore they had to move, under the Carter administration, and since under the Reagan administration, to do it indirectly using surrogates. Israel was able to establish close relations with the neo-Nazi regimes in the southern cone, Argentina and Chile. That's in the American interest, since the United States had to sidestep direct support for them. In Central America the United States relied primarily on Argentine Nazis, but increasingly, and by now primarily, on Israeli forces to support genocidal attacks on the Indian population in Guatemala or to send arms to El Salvador and Honduras to support the contras are two examples.

This is a long and very ugly story, and that's a secondary aspect to the services that Israel is expected to provide for us. All of this is in the public record. If we speculate about what's in the secret record, the United States has major conventional military forces aimed at the Persian Gulf. It's called the Central Command. It used to be called the Rapid Deployment Force. If any unwanted nationalist developments take place in that region, we'll invade. But we need a basing system for that, and we have by now a very elaborate basing system stretching from Turkey all the way around the region to the Indian Ocean. Though there is no public document on this, it's a fair guess, a near certainty, that Israel is regarded as a central part of that basing system.

Much of what I have just said is not only obvious from the way history has evolved but it's expressed in the declassified record. For example, you can see how the American relation to Israel has changed over the years. In the early 1950's it was rather cool and conflicted. In 1956 we ordered Israel out of the Sinai after it had attacked Egypt, the reason being that it had attacked Egypt jointly with France and England. We were then referring to France and England as essentially our enemies. They were attempting to reassert a position from which we had expelled them because we wanted to control that region ourselves. Israel, in its attack on Egypt jointly with them, was essentially conspiring with the enemy, so we threw them out. In the early 1950's at least it wasn't clear who the United States was going to use as the basis for its regional power.

There was some support for using Nasser's Egypt for this purpose. Nasser had some CIA backing at the time and other support. By the mid-1950's it became pretty clear that Nasser was going to be a radical nationalist. That is, he wasn't going to follow American orders, and Nasserite influence began to spread throughout the region. By 1958 a National Security Council memorandum on the Middle East concluded that "a logical corollary" to our opposition to radical Arab nationalism would be support for Israel as the only reliable pro-Western force in the region.

Through the 1960's this increased. American intelligence regarded Israel as a barrier to "nationalist pressure"—Nasserite pressure—in the Arabian Peninsula, and there was a kind of proxy war going on in the southern part of the Peninsula between Egypt and Saudi Arabia. Israel was regarded as a shield protecting the monarchies which controlled the oil and very much subordinated to the United States. Israel's 1967 victory, which really showed that it was the overwhelmingly dominant military force in the region, confirmed its value as a strategic asset. The United States certainly supported Israel in that attack and may actually have participated in it. There's evidence to that effect. It certainly supported it.

At that point American aid to Israel increased enormously and it seemed like Senator Inouye and others recognized that this could be a valuable military force.

In 1970, American aid to Israel quadrupled after Israel had succeeded in doing something that we desperately needed at that time. There was concern that Syria might intervene in Jordan to protect Palestinians, who were being massacred by the Jordanian army. The United States was very much concerned about that and regarded it as a potential threat to the oil-producing region. Israel was able to use its overwhelming military force to block any possible Syrian support for the Palestinians and American aid shot up. It was at that point that the Nixon doctrine was explicitly formulated and Israel's role was more or less formalized regarding the Gulf. When the Shah fell in 1979, Iran lost that role, plainly, and Israel was left the sole reliable militarized base for the United States. Aid to Israel again shot up enormously.

At that time we also carried through what is called here the "peace process," which is kind of an Orwellian term, referring to the fact that we instituted a system whereby Egypt was totally excluded from the conflict through the Camp David agreements. The intent and consequences of that policy were to leave Israel free to extend and intensify its occupation of the occupied territories and also to attack its northern neighbor without any concern for a deterrent force. That's exactly what happened from 1978. The first invasion of Lebanon was in 1978. The repression and expansion of settlements in the occupied territories increased rapidly. Israel continued to attack Lebanon, and in 1982 it invaded directly, and we know the consequences since. All of this flowed quite predictably and directly from the Camp David "peace process." That again is part of the whole system of turning Israel into a militarized state.

By now it's probably the most militarized society in the world. It has probably the highest per capita debt in the world. Its status as a economic entity, for example, is reflected in its credit ratings with international banks, which are below that of Mozambique or Bangladesh, and that's even with the huge American subsidies. Increasingly it's undergoing the kind of internal changes, cultural changes and others, which follow from this debt. This is related to the reason why the United States has consistently blocked any possibility of a diplomatic settlement. There have been many possibilities, at least since 1971, for a peaceful political settlement. The United States has consistently blocked all of them because they would require that Israel be a peaceful member of a region in which relations are conducted by diplomacy rather than violence, and we won't accept that. That won't be the role that we want Israel to play.

Virtually all of this has been very easily documented. I've written about it; there's plenty of material, but it's almost totally suppressed and distorted in the official versions. We talk about the "peace process" and "Israel's search for peace," etc. That's the real story. How much

Senator Inouye actually understands of what he's saying, I don't know. But the people who do the actual planning surely understand this, and it's this evolving conception of Israel's strategic role in the region which accounts for its enormous and rather special kind of subsidy that we provide, one that's guaranteed to maintain it as a military force and to maintain a situation of military confrontation in the region, which is part of this whole thing.

DB: *Indeed, the Camp David process has kind of entered the popular mythology. It has a Nobel Peace Prize mystique about it and we celebrate it as a model, as the proper vehicle for settlement of the Arab-Israeli dispute. Senator John Kerry, in Denver on March 16, 1985, said that he favored "a return to the Camp David process." Why is Camp David so firmly established as the model?*

That's an indication of the marvelous effectiveness of the American indoctrination system. Let's recall that Camp David was an agreement whereby Israel left the Sinai and foreign forces, including American, were placed in the Sinai to ensure that that's not an area of military confrontation. That, in effect, excluded Egypt from the conflict. That's the only thing that was done in Camp David, to exclude the major Arab military force from the conflict. Its exclusion, which they themselves wanted, means that there is no deterrent to Israel's doing whatever it wants. What it felt like doing was obvious: moving towards taking over and integrating the occupied territories and harassing the northern border, expanding towards the north. It has continued to do that until it suffered its first military defeat in the last couple of months at the hands of the Lebanese resistance. Up until that point it was just regular expansion towards the north. In order to ensure that they would do this effectively, we massively increased military aid to Israel at the same time, 1978-79. As already mentioned, the fall of the Shah was a side element in this, that left Israel the sole reliable guardian of the Gulf.

The peace process entailed American aid reaching enormous proportions. In 1979 it was something like 50 percent of total American aid overseas. What was in Jimmy Carter's mind I have no idea, but it was obvious to any rational person that if you free Israel from any deterrent force by eliminating the only substantial Arab military force in the region, and if you then provide it with enormous subsidies, then it will attack as it has done.

The subsidies, incidentally, are unspecified. In the case of every other aid program in the world it's project-oriented; we require specific indications of what the aid is going to be used for. Usually it has to be used for purchase of American exports or something like that. In any case, it's closely supervised. For example, in Egypt, which is the next largest aid recipient, we have something like 125 technicians supervising the aid down to the last detail and making sure it's used for exactly the project we want it used for. Israel is unique: the aid, which is unbelievably high on a per capita basis—off the chart—also happens to be unsupervised. It's just a cash grant. We're telling them, Do whatever you like with it. That's a not too subtle way of telling them, Use it for settlement of the occupied territories, use it for military attacks against Lebanon, etc. That was perfectly predictable, and furthermore it's exactly what happened. Even people who couldn't see it at the time can look back now and see that that's what happened. The expansion into the occupied territories, which had been going on for ten years at that point, then increased very rapidly. Also, the repression in the occupied territories increased. The military occupation, which had always been harsh, became much more brutal especially in 1981 and 1982. And Israel attacked Lebanon. It invaded Lebanon in 1978. Through 1979 there was heavy bombardment against Lebanon with hundreds, maybe thousands of people killed.

Israel repeatedly broke ceasefires to initiate attacks

against Lebanon. In July 1981, in one important case, Israeli planes broke a ceasefire, attacked Lebanon. There was at that point a light rocket response, at which time Israel stepped up the attack and bombed Beirut, killing several hundred people. After that there was a heavier rocket response against the northern Galilee, and even heavier Israeli bombings. These were finally stopped by an American-imposed ceasefire in late July. At the time it was stopped, about 450 Arabs and 6 Israelis had been killed, which are normal proportions reflecting the power balance.

The only thing that's remembered from all that today is that rockets were fired at northern Galilee. That's in the news reports, that's always cited now as a justification for Israel's attack on Lebanon. Yes, rockets were fired on northern Galilee in response to heavy Israeli bombing which killed hundreds of civilians. After this point, the PLO did adhere to the ceasefire scrupulously; there were no attacks across the Lebanese border for eleven months or so. Israel, on the other hand, attempted throughout that period, 1981-82, to elicit some kind of PLO action which could be used as an alleged provocation, a pretext for the further attack on Lebanon, which they began planning in July 1981.

Again, this was completely predictable. The American press either couldn't or pretended not to be able to see it, but it was obvious at the time. Throughout 1981 and 1982 there were repeated Israeli provocations, including bombing of Lebanese towns, to elicit some kind of action, maybe shelling of the north or something, which could then be used as a pretext for the invasion that they had been planning. When no pretext could be found, they simply concocted one and invaded in June 1982. They had full American support, incidentally. That was the Lebanese war.

After that they attempted to consolidate their position in southern Lebanon and would have done so had it not been for the resistance in the south. Here this resistance is called "terrorism." All of that comes out of the Camp David "peace process." It's interesting that these elementary facts can't be perceived by our propaganda system. It parallels the Soviet Union, I suppose, in that the propaganda system pretends or just can't see that the Soviet Union is engaged in severe repression in Eastern Europe and an invasion of Afghanistan. They just can't see it, or at least can't say it. Comparably, we don't see or can't say these things here.

I should mention that one might ask, or any reporter who's even moderately serious would ask, What is the attitude of the indigenous population in the occupied territories? We know that. For example, there are Israeli-run polls concerning the Camp David peace process. It turns out that the population overwhelmingly, over 90 percent, regards the Camp David peace process as detrimental to their interests. It's obvious why, for the reasons discussed previously.

A final comment about Camp David is that on the part of this "peace process" there has been a consistent attempt, which the United States has blocked, on the part of the Arab states and the Europeans to initiate a real peace process. That began clearly in February 1971, when President Sadat of Egypt offered Israel a full peace settlement. In his proposal there was nothing offered to the Palestinians at all; they were simply ignored.

The full peace settlement was to be on the internationally recognized borders, the pre-1967 borders, with recognized borders, guaranteed security, etc. Israel refused it because they wanted to take over the territories. This was the dovish Labor government at the time. The United States backed them in that refusal. That's remained constant until today. For example, just about a year ago Arafat offered Israel negotiations leading to mutual recognition. Of course, Israel immediately rejected it. The United States didn't even bother to respond.

This was virtually blacked out of the American media. Today it's as if it didn't exist. In between that period are numerous similar cases where the United States has vetoed peace offers at the U.N. that came from Syria, Jordan, Egypt and the PLO who called for a two-state settlement. Everyone recognizes this is the only peaceful settlement, which guaranteed recognized borders, etc. Repeatedly over the years the United States has refused to accept any genuine peace offer. So there is something that we might call the "peace process" except that it's been aborted by the United States and of course rejected by Israel consistently. It's out of history, it just doesn't exist. For example, when the *New York Times* runs a news story reporting on the history of peace efforts, as it did a couple of days ago by Thomas Friedman, their reporter in Jerusalem, none of this is mentioned, it's just down the memory hole. The only thing that exists is the American-run system, the Camp David system, which we call the peace process, which in fact is just a war process.

DB: *You've said that the United States and Israel have stood in the way of an international settlement, basically on racist grounds. Although they accept the right of Israel to be a national state, primarily for Jews, they do not accept that the indigenous population has a parallel right. Why?*

I think the American position is strictly racist, there's no question about it. There are two national groups which claim the right of national self-determination in what was once Palestine: there is an indigenous population, the Palestinians, and there are the settlers who partially replaced them, namely the Jewish immigrants. We accept without any question the right of the Jewish immigrants to national self-determination in Palestine and therefore we unequivocally support Israel as an expression of that national right.

However, we deny a comparable right to the indige-

nous population. Our current position, for example, is that
we will only agree even to talk to Palestinians, the indigenous population, if they're not associated with the PLO.
The PLO is plainly the organization which they recognize
as the expression of their national rights. There's no doubt
about this. Returning to these Israeli-run polls, something
like 98 percent of the population in the occupied territories
calls for an independent Palestinian state, that's what
they want. Something like 86 percent of them in the latest
Israeli-run poll want it to be run solely by the PLO. The
rest want to see it run largely by the PLO. The same is
true in Palestinian diaspora. That's more support than
the Zionist organization had among Jews in the 1940's.

If in the 1940's the United States government had
said, Yes, we'll be willing to talk to Jews about Palestine,
but only if they're not connected with the Zionist organization, and of course not permitting any Jewish state, that
would have been regarded as racist, and correctly. I
should say that the Jewish world was divided over this
issue. To refuse to talk to the PLO today is to take the
same stand. Again, it's kind of remarkable that American
commentary cannot perceive the extraordinary racism of
this position.

This racism shows up elsewhere as well. Take the
way in which we react to what's happening today in
Southern Lebanon. The American commentary regards it
as quite legitimate for the Israeli occupying army to use
violence to suppress resistance. In fact, here it's sometimes even called "terror against terror," which is a term
that's chilling. That's the name of an organization set up
by the Gestapo to attack the European resistance. We use
it without any qualms to refer to what's going on in
Southern Lebanon, except we support it. Even when it
reaches the point of Israel murdering CBS reporters, as
happened a couple of days ago, the President gets on
television and says, This is perfectly fine, they were just
doing it in self-defense, etc. There's no comment on this in

the press as yet.

Take the commentary on Israel's forced withdrawal from the south: which is being forced by local resistance. There are anguished stories in the media about the traumatic consequences for the people of northern Galilee, who will once again be under rocket fire from Lebanon. The border was completely peaceful for a year before Israel attacked, and the rocket fire, as I mentioned, was in retaliation to Israeli bombing. Murder of Arabs is considered a perfectly legitimate occupation. Israel killed dozens, maybe hundreds of local people, Lebanese, in its so-called "iron fist" operations in the last months. This included real terrorist acts like breaking into hospitals, taking people away who are trying to give blood to people wounded in Israeli attacks, beating up a hospital director, real barbarism. That's considered legitimate. It's their right to use military force in another country to suppress the local population.

Another aspect of the same racism shows up quite dramatically in our diplomatic stance, our refusal to recognize that the indigenous population has the rights that we naturally accord to the Jewish settlers who immigrated to the country. It's even reached the point that in the United States there's a pretense that the indigenous population didn't exist. There's a rather comical incident in the last year that involves a completely fraudulent book *[From Time Immemorial]* by Joan Peters which became a bestseller in the United States. Virtually every review of it here was extremely laudatory. The book claims that the Palestinians didn't exist. It's a concoction of lies and distortions. As soon as the publishers made a tactical error and allowed it to appear in England where the intelligentsia are not so totally controlled on this issue, it was immediately blasted out of the water. Every review pointed out grotesque errors and ridiculous fabrications. But here it was accepted as gospel truth because it says what we want to hear. If the Palestinians didn't exist, that justifies our racist attitudes towards them.

DB: *June 1985 is the third anniversary of the "Peace for Galilee," the Israeli invasion of Lebanon. What has Israel accomplished in Lebanon?*

It accomplished quite a bit. The main purpose of Israel in Lebanon is revealed by their own statements. For example, Prime Minister Shamir pointed out that Israel faced a real danger in Lebanon before 1982. He then went on to explain that it was not a military but a political danger, that the PLO had scrupulously adhered to the ceasefire and had increased its attempts to lay the basis for a political settlement. That's a danger, because if there is to be a political settlement and the Palestinians are to be recognized as participants, then Israel will not be able to maintain its control over the occupied territories and will have to settle for peace and peaceful integration into the region, which it does not want to do. So there was a political danger, as Shamir pointed out. One of the best Israeli journalists, a well-known Israeli satirist, B. Michael, had an article right after Shamir's statement in which he stated, "Thank God there's no one to talk to." Israel did succeed in eliminating this political threat. The attack on the Palestinians, which meant the destruction of organized Palestinian society, that was the purpose of the war, was successful. Organized Palestinian society was destroyed, the PLO was somewhat marginalized, and the danger of a political settlement reduced.

Israel had further goals, namely to essentially take over Lebanon and install there what they called a "new order" which would mean a client regime based on right-wing Christians and selected privileged Muslim elites. This is sometimes called Sharon's plan, and now people denounce it because Sharon was so terrible. But it should be remembered when it looked as though that plan was going to be successful, in late August 1982, after the savage bombings of Beirut and the destruction of southern Lebanon, the popular support for it in Israel was enormous. Support for Likud, Begin and Sharon reached about 80 percent, which was totally unprecedented in Israel. It was only when the plan began to fall apart that opposition developed. That was the large plan, namely the establishment of a client state based on those Christian and selected Muslim elements. That failed. They were unable to do that, for a number of reasons, one of them being the intense resistance in the south.

In fact, in the south Israel has suffered its first military defeat ever. It has been compelled by local resistance to partially withdraw from southern Lebanon. I don't believe it really intends to withdraw. What they're intending to do is to hold on to as much of southern Lebanon as they can, and that will take violence, because the local population does resist. But they'll do that. There may be moves towards trying to depopulate southern Lebanon if that's necessary, as they did along the Jordan Valley in the late 1960's. They'll maintain a toothold there, I would imagine, at least if the United States supports them.

DB: *Can you talk about the problems of discussing Israeli policies in the United States without being labelled "anti-Semitic"? You, for example, speak out frequently, and you've written many books. Have you personally encountered any difficulties?*

I can't be called "anti-Semitic," because I'm Jewish, so there's another label that's used. These are used by people who call themselves "supporters of Israel." Actually they are the real enemies of Israel. They're supporting the development of what I have described, the development of a militarized, unviable society geared towards war and subservient to American interests. That's not support for Israel in any meaningful sense. People who call themselves "supporters of Israel" have two categories with which they try to silence criticism. One is "anti-Semite," the other is "self-hating Jew." That takes care of everyone. You're either an anti-Semite or a self-hating Jew if you don't follow the party line strictly.

These tactics run across the board, so it's not just right-wing extremist Israeli circles, or supporters of Israel here that adopt that position, but also people like Abba Eban, a Labor dove, who have explicitly stated that the task of Israeli agitprop is to make it clear that any criticism of Israel is either anti-Semitism or the position of self-hating Jews. In the United States a rather effective system of intimidation has been developed to silence critique. Let me just give you one example: Take the Anti-Defamation League of the B'nai Brith, which is reputed to be a civil rights organization.

It's rather comical. It's actually an organization devoted to trying to defame and intimidate and silence people who criticize current Israeli policies, whatever they may be. For example, I myself received, through a leak in the New England office of the Anti-Defamation League, a copy of my file there. It's 150 pages, just like an FBI file, interoffice memos warning that I'm going to show up here and there, surveillance of talks that I give, comments and alleged transcripts of talks. They're mostly fabricated because people don't hear or can't understand. This material has been circulated. If I'm going to give a talk somewhere, this material would be sent to some local group which would use it to extract defamatory material which would then be circulated, usually in unsigned pamphlets outside the place where I'd be speaking.

I happened to get this material when it was being sent to Harvard law professor Alan Dershowitz in preparation for a debate that we were to have a few days later, so that he would be able to extract from it defamatory material concocted by the Anti-Defamation League surveillance system. Which is in fact exactly what he did. This is typical of the way they act. If there's any comment in the press which they regard as insufficiently subservient to the party line, there'll be a flood of letters, delegations, protests, threats to withdraw advertising, etc. The politicians of course are directly subjected to this, and they are also subjected to substantial financial penalties if they don't go along. The Israeli press is very open about this.

For example, after the last election, there was an article in one of the major Israeli journals by a very good journalist named Yoav Karni. The headline of the article was actually a pun. It reads in Hebrew "Jewish money buys the vote," but it could also be read as "Jewish money buys everything." That was the headline. Then came a report of a speech by Thomas Dine, head of the Israeli lobbying group in Washington, AIPAC [American Israel Public Affairs Committee], in which he just gloated over the successes of the Jewish political lobby, the Israeli political lobby here, in controlling the American Congressional elections. He said that their major achievement was to eliminate Senator Charles Percy, who was too critical of Israel. He went on to say that they felt that, through electoral victories, they had Congress in their pocket until the year 2000. If this appeared somewhere in the United States it would be regarded as some kind of fanatic, anti-Semitic publication, sort of like the *Protocols of the Elders of Zion*. But this is a Hebrew article in the Hebrew press. I should mention that the journalist was appalled by all of this. He said it was a real threat to American democracy. But here the Israeli lobbying groups regard it as a great success and they are quite proud of it, though, of course, they don't publicly say the things that they say privately.

This is a very effective system, particularly since there's no counterweight to it. There's no pressure on the other side. There is a very broad international consensus, and there has been for many years, over a political settlement to the dispute. It's essentially a two-state settlement which would recognize the national rights of both Jews and Palestinians. It's supported by most of the world. It's blocked by the United States, who leads the rejectionist camp. But the point is that there's no articulate voice here expressing anything like the international consensus. There's no articulate voice here opposing repression and atrocities conducted quite freely by Israel, which encourages them to go on and do more of it. That's one of the reasons why they're capable of such really barbaric actions in south Lebanon. They've never been criticized in the past, why should it begin now? There's occasional criticism when things really get out of hand, like the Sabra and Shatila massacres, but that's quickly silenced and things return to their norm. This is a totally one-sided pressure and system of vilification, lying, defamation, and judicious use of funds in the political system, that has created a highly biased approach to the whole matter and is why the United States can continue to block a political settlement. The system of military confrontation, a very dangerous one that repeatedly threatens global war, is maintained with complete impunity. There's no internal criticism here.

DB: *What about genuine Israeli fears? You're quite familiar with the level of lexical violence from Arabs and others talking about Israel as a "cancer in the Middle East" that needs to be "exterminated" and "eliminated."*

First of all, I'm not familiar with those, because they're mostly fabricated. They did exist, primarily in the 1960's, but since early 1970, most of the Arab world has been quite willing to reach an accommodation with Israel. This was explicit in the case of Egypt in 1971; Jordan in 1971 made a similar proposal. I don't want to bother going through the whole diplomatic record here, which I reviewed in *The Fateful Triangle,* not too long ago. Through the 1970's there were repeated Arab offers, Egypt, Syria, the PLO, Saudi Arabia and others, to arrange for a political settlement in accord with the international consensus. There is talk about a "cancer," and so on, but that typically comes from Israeli sources. Israel typically refers to the PLO as a "cancer" which is "metastasizing" and a "disease which has to be stamped out," etc.

DB: *Gideon Hausner said that.*

Yes, who was the prosecutor in the Eichmann trial, the person who used this terminology which is in fact rather reminiscent of Eichmann himself. However, I wouldn't downplay the threat to Israel, I think it's real. As long as military confrontation persists, Israel is in real danger of destruction, there's no doubt about that. My own feeling is that they're heading for destruction. They happen to be the dominant military force in the region now, but there's no guarantee that that will persist. In a system of continued and unending military confrontation, sooner or later they're going to lose. Military intelligence is a very low-credibility operation. It rarely knows what it's talking about. Modern history shows that quite well. They may think that they're in a position of military dominance, and they may find that they're wrong. Unexpected things do happen in the case of war. They came close to being destroyed in 1973 after two years of rejecting Sadat's peace offers. However, they have not learned the lesson from that. The lesson plainly is that if they want to maintain control of the occupied territories and they want to keep harassing the northern border, then they're going to be in a situation of permanent military confrontation. That's going to mean repeated chance of war and sooner or later destruction. So the threats are very real, except that I think that by now a lot of these threats are self-generated.

DB: *A central thesis of your book* The Fateful Triangle *is that although the United States claims to be the friend of Israel, the* *policy it's pursuing will ultimately destroy it.*

I think that's true. I think it's even more dramatically true of the people who call themselves supporters of Israel. I should say that this view is shared very widely by the small group of Israeli doves. They put things in terms much more extreme and harsh than I would use. For example, take Meir Pail, who's a real member of the Israeli establishment. He's a retired colonel, a well-known military historian, formerly a leading military strategist in the army. He was head of the officer's training school in the Israeli army, straight out of the establishment. He had an article about a year ago in which he was attacking the American Jewish community. I think he was targeting it too narrowly. The title of the article was "Zionism and the Danger of Cancer." He said that the danger was coming from the American Jewish community, that what they want is an Israel which is a "war god similar to Mars." They get their psychological thrills from seeing Israel, a superman, stomping on people's faces. He went on to say that the attitude of the American Jewish community and their monolithic support for these tendencies in Israel and their intolerance of any discussion and debate of them are going to create an Israel which "will be a new development in political history, a combination of the worst features of South Africa and Northern Ireland." He virtually pleaded with the American Jewish community to stop what they call support for Israel, which is, in fact, driving it in this direction.

As I say, those are terms much more extreme than I would use, and they come from a mainstream Israeli establishment figure who happens to be a dove. I think he's much too narrowly focused when he talks about the American Jewish community. That's what they tend to see. In fact, the support for that kind of policy in the United States is only very partially based on the American Jewish community. It's far broader than that.

DB: *There seems to be much more pluralism and political diversity in Israel on some of these issues than in the United States itself.*

There's no doubt of that. For the Jewish population of Israel, let's put aside the Arab citizens, it achieves a level of democracy that's well beyond that of the United States. These issues in particular are commonly debated in Israel. In the United States they're so marginalized as to be non-existent. Again, to take a personal case, I can virtually not publish in the United States on these topics, but I've been asked by mainstream Israeli journals to write regular articles for them.

DB: *You read Hebrew and you closely follow Israeli press and politics. Do you see any signs in Israel today that point toward a two-state settlement?*

There can be no signs in Israel, for a very simple reason. Israel is so utterly dependent on the United States at this point that no group can attain any degree of credibility in Israel unless it has substantial American support. That's one of the reasons that people like Meir Pail and others like him are so upset by the monolithic and chauvinistic and rather hysterical tendencies in the United States on this issue. They know that unless some American support develops for a political settlement, then those groups within Israel, and they certainly exist, that regard current developments as dangerous and intolerable, will have no domestic support. In fact, that's correct. Let's take a look at the current Knesset, the Parliament. I'd suppose maybe 10 percent of its members would tend to support some sort of political settlement of the kind that corresponds to the international consensus. That's a rather optimistic appraisal. It may be much less than that. Explicitly committed to that are a smaller group. If American support, however, developed for a political settlement, then such tendencies would develop in Israel in this direction too.

DB: *Can you make some suggestions as to what people can do to become aware of this issue and effect some movement in United States foreign policy vis-à-vis Israel?*

This is one of the easier questions. To change American policy with regard to, say, Central America, would be extremely difficult because the United States has a long-time historic interest in violence and repression in Central America and we're not going to give it up easily. But in the case of the Middle East I think it would be quite an easy thing to do. Even though there's virtually no articulate voice in the United States in support of the international consensus on a political settlement, polls nevertheless indicate that a large percentage of the population—in many polls up to two-thirds or three-quarters of the population—support a Palestinian state. That is, they believe that the indigenous population should have the right of national self-determination alongside of Israel. That means that there's a potential popular support. Within elite planning groups there's a real sharp division on this topic.

There are people who feel that we should maintain Israel as a strategic asset and a base for projection of American power and a source of violence and threat to intimidate the region. There are many other people, including people who represent quite powerful economic and political interests in the United States, who believe to the contrary that we should go along with the international consensus and try to reach an authentic political settlement. George Ball is a good example of a spokesman for this point of view. A recent book of his, *Error and Betrayal in Lebanon,* which I'm sure will never be reviewed here, is a good, clear, lucid and I think quite persuasive exposition of this point of view. This is not an open political issue in the United States, and I think this is one of the rare cases where virtual domination, total domination of articulate expression of the media, the books, schools, the whole ideological system, the domination of that by one extremist position has in fact shifted the political balance very radically.

The potential split among dominant American elites has not even emerged into policy, because the ones who support the hawkish, extremist, violent policy have almost total support in articulate opinion. That can be changed if people are willing to face the intimidation apparatus which will be unpleasant. It's unpleasant to have mud thrown at you and be denounced, etc. But if you're willing to face that and to do some self-education, and the facts are available, and then some real education of others, organizing and so on, I think that political pressures can be developed to make it possible for Congressional representatives and for the press, this means pressure on the press, too, to take a stance which at least recognizes reality. And also to effect political decisions and to move the United States towards joining what is a very broad international consensus on this issue. That could happen. It's easily within range. It would have large-scale support even among powerful American interests. In this respect it's quite different, an easier task, than what faces people who are trying to change the American policy of organized violence in Central America.

Terrorism:
The Politics of Language

October 24, 1986

DB: *To what extent does the control of language shape and form our perceptions and understanding of reality?*

There are obvious examples. One important fact to bear in mind when one listens to or is subjected to political discourse is that most terms are used in a kind of a technical meaning that's very much divorced from their actual meaning, sometimes even the opposite of it. For example, take a term like "national interest." It is commonly used as if it's something good for us, and people are supposed to understand that. So if a political leader says that "I'm doing this in the national interest," you're supposed to feel good because that's for you. However, if you look closely, it turns out that the national interest is not defined as what's in the interest of the entire population; it's what's in the interests of a small group of dominant elites who happen to be able to command the resources that enable them to control the state—basically, corporate-based elites. That's what's called the "national interest."

Correspondingly, the term "special interests" is used in a related way, to refer to the general population. The population are called the "special interests" and the corporate elite are called the "national interest." You're supposed to be in favor of the national interest and against the special interests.

This became very clear in the last few presidential campaigns. The Reagan administration is largely a figment of the public relations industry. The public relations aspects of it, including control over language, are very striking—it's a professional public relations outfit. It was interesting to see how the choice of terms they use was carefully crafted. In both the 1980 and 1984 elections, they identified the Democrats as the "party of special interests," and that's supposed to be bad, because we're all against the special interests. But if you look closely and ask who were the special interests, they listed them: women, poor people, workers, young people, old people, ethnic minorities—in fact, the entire population. There was only one group that was not listed among the special interests: corporations. If you'll notice the campaign rhetoric, that was never a special interest, and that's right, because in their terms that's the *national* interest. So if you think it through, the population are the special interests and the corporations are the national interest, and since everyone's in favor of the national interest and against the special interests, you vote for and support someone who's against the population and is working for the corporations.

This is a typical case of the way the framework of thought is consciously manipulated by an effective choice and reshaping of terminology so as to make it difficult to understand what's happening in the world. A very important function of the ideological institutions—the media, the schools, and so on—is to prevent people from perceiving reality, because if they perceived it they might not like it and might act to change it. That would harm privileged people who control these things.

DB: *Perhaps it's as George Orwell wrote in his essay "Politics and the English Language," that "In our time, political speech and writing are largely the defense of the indefensible."*

Yes, he gave interesting examples which are now classic, like the term "pacification." It is used for mass murder; thus we carried out "pacification" in Vietnam. If you look at what the pacification programs were, they were literally programs of mass murder to try to suppress and destroy a resisting population. Orwell wrote long before Vietnam, but he already noted that pacification was being used that way; by now it's an industry.

It's the same with every term you can think of. Take the term "conservative." Conservative is supposed to be a good thing, and this is supposed to be a conservative administration. A true conservative like, say, Robert Taft, would turn over in his grave to see what's being called conservative. Everything the conservatives have always fought against is being advanced by this administration. It's in favor of extending the power of the state and increasing the intervention of the state in the economy. State power has increased faster under this administration than under any since the Second World War. It's also interested in protecting the state against its citizens, cutting down access to the state, controlling thought, controlling expression, attacking civil liberties, attacking individual rights. It's the most lawless administration we've ever had. All of these things are anathema to conservatives. Conservatives want the opposite in every respect, so naturally they call the administration conservative, and if you like it you're supposed to be conservative.

These are all ways of undermining the possibility of independent thought, by eliminating even the tools that you can use to engage in it.

DB: *The power of naming seems to be crucial in this whole process.*

These are all examples of it. Language is, after all, a tool for thought. If you debase the language, you debase the thought. I don't want to exaggerate this element of it, but it is one element, and one that's certainly consciously manipulated in order to introduce confusion and lack of perception.

DB: *In recent years, starting in the 1970s, continuing through the 1980s and for the foreseeable future, the term "terrorism" has become a dominant issue, a theme and focus for the media and politicians. I wonder if you could talk about the word itself. It seems to have undergone a curious transformation in the last couple of centuries.*

It definitely has, it's a very interesting case. The word "terrorism" came into general use at the end of the 18th century, and it was then used to refer to acts of violent states that suppressed their own populations by violence. Terror was the action of a state against its own citizens. That concept is of no use whatsoever to people in power. So, predictably, the term has come to be changed. Now it's the actions of citizens against states; in fact, the term "terrorism" is now almost entirely used for what you might call "retail terrorism": the terrorism of small, marginal groups, and not the terrorism of powerful states.

We have one exception to this: if our enemies are involved in terrorism, then you can talk about "state terrorism." So there are really two things that define terrorism. First, it's done against states, not by states against their citizens, and it's done by them, not us. So, for example, take Libya. Qaddafi is certainly a terrorist. The latest edition of the Amnesty International publication, *Political Killings by Governments*, lists Qaddafi as a terrorist; he killed fourteen people, Libyans, mostly in Libya, in the 1980s. There may be a handful of others, but even taking the most extreme estimate it couldn't be more than several dozen, probably less. That's terrorism, and he's therefore the "Mad Dog of the Middle East" and the "King of International Terrorism." That's because he meets our criteria: he's them, not us, and the terrorism that one talks about is carried out generally by small groups, not by one of our major states.

Let's compare it with El Salvador. In the same years in which Libya killed fourteen, maybe 20 people, mostly Libyans, the government of El Salvador slaughtered about 50,000 people. Now that's not just terrorism, that's international terrorism, because it was done by us. We instituted the government as much as the Russians instituted the government in Afghanistan. We created the army, a terrorist army; we supplied, organized and directed it. The worst atrocities were carried out by American-trained elite battalions fresh from their training. The U.S. Air Force participated directly in coordinating bombing strikes—the terror was not ordinary killing. Libyan terror is bad enough; they kill people. But our terrorists first mutilate, torture, rape, cut them to pieces—it's hideous torture, Pol Pot-style. That's not called terrorism. El Salvador is not called a terrorist state. José Napoléon Duarte has presided over all this, who has perceived his role from the beginning as ensuring that the murderers are supplied with weapons, and that nothing will interfere with the massacre which he knew was coming when he joined the military junta. He's called a great liberal hero, and El Salvador is considered a kind of magnificent triumph of democracy. Here's a major terrorist state—Libya is a very, very minor terrorist state—but we see it the other way around. "Terrorism" is used for them, not us. In the case of El Salvador it's plainly being done by a major state against its own citizens—in fact a state that we established, a client state of the United States. Therefore it can't be terrorism, by definition.

This is true in case after case. My book about it, *Pirates and Emperors,* takes its title from a rather nice story by St. Augustine in his *City of God.* St. Augustine describes a confrontation between King Alexander the Great and a pirate whom he caught. Alexander the Great asks the pirate, "How dare you molest the sea?" The pirate turns to Alexander the Great and says, "How dare you molest the whole world? I have a small boat, so I am called a thief and a pirate. You have a navy, so you're called an emperor." St. Augustine concludes that the pirate's answer was excellent. That's essentially the story. Retail terrorism directed against our interests is terrorism; wholesale terrorism carried out for our interests isn't terrorism.

The same is true in the Middle East region. In case after case, this is the way the term is used, and very effectively. In fact, it was very predictable that the Reagan administration would take international terrorism to be the core of its foreign policy, as it announced right off. The reason was that the administration made it very clear that it was going to be engaged in international terrorism on a massive scale, and since it's going to be engaged in international terrorism, naturally, in a good public relations-directed world, you start off by saying that you're opposed to international terrorism. That shifts attention away from the crucial issue: that you're going to maximize international terrorism.

DB: *Why the tremendous fascination with terrorism—the TV specials, the articles, the documentaries, the symposia, the conferences, and on and on—is there something deeper that's being touched by this?*

Oh, yes, very deep. It's very close to the Reagan administration's domestic policies. It's important to remember that the Reagan administration's policies are extremely unpopular, and for obvious reasons. The polls show this very clearly; on just about every major issue the public is strongly opposed to the Reagan programs. Take, say, social spending vs. military spending. When the question is asked in polls: Would you prefer to have a decrease in welfare payments or in military spending?, the overwhelming majority of the population supports social spending and opposes military spending. In fact, much of the population is quite willing to see taxes raised to improve social spending. The same is true on just about every issue. On intervention abroad (in other words, international terrorism, if we were to be honest), the population is strongly against it, by large majorities. The Reagan administration is for it. On the nuclear freeze, the public is overwhelmingly in favor of it; the figure is something like three to one. The administration is against it. And so on. As you go down the line, every major policy program is unpopular. This is a problem, of course; you've got to control the population. There is a classic answer to this problem: you frighten them.

Let me just go back to another step of the Reagan program which is even more obvious: an essential part of the Reagan program was to try to transfer resources from the poor to the rich. Now, that's going to be unpopular, and the attack on social spending is a part of it. Much of the Reagan program is turning an increasingly powerful state into a welfare state for the rich. The military program is very largely for that purpose. That's a forced public subsidy to advanced industry, again unpopular, and you can't present it in these terms. What do you do? You have to get the public lined up. They oppose your policies. There's only one way to deal with this; every leader throughout history has understood it. You've got to frighten them, make them think their lives are at stake, that they've got to defend themselves, and then they'll accept these programs that they despise or dislike as an unfortunate necessity.

How do you terrify people? Again, there's a classic answer: you find some "Evil Empire" that's threatening to destroy them. In our case, it's now the Soviet Union; it used to be the Huns, before that, the British, and so on. But since the Bolshevik Revolution it's been the Soviet Union that's threatening to destroy us. So that's the Evil Empire. But here you run into a problem. Confrontations with the Evil Empire are dangerous. That's a big, powerful state; it can fight back, and you don't want to get involved with them because you might get hurt. So what you have to do is have confrontations, but not with the Evil Empire—that's too dangerous. The best way is to have confrontations with groups that you designate as "proxies" of the Evil Empire. What you try to do is to find essentially defenseless countries or groups that can be attacked at will, and designate them to be proxies of the Evil Empire, and then you can defend yourself against them by attacking them. Libya, for example, is perfect for this purpose. It has loose associations with the Soviet Union. It's a minor actor in the world of international terrorism. Against the background of anti-Arab racism, which is rampant in the United States—it's the last legitimate form of racism—you can easily talk about the Mad Dog and how he ought to get down from the trees and all this kind of stuff. That works, that scares people.

Furthermore, if you can manage to elicit terrorism, which some of our acts have done, that will really frighten people, since that strikes at home. In fact, actual terrorism is very slight; you're much more likely to be hit by lightning. But people can get scared, and a confrontation with Libya is cheap. You can kill Libyans at will; they can't fight back, it's a tiny, defenseless country, we can beat them up every time we feel like it. It will make people here feel that somehow our courageous cowboy leader is defending us from these monsters who are going to destroy us, most of which is a public relations concoction. In fact, throughout the history of the Reagan administration there has been a sequence of carefully concocted, fraudulent incidents created to give us an opportunity to attack and kill Libyans, always for some specific political purpose at home, like building up support for the rapid deployment force, an intervention force in the Middle East or gaining support for contra aid, or one thing or another. They're very carefully timed, as I said; this is a public relations administration. Their genius is manipulation of the public; that's what they're good at. The spring of 1986, for example, was a brilliant exercise in public relations—

DB: *The bombing of Libya...*

—and the impact, the pretext for it was fabricated. It was covered up by the media, which know the true story but will not report it. It terrified the domestic population—people wouldn't even go to Europe, they were so scared, which is ludicrous. You're a hundred times as safe in any European city as in any American city—but people were so terrified they stayed at home. If you can terrify the domestic population then they'll support things like Star Wars or whatever lunacy comes along in the belief that you have to defend yourself. Crucially, you can't have confrontations with the Russians; they can fight back. So you've got to find somebody you can beat up at will: Grenada, Libya, Nicaragua, anybody who can't fight back. That's what you need.

This is, incidentally, understood very well abroad. When you read the foreign press, they regularly comment on the thuggishness and the cowardice of this administration, the sort of "bully on the block mentality": you find somebody little enough to beat up and you go send your goon squads to beat him up, that's essentially their style. But here somehow people can't see it.

DB: *This retail minor-actor terrorism you've been talking about—when it's presented in the media it occurs ahistorically: it has no context, it's totally irrational, so it seems that the logical response would be one of loathing and fear, and it's very effective.*

That's right. Most of the retail terrorism—what is called "terrorism" in the United States—comes out of Lebanon, and that started in 1982. It was a very marginal phenomenon before that, a major phenomenon, mainly in Europe, after 1982; so plainly something must have happened in 1982 to cause terrorism to start coming out of Lebanon. During that year, with enthusiastic American support, Israel attacked Lebanon. The purpose of the Israeli attack was to demolish the civilian society of the Palestinians so as to ensure Israeli control over the West Bank, and in the process the Palestinian community was destroyed, and Lebanon, already in bad shape, got the final blow.

The United States supported it all the way. We vetoed U.N. resolutions trying to stop the aggression, we supplied Israel with arms, diplomatic support, the whole business, and naturally it was perfectly predictable that that was going to evoke international terrorism. You cut off every political option for people and they are going to turn to terrorism. And I should say that this was well understood in Israel. Here you can't talk about it, because we're a much more indoctrinated country, but in Israel, which is a more democratic society—at least for the Jewish majority—this was openly discussed. For example, the current prime minister, Yitzhak Shamir, pointed out that there was a threat to Israel from the Palestinians, but said it was a political, not a military threat. The threat was that they would compel Israel to enter into a political settlement that it didn't want, and that had to be stopped.

Israel's and perhaps the world's leading specialist on the Palestinians, a professor at Hebrew University named Yehoshua Porath, wrote an analysis shortly after the invasion, a long, detailed article in *Ha'aretz,* Israel's major newspaper (kind of like the *New York Times),* in which he explained what he thought, very plausibly, the invasion was about. He said, and I'm paraphrasing: Look, here's the situation. For the last year, the PLO has not engaged in any cross-border terrorism. Israel has tried to get them to do it, we have continually bombed them and murdered them and so on to try to evoke some response across the border, but they haven't done it. They've kept discipline despite the fact that we've bombed them, killing dozens of people and so forth. This is a veritable catastrophe for the Israeli leadership, since if the PLO continues to maintain this posture of not engaging in cross-border terrorism and demanding a diplomatic settlement, Israel might be driven to a political settlement, which it does not want. In a political settlement it would have to give up control of the occupied territories. What the Israeli leadership wants is to return the PLO to much earlier days when it engaged in random terrorism, a PLO that will hijack airplanes, kill many Jews and be a source of loathing and horror throughout the world. They don't want a peaceful PLO that refuses to respond to Israeli terrorist attacks and insists on negotiation. That's what the invasion will achieve.

Others also commented in the same way, and that's a very plausible analysis. I presume that's what the planners in the Reagan administration wanted, too. From their point of view, terrorism coming out of Lebanon is very beneficial. It frightens the American population. Terrorist acts are indeed loathsome, and if you cut people off from every possible option, you can predict pretty well that that's what they're going to do. So let's take, for example, the Karachi hijacking. It appears—we don't know for sure—as if the hijackers were victims of the Sabra Shatila massacre. Everybody knows what that was. That's what happens—you send killers into a defenseless civilian area for the purpose of slaughtering and torturing people, and those who survive are very likely to turn to terrorism, and that's in effect what happened. People pretend they don't understand, but anyone who can look at dates can figure it out. The Lebanese-based terrorism, mainly in Europe, since 1982 is a direct, predictable and probably desired effect of the U.S.-backed Israeli aggression in Lebanon, which eliminated the hope of a political settlement, demolished the civilian society and the PLO—brutally, I should say—and smashed to pieces what was left of Lebanon. Every time we look at terrorism there's a context, though virtually unreported here.

There's an interesting reaction here when this is

brought up: "You're justifying terrorism." I'm not justifying terrorism; justification and explanation are two different things. What you're pointing out is that there's an explanation for terrorism, and if you want to stop it you look at the explanation. When you look at the explanation you quite often find that violent, powerful states try to evoke terrorism because it's in their interest. That's no justification; it's an explanation. Terrorist acts are indeed loathsome. It was loathsome when Leon Klinghoffer was thrown off a boat in a wheelchair and killed on October 7, 1985. It was also loathsome when, a week earlier, Israel bombed Tunis and killed about 75 people using "smart" bombs that the United States probably supplied them. That's loathsome too. We regard one, but not the other, as terrorism, because one was retail terrorism on their side and the other wholesale terrorism on our side.

DB: *That particular attack, the Tunis bombing, is, of course, always framed in the concept of retaliation; it was a response, not initiated.*

Every terrorist act is *always* called retaliation. The sequence is as follows: first came a PLO attack in Larnaca, Cyprus, where three Israelis were killed. The killers were immediately caught and placed on trial; they're now in jail. About a week later came the Israeli bombing of Tunis in which, according to Israeli correspondents, about 75 people were killed, 20 Tunisians and 55 Palestinians, mostly civilians. Then, a week after that came the Achille Lauro hijacking with the Klinghoffer assassination. All three of these things were called retaliations by the people who did them. The Larnaca, Cyprus operation was called a retaliation for a fact which is suppressed here. Namely that the Israeli navy, apparently using agents based on Cyprus, has been hijacking boats for over ten years— that's called terrorism when the other guy does it—hijacking boats in transit between Cyprus and various parts of northern Lebanon. In fact, they have often taken Palestinians off those boats and handed them over to their own Maronite allies in Lebanon, who then killed them. The PLO claimed that Larnaca was in retaliation for the many years of hijacking, which certainly happened, there's no doubt. We didn't call that retaliation, we just called it terrorism.

Then came the Israeli bombing, which they called retaliation, except with one slight problem: it was not directed against the people who carried out the terrorist attack. In fact, Israel had conceded that the people they were bombing in Tunis apparently had nothing to do with the Larnaca attack. But it was a cheap target. The people who had to do with the attack probably came from Syria, but that's not a cheap target; they can fight back. Tunis, on the other hand, is a defenseless target, so you attack it. That's the way it's done. It was done, incidentally, with the complicity of the United States. The U.S. Sixth Fleet in the Mediterranean certainly had the Israeli bombers under surveillance. They claimed they couldn't see them, which was ridiculous. The Israelis had to fly all the way across the Mediterranean; they were refueled in flight, they passed by the most sophisticated radar and surveillance systems that the U.S. government and military can establish, and somehow we claimed that they were invisible. That's nonsensical; we obviously knew they were coming, and we didn't warn Tunis. Tunis is a loyal American ally, but we didn't warn them that the killers were on the way. Anyhow, they called that a retaliation, but of course it wasn't. It had nothing to do with the attack. Then came the Achille Lauro hijacking. They called that a retaliation, namely for the Tunis bombing, and you can trace it back as far as you like, go back to the first interaction, and every step is called by the terrorists a retaliation for what came before, and in a certain sense it is. That's the cycle: repression, violence, retaliation, more retaliation, preemption, etc.

In our ideological system, we have a very simple way to handle it. When the guys we don't like do it, it's terror. When the guys we do like do it, it's retaliation.

The Propaganda System

October 24, 1986

DB: *You've talked extensively about the politics of language and semantics, and you've said, "We have to peel away veil after veil of distortion to see the truth." My question is, in the age of Orwell, and given the U.S. educational system, what intellectual tools is that system providing to students to decode, decipher and translate those Orwellian terms?*

Let me first comment that, although we always, I too, call this the age of Orwell, the fact is that Orwell was a latecomer on the scene. The American public relations industry, which is a very sophisticated industry, already in the early 1920s was developing these tools, writing about them, and so on. In fact, even earlier, during the First World War, American historians offered themselves to President Woodrow Wilson to carry out a task that they called "historical engineering," meaning designing the facts of history so that they would serve state policy. That's Orwell, long before Orwell was writing. Shortly after that, American journalists like Walter Lippmann, the famous American journalist, said in 1921 that the art of democracy requires what he called "manufacture of consent," what the public relations industry calls "engineering of consent," another Orwellism meaning "thought control." The idea was that in a state in which the government can't control the people by force it had better control what they think. So, well before Orwell this was understood; the techniques were designed and had been implemented extensively.

As to what the schools teach to defend people against this, the answer is simple: zero. The schools are quite on the opposite side: they are part of the disinformation apparatus. In fact, this is well understood, too. It's even well understood by liberal intellectuals, democratic theorists, and so on. We've discussed in another interview the example of the important study called *Crisis of Democracy*, another Orwellism meaning "beginnings of democracy," published by the Trilateral Commission, a group of international, essentially liberal elites. They are people of whom Carter was a kind of representative, along with the ones who staffed his administration. They refer to the schools as institutions responsible for "the indoctrination of the young." Of course, they're talking to one another there; that's not what you say in public. But that's the way they're understood. They are institutions for indoctrination, for imposing obedience, for blocking the possibility of independent thought, and they play an institutional role in a system of control and coercion. *Real* schools ought to provide people with techniques of self-defense, but that would mean teaching the truth about the world and about the society, and schools couldn't survive very long if they did that.

DB: *C.P. Otero, who has edited a collection of your essays entitled* Radical Priorities, *has written in its preface, "The totalitarian system of thought control is far less effective than the democratic one, since the official doctrine parroted by the intellectuals at the service of the state is readily identifiable as pure propaganda, and this helps free the mind." In contrast, he writes, "the democratic system seeks to determine and limit the entire spectrum of thought by leaving the fundamental assumptions unexpressed. They are presupposed but not asserted."*

That's quite accurate. I've also written about that many times. Just think about it. Take, say, a country which is at the opposite end of the spectrum from us domestically, the Soviet Union. That's a country run by the bludgeon, essentially. It's a command state: the state controls, everybody basically follows orders. It's more complicated than that, but essentially that's the way it works. There, it's very easy to determine what propaganda is: what the state produces is propaganda. That's the kind of thing that Orwell described in *1984*. In a country like that, where there's a kind of Ministry of Truth, propaganda is very easily identifiable. Everybody knows what it is, and you can choose to repeat it if you like, but basically it's not really trying to control your thought very much; it's giving you the party line. It's saying, "Here's the official doctrine; as long as you don't disobey you won't get in trouble. What you think is not of great importance to anyone. If you get out of line we'll do something to you because we have force."

Democratic societies can't really work like that, because the state can't control behavior by force. It can to some extent, but it's much more limited in its capacity to control by force. Therefore, it has to control what you think. And again, democratic theorists have understood this for 50 or 60 years and have been very articulate about it. If the voice of the people is heard, you'd better control what that voice says, meaning you have to control what they think. The method Otero mentions there is one of the major methods. One of the ways you control what people think is by creating the illusion that there's a debate going on, but making sure that that debate stays within very narrow margins. Namely, you have to make sure that both sides in the debate accept certain assumptions, and those assumptions turn out to be the propaganda system. As long as everyone accepts the propaganda system, then you can have a debate.

The Vietnam War is a classic example. In the major media, the *New York Times* or CBS or whatever—in fact, all across the spectrum except at the very far-out periphery which reaches almost no one—in the major media which reach the overwhelming majority of the population, there was a lively debate. It was between people called "doves" and people called "hawks." The people called hawks said, "If we keep at it we can win." The people called doves said, "Even if we keep at it we probably can't win, and besides, it would probably be too costly for us, and besides maybe we're killing too many people," something like that. Both sides, the doves and the hawks, agreed on something: we have a right to carry out aggression against South Vietnam. In fact, they didn't even admit that it was taking place. They called it the "defense" of South Vietnam, using "defense" for "aggression" in the standard Orwellian manner. We were in fact attacking South Vietnam, just as much as the Russians are attacking Afghanistan. Like them, we first established a government that invited us in, and until we found one we had to overturn government after government. Finally we got one that invited us in, after we'd been there for years, attacking the countryside and the population. That's aggression. Nobody thought that was wrong, or rather, anyone who thought that was wrong was not admitted to the discussion. If you're a dove, you're in favor of aggression, if you're a hawk you're in favor of aggression. The debate between the hawks and the doves, then, is purely tactical: "Can we get away with it? Is it too bloody or too costly?" All basically irrelevant.

The real point is that aggression is wrong. When the Russians invaded Czechoslovakia, they got away with it. They didn't kill many people, but it was wrong because aggression is wrong. We all understand that. But we can't allow that understanding to be expressed when it relates to the violent actions of our state, obviously. If this were a totalitarian state, the Ministry of Truth would simply have said, "It's right for us to go into Vietnam, period. Don't argue with it." People would have known that's the propaganda system talking and they could have thought what they wanted. They could have seen that we were attacking Vietnam just like we can see that the Russians are attacking Afghanistan.

You couldn't permit that understanding of reality in

this country; it's too dangerous. People are much more free, they can express themselves, they can do things. Therefore, it was necessary to try to control thought, to try to make it appear as if the only issue was a tactical one: can we get away with it? There's no issue of right or wrong. That worked partially, but not entirely. Among the educated part of the population it worked almost totally.

There are good studies of this that show, with only the most marginal statistical error, that among the more educated parts of the population the government propaganda system was accepted unquestioningly. On the other hand, after a long period of popular spontaneous opposition, dissent and organization, the general population got out of control. As recently as 1982, according to the latest polls I've seen, over 70 percent of the population still was saying that the war was, quoting the wording of the Gallup poll, "fundamentally wrong and immoral," not "a mistake." That is, the overwhelming majority of the population is neither hawks nor doves, but opposed to aggression. On the other hand, the educated part of the population, they're in line. For them, it's just the tactical question of hawk *vs.* dove.

This is, incidentally, not untypical. Propaganda very often works better for the educated than it does for the uneducated. This is true on many issues. There are a lot of reasons for this, one being that the educated receive more of the propaganda because they read more. Another thing is that they are the agents of propaganda. After all, their job is that of commissars; they're supposed to be the agents of the propaganda system so they believe it. It's very hard to say something unless you believe it. Other reasons are that, by and large, they are just part of the privileged elite so they share their interests and perceptions, whereas the general population is more marginalized. It, by and large, doesn't participate in the democratic system, which is overwhelmingly an elite game. People learn from their own lives to be skeptical, and in fact most of them are. There's a lot of skepticism and dissent and so on.

Here's a case which is an interesting one because, while the technique of thought control worked very effectively, in fact to virtually 100 percent effectiveness among the educated part of the population, after many years of atrocities and massacres and hundreds of thousands of people killed and so on, it began to erode among the general population. There's even a name for that: it's called the "Vietnam Syndrome," a grave disease: people understand too much. But it's very striking, very illuminating to see how well it worked among the educated. If you pick up a book on American history and look at the Vietnam War, there is no such event as the American attack against South Vietnam. It's as if in the Soviet Union, say, in the early part of the 21st century, nobody will have ever said there was a Russian invasion of Afghanistan. Everyone says it's a Russian defense of Afghanistan. That's not going to happen. In fact, people already talk about the Russian invasion of Afghanistan—maybe they defend it, maybe not—but they admit that it exists. But in the United States, where the indoctrination system is vastly more effective, the educated part of the population can't even see that it exists. We cannot see that there was an American invasion of South Vietnam. It's out of history, down Orwell's memory hole.

DB: *Who engineers this, who pulls this off, who are the mandarins, or to use Gramsci's term, the "experts in legitimation"?*

The experts in legitimation, the ones who labor to make what people in power do seem legitimate, are mainly the privileged educated elites. The journalists, the academics, the teachers, the public relations specialists, this whole category of people have a kind of an institutional task, and that is to create the system of belief which will ensure the effective engineering of consent. And again, the more sophisticated of them say that. In the academic social sciences, for example, there's quite a tradition of explaining the necessity for the engineering of democratic consent. There are very few critics of this position. Among them is a well-known social scientist named Robert Dahl who has pointed out—as is obviously true—that if you have a political system in which you plug in the options from a privileged position, and that's democracy, it's indistinguishable from totalitarianism. It's very rare that people point that out.

In the public relations industry, which is a major industry in the United States and has been for a long time, 60 years or more, this is very well understood. In fact, that's their purpose. That's one of the reasons this is such a heavily polled society, so that business can keep its finger on the popular pulse and recognize that, if attitudes have to be changed, we'd better work on it. That's what public relations is for, very conscious, very well understood. When you get to what these guys call the institutions responsible for "the indoctrination of the young," the schools and the universities, at that point it becomes somewhat more subtle. By and large, in the schools and universities people believe they're telling the truth. The way that works, with rare exceptions, is that you cannot make it through these institutions unless you've accepted the indoctrination. You're kind of weeded out along the way. Independent thinking is encouraged in the sciences but discouraged in these areas. If people do it they're weeded out as radical or there's something wrong with them. It doesn't have to work 100 percent, in fact, it's even better for the system if there are a few exceptions here and there. It gives the illusion of debate or freedom. But overwhelmingly, it works.

In the media, it's still more obvious. The media, after all, are corporations integrated into some of the major corporations in the country. The people who own and manage them belong to the same narrow elite of owners and managers who control the private economy and who control the state, so it's a very narrow nexus of corporate media and state managers and owners. They share the same perceptions, the same understanding, and so on. That's one major point. So, naturally, they're going to perceive issues, suppress, control and shape in the interest of the groups that they represent: ultimately the interests of private ownership of the economy—that's where it's really based. Furthermore, the media also have a market: advertisers, not the public. People have to buy newspapers, but the newspapers are designed to get the public to buy them so that they can raise their advertising rates. The newspapers are essentially being sold to advertisers via the public. Since the corporation is selling it and its market is businesses, that's another respect in which the corporate system or the business system generally is going to be able to control the contents of the media. In other words, if by some unimaginable accident they began to get out of line, advertising would fall off, and that's a constraint.

State power has the same effect. The media want to maintain their intimate relation to state power. They want to get leaks, they want to get invited to the press conferences. They want to rub shoulders with the Secretary of State, all that kind of business. To do that, you've got to play the game, and playing the game means telling their lies, serving as their disinformation apparatus. Quite apart from the fact that they're going to do it anyway out of their own interest and their own status in the society, there are these kinds of pressures that force them into it. It's a very narrow system of control, ultimately.

Then comes the question of the individual journalist, you know, the young kid who decides to become an honest journalist. Well, you try. Pretty soon you are informed by your editor that you're a little off base, you're a little too emotional, you're too involved in the story, you've got to be more objective. There's a whole pile of code words for this, and what those code words mean is "Get in line, buddy, or you're out." Get in line means follow the party line. One thing that happens then is that people drop out. But those who decide to conform usually just begin to believe what they're saying. In order to progress you have to say certain things; what the copy editor wants, what the top editor is giving back to you. You can try saying it and not believing it, but that's not going to work, people just aren't that dishonest, you can't live with that, it's a very rare person who can do that. So you start saying it and pretty soon you're believing it because you're saying it, and pretty soon you're inside the system. Furthermore, there are plenty of rewards if you stay inside. For people who play the game by the rules in a rich society like this, there are ample rewards. You're well off, you're privileged, you're rich, you have prestige, you have a share of power if you want, if you like this kind of stuff you can go off and become the State Department spokesman on something or other, you're right near the center of at least privilege, sometimes power, in the richest, most powerful country in the world. You can go far, as long as you're very obedient and subservient and disciplined. So there are many factors, and people who are more independent are just going to drop off or be kicked out. In this case there are very few exceptions.

Let me just give you one example. In March 1986, came the major vote on contra aid. For the three months prior to that, the administration was heating up the atmosphere to try to reverse the congressional restrictions on aid to the terrorist army that's attacking Nicaragua, what they internally call a "proxy army," a proxy terrorist army attacking Nicaragua, which is of course what it is.—

DB: *Also called "freedom fighters."*

—To the public they call them freedom fighters. If

you look at the internal documents they're a proxy army engaged in terrorism, but that's internal, so I'll call them by the accurate internal terms: proxy terrorist army.

The question is: Could we reverse the congressional restrictions on this? That was the government's problem. The first three months of that year were very interesting in that respect: how were the media going to respond to the government campaign to try to reverse the congressional vote on contra aid. I was interested, so I took the two national newspapers, the *Washington Post* and the *New York Times,* and I went through all their opinion pieces, every column written by one of their own columnists, every authored submitted opinion piece and so on for January, February and March. There were 85. Of the 85, all were anti-Sandinista. On that issue, no discussion was even tolerable. So, 85 out of 85 followed the party line: Sandinistas are bad guys. Incidentally, it's interesting that there is one person of those 85 who has written elsewhere, in a more nuanced fashion, but not here. Perhaps he knows that he never could have gotten in unless he took that position. So on the major issue, Are we against the Sandinistas?: 100 percent control. Not a whisper of debate.

Now comes the next point. There are two very striking facts about the Sandinista government as compared with our allies in Central America: Honduras, Guatemala, El Salvador. These facts are undeniable, whatever you think about them. One is that the Sandinistas, among these Central American countries, are unique in that the government doesn't slaughter its population. That's just not open to discussion. That's a fact. Second, it's the only one of those countries in which the government has tried to direct services to the poor, has in fact diverted resources to social reform. Again, that's not under discussion. You can read that in the Inter-American Development Bank reports or anywhere you like. So these are two rather striking facts that differentiate Nicaragua from Guatemala, El Salvador and in fact even Honduras, where about half the population is starving to death. Those three countries, especially Guatemala and El Salvador, are among the world's worst terrorist states. In the 1980s, they have slaughtered maybe over 100,000 of their own citizens with ample U.S. support and great enthusiasm. They are simply violent, terrorist states. They don't do anything for their population except kill them. Honduras is more like a government where the rich rob the poor. They do some killing, but not on the scale of their major allies. Maybe half the population is starving.

In contrast, the Sandinista government, whatever you think about them, has not slaughtered the population and has diverted resources to them. That's a big difference. So the next thing I looked at was: How often were those two facts mentioned in these 85 editorials? The fact that the Sandinistas are radically different from our allies in that they don't slaughter their population was not mentioned once. No reference to that fact. The fact that they have carried out social services for the poor was referred to in two phrases in 85 columns, both sort of buried. One was an oblique reference which said that because of the contra war they can't do it any more. It didn't say what they were doing. The other was a passionate attack against the Sandinistas as totalitarian monsters and so forth and so on, which said that well, of course, they did divert resources to the poor. So, two phrases in 85 columns on that crucial issue. Zero phrases in 85 columns on the not-insignificant fact that, as distinct from our allies, they haven't slaughtered their population, they haven't killed 100,000 people. Again, that's really remarkable discipline.

After that, I went through all the editorials in the *New York Times* from 1980 to the present—just editorials—on El Salvador and Nicaragua, and it's essentially the same story. For example, in Nicaragua on October 15, 1985, the government instituted a state of siege. This is a country under attack by the regional superpower, and they did what we did in the Second World War in Hawaii: institute a state of siege. Not too surprising. There was a huge uproar: editorials, denunciations, it shows that they're totalitarian Stalinist monsters, and so on. Two days after that, on October 17, El Salvador *renewed* its state of siege. This is a state of siege that had been instituted in March 1980 and has been renewed monthly since, and it's far more harsh than the Nicaraguan state of siege. It blocks freedom of expression, freedom of movement, virtually all civil rights; it's the framework for mass slaughter within which the army we organized has carried out massive torture, slaughter, and is still doing it, in fact. All you have to do is look at the latest Amnesty International report.

So here, within two days, Nicaragua instituted a state of siege, and El Salvador renewed its state of siege under which they had carried out a major mass slaughter and torture campaign. The Nicaragua state of siege was a great atrocity; the El Salvador state of siege, which was far harsher in its measures and its application, literally was not mentioned. Furthermore, it has never been mentioned. There is not one word in about 180 editorials which mentions it, because that's our guys, so we can't talk about it. They're a budding democracy so they can't be having a state of siege. In fact, the editorial comment and the news reporting on El Salvador is that this is somehow a moderate centrist government which is under attack by terrorists of the left and terrorists of the right. It's complete nonsense. Every human rights investigation, the church in El Salvador, even the government itself in its own secret documents, concedes that the terrorism is by the centrist government; they are the terrorists. The death squads are simply the security squads. Duarte is a front for terrorists, as he knows. But you can't say that publicly because it gives the wrong image. You can go on and on, but these are very dramatic examples of the utter servility of the media right at the top. They will not even permit opinion pieces, not only editorials, even opinion pieces won't be permitted which stray from the party line, because it's just too dangerous.

Similarly, throughout the whole Vietnam War there was never an opinion piece in the *New York Times* or any other newspaper that I know of that said that the United States was wrong to attack South Vietnam. Here's a research project for someone: if you can find one word in any opinion piece in any American newspaper or in the media, I'd be very surprised. I haven't read everything, of course, but I've been following it pretty closely for years, and I've never seen it.

DB: *Is the control of capital the source, the bedrock of power in the American state?*

Certainly, there's no doubt of it. The first Chief Justice of the Supreme Court and the President of the Constitutional Convention, John Jay, expressed it very accurately: he said, "The people who own the country ought to govern it." And that's the way it works. There are all sorts of mechanisms. For one thing, they have the resources to participate in politics. They can get information, they can put pressure, they can lobby, they can build platforms. They, in fact, are the real market for the political parties, they allow the parties to survive. They staff the executive, by and large. They staff Congress even. Furthermore, if any government ever got out of line, even in the slightest way, they could stop it simply by cutting back investment, by capital flight, and so on. Here this isn't a problem, because the corporations so totally own the government that it never gets out of line. But in other countries, especially third world countries, that problem sometimes arises, and then very quickly, if the government tries to carry out social reform, it's stopped. Why? Just a little bit of capital flight is enough to do it, and it means the country grinds to a halt. So an effective control over the basic decisions in the society is in private hands, narrowly concentrated, that's going to control the state.

Historical Engineering

October 24, 1986

DB: *The rewards for playing ball with the system in this society and this culture are very clear. The financial rewards are obvious. We've talked about the prestige and class rewards as well. What about the other side of the coin? What about the punishments?*

Societies differ. For example, in the Soviet Union the punishments for honest dissidence are that you may very well end up in a psychiatric prison or in exile under ugly conditions. If you're a dissident in a typical American satellite like El Salvador, you're likely to find yourself in a ditch tortured after hideous mutilation. In the United States those are not the punishments. Here again we still have to make distinctions. If you're a black organizer in the ghetto you can be assassinated by the national political police or at least with their complicity, as happened with Fred Hampton in Chicago in 1969, a straight Gestapo-style assassination of a sleeping man, probably drugged, in a 4 a.m. attack by the police, coordinated with the FBI. In fact the black movement was decimated by government terrorism, a lot of that's pretty well documented. If you're essentially defenseless you can be subjected to a fair amount of violence, nothing like El Salvador, of course, but not so trivial either.

DB: *Or there's the example in your home town of Philadelphia, the first domestic air raid in American history.*

Yes, that's another one. It can happen, but it's not on the scale of a state that really terrorizes its own citizens. If you come from the more privileged classes, if you're a white middle-class person, then the chances that you are going to be subjected to literal state terror are very slight. It could happen, but it's slight. What will happen is that you'll be marginalized, excluded. Instead of becoming part of the privileged elite, you'll be driving a taxi cab. It's not torture, but very few people are going to select that option, if they have a choice. And the ones who do select it will never be heard from again. Therefore they are not part of the indoctrination system. They don't make it. It could be worse, but it's enough to discipline people.

DB: *Generally speaking your books are ignored. They're not reviewed. You're not invited on* Face the Nation *or the evening news with Dan Rather, nor are you interviewed on* National Public Radio. *The few times that your books are reviewed, they are neither favorable or accurate. An example here, one is a* New York Times *review of* Turning the Tide *written by Alan Tonelson, who is the associate editor of* Foreign Policy *magazine. He begins the review by calling you a "new left stalwart" and then he says that the evidence that you present in your book is a "clip job drawn from secondary sources, source histories, from news articles and reports from the usual assortment of liberal and left-leaning, Latin American human rights groups." Is that typical?*

It's surprising it was reviewed at all, but that's a typical sort of putdown. All you have to do is to look at the footnotes to see how false it is. First of all, the "left-leaning human rights groups" are the standard human rights groups. There's nothing "left-leaning" about Americas Watch. From his point of view they are "left-leaning" because they criticize Western as well as Eastern atrocities. And that, of course, is "left-leaning." As for it being a "clip job," like every scholarly work, I deal with original sources, which are press reports of ongoing events. Exactly the same is true in the most honored works of scholarship.

Furthermore, there is plenty of use made of unused primary sources, suppressed primary sources. For example, government documents that would never be used in the mainstream because they tell the wrong story. It's not because it's me. Any critic of the party line must meet very high standards. If you're following the party line you don't have to document anything; you can say anything you feel like. There are major books, well reviewed, highly regarded, which are just an expression of opinion. There is nothing in them that you can even trace to its source, but that doesn't matter as long as you're producing the party line. That's one of the privileges you get for obedience.

On the other hand, if you're critical of received opinion, you have to document every phrase. He also later in the review calls my writing "turgid." That's correct; part of the reason it's turgid is because every three words I have to have a footnote with big documentation explaining it. On the other hand, if you're on the other side you can just pay attention to style, because it doesn't matter what you say.

I should say, incidentally, that I benefit from that privilege, too. So that when I write critically of the Soviet Union I don't have to document anything, nobody ever cares. They think it's fine. Since you're attacking the enemy, why do you have to document anything? And if you're always within the party line you never have to document anything. But the main point of interest about the review is his total incapacity to perceive the words. In fact, if you read through the review he never takes issue with any thing I say, this looks correct, and so on. But he says I'm missing the point because I don't explain how the United States should defend the national interest. He says something like, "Since he doesn't offer an alternative to defending the national interest, there's something missing, missing the point."

In fact I discussed that matter at great length. I pointed out that the phrase "national interest" is an Or-wellism used to refer to the interests of corporate elites. If I had more space there I'd give a lot of documentation of it, and I said that of course in that sense of national interest the citizens of the country shouldn't want to defend it. It's often opposed to their interests. But he cannot understand that. A deeply indoctrinated person, a real sign of deep indoctrination is that you can't understand elementary thoughts that any 10-year-old can understand. That's real indoctrination. So for him it's kind of like a theological truth, a truth of received religion, that the national interest is what we should defend. Suppose I say "everyone like you is using the term 'national interest' in a very deceitful way, it's not in the interest of the nation. It's the interest of a powerful privileged group, maybe this is the right way to defend their interests, but I'm not interested in defending their interests. I'm interested in defending the interests of the population of the United States, in fact the world, so I don't have to answer to your question. I don't have to provide a better way to serve the interests of the corporate elite. I'm just not interested in that question." He cannot understand that. It's not that he has an answer. He cannot understand the point. It's too far out of the way of thinking.

In this respect there's been a very sharp decline since the Middle Ages. In the Middle Ages, when you read Thomas Aquinas, he felt that he had to deal with heresy. He wanted to defend the doctrines of the faith against heresy, but he felt he had to understand it. Medieval theology had some aspects of an honest intellectual atmosphere: if people had heretical arguments you had to pay attention to them, think about them, find answers to them.

We've degenerated far below that in modern culture. Here you don't have to understand heresy, you just point to it, you just say, "Look, this guy's involved in heresy," and that's the end of that discussion. Now we go on. That wouldn't have been tolerated in more honest and intellectually advanced societies such as medieval theology. And this is another sign of the dramatic decline of the intelligentsia as they become the commissars for external power, state or private. The review is a fine example of it.

DB: *Another example was Michael Mandelbaum's 1982* New York Times *review of your book* Towards a New Cold War. *This book is one of the most heavily and carefully documented books I've ever read. Mandelbaum really doesn't deal with any of the substantive issues you raise, but he accuses you by saying "if the book has a consistent theme at all, it's one of anger." So you're an angry person, and we know how to deal with angry people, just dismiss them.*

That incidentally is true. I don't pretend not to be angry. When I'm talking about torture, mass murder and slaughter and so on, I am angry. If I have to express it, fine. I'm not trying to deceive anyone. But the point you make is quite accurate: Somehow they have to get rid of the stuff. You can't deal with the arguments, that's plain, for one thing you have to know something, and most of these people don't know anything. Secondly, you wouldn't be able to answer the arguments because they're correct. Therefore what you have to do is somehow dismiss it. So that's one technique, "It's just emotional, it's irresponsible, it's angry." In fact, it's a very striking fact that books that really are emotional, that don't try to document, get a much better press. Those are honest and important books. If somebody comes out with a sermon, saying "I hate the war in El Salvador, it drives me up the wall, I don't want to see any more people tortured," that book will get a good review, because it's very unthreatening.

DB: *Joan Didion's book* Salvador *was precisely like that.*

Yes, that gets good reviews because it's unthreatening. It doesn't direct attention to the reality of what's happening. It's something over there, you know, some atrocities going on over there. Oh, it's horrible. It makes me feel awful. But that atrocity is not going on over there, it's going on in Washington, in New York and Chicago, just as the atrocities in Afghanistan are going on in Moscow, not in Kabul. As long as you don't get people to understand that, you're all right, but as soon as you point out that those atrocities are systematic, they have happened over and over again, they've happened in the same ways, we have a lot of documentation to explain why American planners want those atrocities to go on in that way. As soon as you put it in the framework of consistent systematic history and institutional structure that leads to it, especially when you give them the documentation to prove it, then you've got to be eliminated, because that might get people to understand something.

On the other hand, it's interesting, they especially do this with women, like Joan Didion. If a woman writes a book which has an emotional character to it, that's terrific, like "Oh well, look at this, we understand about women, so emotional, so they get upset about these things, but that's because they don't understand the harsh realities, and so on, so that's fine."

DB: *Let's talk about the peace and student movements of the 1960s. You've made a number of statements about them and I'd like you to further explain them. You say that the peace and student movements of the 1960s "changed consciousness and raised the cultural and moral level of the country. It changed the character of the country, probably permanently." In what ways?*

There was a very striking improvement in the intellectual, cultural and moral climate of the country. You can see this in all kinds of ways. It wasn't just the student movement. There were also all the popular movements that developed in that period—the women's movement, the environmental movement, this whole complex of groups of which the students and the youth were a central and early component. For one thing, we are now able to face, at least, certain forms of repression and coercion and atrocities that we couldn't face before. The women's move-ment is a perfect example of that. Sexist oppression ex-isted before 1970, but it wasn't an issue to the extent it is now. It still exists but it's a big issue, and undoubtedly consciousness has been changed on that.

Take something more remote, the treatment of na-tive Americans. Here's an interesting fact if you think about it. The United States is founded on the destruction of the native population. Before Columbus the population north of the Rio Grande was maybe 12-15 million. At the turn of the century it was 200,000. The whole history of the conquest of the continent from the time that the saintly Pilgrims landed is destruction of the native popu-lation by various means, sometimes just plain mass slaughter, like the Pequot Massacre by the Puritans or George Washington's destruction of the Iroquois civiliza-tion right in the middle of the War of Independence, and many later events running through the conquest of the national territory. Sometimes it was criminal expulsion like Jackson's expulsion of the Cherokees, really hard-line things. Anyway, that's the history. That was not under discussion, it's hard to remember now, but it was dis-cussed in the context of cowboy and Indian movies. The Indians were the bad guys, the cowboys were the good guys. That's two hundred years, three hundred years in fact, that we couldn't come to terms with it. Even scholar-ship couldn't.

Incidentally, this changed in the 1970s. For the first time it has become possible to give a relatively honest account of the interaction between the European conquer-ors and the native population whom they destroyed. There is still a long way to go, but it's beginning. While you can find occasional examples over the past few centuries, a book here and there, the mythology was intact in the scholarly world and popular consciousness until the rise in cultural level. Sometimes this is true in an astonishing fashion. For example, the Declaration of Independence, which we print on a full page every July 4th and everyone reads in elementary school and so on. We went 200 years, as far as I know, before anyone, at least anyone I can find, noticed a rather amazing fact about that document. In the Bill of Indictment against King George of England, he is accused of "unleashing the merciless Indian savages against us with their known methods of warfare," which are extermination and so on. That's a statement of astonishing cowardice and fantastic deceit. As the framers of the Constitution well knew, it was the merciless European savages, and their ancestors and descendants, with their methods of warfare—destruction of men, women and children—that was unleashed against the native population. This inversion went on unnoticed. I don't know anything in the American literary or historical tradition that even commented on it. Probably there's something somewhere, but I can't find it.

In the 1970s people finally noticed that for 200 years we had been living a violent, cowardly lie, not a marginal one. It's not marginal that the native population was wiped out in the course of the conquest of the national territory.

The same awareness of lies happened on other historical issues. It became possible to have a more honest look at the Philippine war, a war of slaughter, hundreds of thousands killed, not a great victory. It became possible for the first time to begin to look at Woodrow Wilson's war in Haiti and the Dominican Republic, brutal murderous counterinsurgency wars. The counterinsurgency war in Greece in the late 1940s, with tens of thousands of people killed and 60,000 sent to what were then called re-education camps where they were tortured or executed, and the political system destroyed and the labor unions destroyed. That was a hidden story until the late 1970s. We could go on in case after case. There was an awakening, a willingness to face some of the realities of the world.

DB: *What do you attribute that to?*

I attribute it to the rise in the cultural level caused by the student movement and other associated movements. It just broke down a lot of barriers and made it possible for people to think.

DB: *Has not the American state attempted to reconstruct the past and destroy that memory?*

Very definitely, absolutely. There has been a major campaign on every issue to try to restore order and obedience. Among the educated elites it has basically worked, but of course they have never deviated very much either, so there wasn't far to go. Among much of the population it's worked partially but not too much. For example, they have finally succeeded in reconstituting a kind of jingoist consensus, an atmosphere of fear and terror in which people say, "Let's go out and kill the bastards." They have succeeded in instituting that.

But they haven't overcome the understanding or even the sympathy for oppressed people or even the opposition to atrocities. The population is just a lot more sophisticated. I can see that myself in the talks that I give. I've been doing this for a long time. During the 1960s and early 1970s, at the peak activity of the peace movement, if I was talking to selected peace movement audiences, radicals, I could not say the things that I say to general audiences today. The kind of things I'm saying now, for example, I could never have said to a public audience or even for that matter to most peace movement audiences, even at its height. What's happened is that there's been a general change; you can approach people much more honestly, especially those who are not part of the tiny educated, privileged elite who are immune—you can't talk to them. But apart from that, much of the population has changed significantly, and I think and I hope that that's a permanent thing.

DB: *After the Vietnam War ended you wrote a number of essays predicting the attempts of the American state to reconstruct what had happened in Indochina. Have those attempts been successful?*

I think they have been successful among the educated elite. In the general population, I think much less so, but they don't matter much. It's important to bear in mind that most of the population is marginal; they're not part of the system, they just watch. The politically active parts of the population are the ones who are really dangerous. As long as the population is unorganized, apathetic, marginalized, doesn't do anything—

DB: *Watching TV.*

Nobody really cares what they think. They're just not part of the system. It's the articulate, educated elites, the groups that are politically active, that can make a difference. Those are the ones you have to watch. Among them, the reconstruction of history has been very successful, but then, it didn't have far to go.

DB: *In an op-ed article in the August 10, 1986* New York Times, *George McGovern, very much associated with opposition to the Vietnam War, wrote, "I am anguished over our disastrous involvement in Vietnam. Only history and providence will know finally who was right or wrong on that tragic issue." What do you think of that?*

That's rather consistent throughout. McGovern was not an early opponent of the Vietnam War. In the hard, early years of opposition, before it became a popular issue, before even much of the business community turned against it on grounds of cost, he wasn't particularly visible. He was in fact marginal in the hard years. Later he came along, I'm sure honestly, but I think that his position probably expresses his feeling quite accurately. For him it's a question of who was right.

DB: *And if it's left for history, given what we've been talking about, the engineering of history...*

They'll take care of it.

DB: *Don't you find it odd that there's little expression of anguish for the peoples of Vietnam, Laos and Cambodia, whose countries were turned into free-fire zones?*

That's true of all the discussion. There's a big fuss, and there should be, about American veterans who have suffered under Agent Orange. However, there's a slight observation that might be made, and that is that the people of Vietnam suffered a thousand times as much, and we're certainly not trying to help them, in fact we want to increase their suffering.

DB: *What did you think of the PBS series on Vietnam?*

I thought it was cheap propaganda and vulgar nonsense. On the early parts of the war, the French parts, it was pretty accurate. They were able to deal with a French war.

DB: *That's safe.*

That's safe. As soon as it got to the American war, it shifted over into the mainstream propaganda system. Some talk about atrocities, individual atrocities, which is not terribly important. Individual soldiers in the field who are fighting under horrible conditions are almost certain to conduct atrocities in every war. It's easy to blame them, we sit here in comfort and the grunts in the field kill somebody and we get all upset.

The real atrocities were carried on in Washington, and they were basically two: First was a war crime, the crime for which people were hanged at Nuremberg, namely aggression. Second was crimes against humanity, that is, planned attacks, organized in Washington, with the purpose of mass murder and slaughter. Crimes for which people were hanged at Nuremberg. Those weren't discussed, and there was no political context for it. Actually, I wrote a long review of the book that was the companion for it, by Stanley Karnow. In his view it was a noble cause, failed effort, only history will tell, etc. The whole thing is falsified. In fact, incident by incident, even the particular incidents are falsified, case by case after case. The truth doesn't matter. And also there's no documentation, no support, no nothing. The arguments are often ridiculous.

If a book of that caliber were written critical of the United States, it would be demolished across the board as communist propaganda of the most absurd sort. But here it's considered a sober, careful analysis, somewhat on the liberal side. In fact the whole thing had to be attacked from the right because it was too liberal. It's very interesting that the series and the book were subjected to two attacks: one from the right and one from the left. The one from the right was real nonsense, even worse than the original series.

DB: *By the organization Accuracy in Media.*

It was childish, in fact, it was embarrassing. I've gone through the transcript and will write about it some day [see *Manufacturing Consent,* 1988]. But it was really infantile and embarrassing. Nevertheless it had to be aired. The critique on the other side, what is called the "left," although I don't like the word, said, "Look, this thing is biased toward government propaganda." That one was honest, accurate, very well documented, but didn't have to be answered. There was a reason for that. Power lies on the right. That's where the takeover bids are. That's where the control over capital is. So that argument you've got to deal with. The argument on the other side has no power behind it, and since truth and honesty are total irrelevancies, you can forget about it.

DB: *You just mentioned the left and being a bit uncomfortable using that term; in a lecture at Oberlin in 1969 you quoted Orwell as saying, "Political thought, especially on the left, is a sort of masturbation fantasy in which the world hardly matters." You added, "That's true, unfortunately, and it's part of the reason that our society lacks a genuine left-wing movement." Do you still feel that way?*

I don't like terms like "right" and "left," especially in the United States. I don't think they mean very much. But if we mean by the left what it historically meant, that is, that component of the body politic which is concerned with defending human rights, increasing democracy, increasing public control over the major decisions in the society, including democratization of the private economy, placing it under public, democratic control, workers' control of production, community control over their affairs. If we are talking about left in that sense, that is, an extension of the movement towards popular democracy and popular control to new and other spheres, overcoming authority and repression and autocratic structures and so on, if that's what we mean by the left, there isn't much of it in the United States. And it doesn't have a well-established intellectual tradition and has no institutions to speak of. But there's a good reason for that: they have no power. They have no control over resources. They essentially have no wealth, and therefore they cannot develop institutions of a sustaining nature. They can't develop a literature. They can't learn, they can't improve over time. Everything starts from the beginning all the time. That's the genius of a society in which power is overwhelmingly in the hands of the owners of the private economy and all the institutions, including the political parties, are subservient to them.

The comment that Orwell made remains true to a certain extent, perhaps not as strong as those words indicate, and that again is a reflection of the nature of power. You can have brilliant works produced on the left, and there have been some, but they're kind of irrelevant. They're down the memory hole, too. They can't reach people, people can't use them and can't understand them. They're just too far off the received doctrinal position that's associated with real power.

Israel, the Holocaust and Anti-Semitism

October 24, 1986

DB: *One of your books,* The Fateful Triangle, *focuses specifically on the Middle East, and I was wondering if you could talk about your position on a possible two-state solution to the Palestinian question.*

I don't think that's the optimal solution, but it has been the realistic political settlement for some time. We have to begin with some fundamentals here. The real situation is: there are plainly two national groups that claim the right of self-determination in what used to be Palestine, roughly the area now occupied by Israel minus the Golan Heights, which is part of Syria. One group is the indigenous population, or what's left of it—a lot of it's been expelled or driven out or fled. The other group is the Jewish settlers who came in, originally from Europe, later from other parts of the Middle East and some other places. Both groups claim the right of national self-determination.

Here we have to make a crucial decision: are we racists or aren't we? If we're not racists, then the indigenous population has the same rights of self-determination as the settlers who replaced them. Some might claim more, but let's say at least as much right. Hence if we are not racist, we will try to press for a solution which accords them—we'll say they are human beings with equal rights, therefore they both merit the claim to national self-determination. I'm granting that the settlers have the same rights as the indigenous population; many do not find that obvious but let's grant it.

Then there are a number of possibilities. One possibility is a democratic secular society. Virtually nobody is in favor of that. Some people say they are, but if you look closely they're not really. There are various models for multi-ethnic societies, Switzerland, for example. And maybe in the long run these might be the best idea, but they're unrealistic. The only realistic political settlement, for the time being, in the past ten or twelve years, that would satisfy the right of self-determination for both national groups is a two-state settlement. Everybody knows what it would have to be: Israel within approximately the pre-June 1967 borders and a Palestinian state in the West Bank and the Gaza Strip, and a return of the Golan Heights to Syria, or maybe some other arrangement. This would be associated with maybe demilitarized zones and international guarantees of some sort or another, but that's the framework of a possible political settlement.

As I say, I don't think it's the best one, but that's the realistic one, very realistic. It's supported by most of the world. It's supported by Europe, by the Soviet Union, by almost all the non-aligned countries. It's supported by all the major Arab states and has been for a long time, supported by the mainstream of the PLO and again has been for a long time. It's supported even by the American population, by about two to one according to the polls.

But there are also people who oppose it. It's opposed by the rejection front in the Arab world, the minority elements of the PLO, Libya, a few other minority rejectionist elements. But crucially it's opposed by the leaders of the rejection front, namely the United States and Israel. The United States and Israel adamantly oppose it. The United States will not consider it. Both political groupings in Israel reject it totally. They reject any right of national self-determination for the indigenous population in the former Palestine. They can have Jordan if they want, or the former Syria, or something, but not the area that they now hold under military occupation.

In fact they're explicit about it. There are carefully fostered illusions here that the Labor Party is interested in compromise over the issue. But if you look closely, there's no meaningful compromise. The position of the Labor Party remains what was expressed by their representative, who is now President, Chaim Herzog, who said that "no one can be a partner with us in a land that has been holy to our people for 2000 years." That's their position. They're willing to make minor adjustments. They don't want to take care of the population in the West Bank, because there are too many Arabs. They don't want a lot of Arabs around. So what they would like to do is take the areas and the water and the resources they want from the West Bank but leave the population either stateless or under Jordanian control. That's what's called a "compromise solution." It's a very cynical proposal, even worse in many respects than annexation.

But here that's called compromise and the reason is that we are educated elites in the United States and national discussion takes a strictly racist view of this. The Palestinians are not human. They do not deserve the rights that we accord automatically to the settlers who displaced them. That's the basis of articulate American discussion: pure, unadulterated racism. Again, that's not true of the population, as usual, but it is of the politically active and articulate parts of it and certainly the government. As long as the United States and Israel reject the political settlement, there can't be one.

There certainly have been very plausible opportunities for a political settlement over many years. Just to mention a few which have disappeared from history because they're too inconvenient:

● In February 1971 President Sadat of Egypt offered a full peace treaty to Israel on the pre-June 67 borders. In accordance with official American policy, incidentally, but not operative policy, offering nothing to the Palestinians, he didn't even offer them a Palestinian state, nothing. Nevertheless Israel rejected it, and the United States backed them in that rejection.

● In January 1976 Syria, Jordan and Egypt, the so-called "confrontation states," made a proposal in the U.N. Security Council for a two-state settlement with international guarantees and territorial rights secured and so on. That was backed and even prepared by the PLO, supported by the Soviet Union and most of the world. It was vigorously opposed by Israel, which even boycotted the session. In fact, it bombed Lebanon in retaliation against the United Nations, killing about 50 people, with no excuse at all, in a fit of anger, "We're going to kill anybody who gets in our way if you push this," and the United States vetoed it.

There have been a series of such things ever since. The United States has always blocked them and Israel has always refused them, and that means there's no political settlement. Rather there is a state of permanent military confrontation. Aside from what it means to the Palestinians, which is obvious and terrible, it's very bad for Israel. It's leading to their own destruction, in my view, certainly to their economic collapse and moral degeneration and probably sooner or later their physical destruction. You can't have a state of military confrontation without a defeat sooner or later. It's leading the world very close to nuclear war, repeatedly. Every time we have an Arab-Israeli conflict—and there will be more of them, as long as we maintain a military confrontation—the Soviet Union and the United States come into confrontation. Both are involved. The Soviet Union is close by, not like in Central America. It's a strategic region right near their border and they're involved. It's very far from us but it's a strategic region for us because of the oil nearby, primarily. So we're involved. The fleets come into confrontation, it's very close. In 1967 it came very close to nuclear war and it will again. So it's very dangerous, it's the most likely spot where a nuclear war would develop, but we are pursuing it, because we don't want a political settlement. The United States is intent on maintaining a military confrontation.

DB: *You've mentioned racism vis-à-vis the Palestinians. To what extent, if any, have Israelis of Ashkenazic origin absorbed German racial attitudes toward not just Arabs but even to the Oriental Jews, the Sephardim?*

I wouldn't call it particularly German—

DB: *European?*

Yes. It's part of European culture to have racist attitudes toward the Third World. We're part of Europe in that respect. Naturally the Jewish community shared the attitudes of the rest of Europe, not surprising. There certainly are such things inside Israel. My feeling is they could be overcome in time under a situation of peace. I think they're real, but I don't think they're lethal. Through slow integration they could probably be overcome.

The one that probably can't be overcome is the anti-Arab racism, because that requires subjugation of a defeated and conquered people and that leads to racism. If you're sitting with your boot on somebody's neck, you're going to hate him, because that's the only way that you can justify what you're doing, so subjugation automatically yields racism, and you can't overcome that. Furthermore, anti-Arab racism is rampant in the United States and much of the West. There's no question about that. The only kind of racism that can be openly expressed with outrage is anti-Arab racism. You don't put caricatures of blacks in the newspapers any more; you do put caricatures of Arabs.

DB: *But isn't it curious that they're using the old Jewish stereotypes, the money coming out of the pockets, the beards, the hooked nose?*

I've often noticed that the cartoons and caricatures are very similar to the ones you'd find in the Nazi press about the Jews, very similar.

DB: *What dimension does the Holocaust play in this equation? Is it manipulated by the Israeli state to promote its own interests?*

It's very consciously manipulated. I mean, it's quite certainly real, there's no question about that, but it is also undoubted that they manipulate it, in fact they say so. For example, in the *Jerusalem Post,* in English so you can read it, their Washington correspondent Wolf Blitzer, I don't recall the exact date but it was after one of the big Holocaust memorial meetings in Washington, wrote an article in which he said it was a great success. He said, "Nobody mentioned arms sales to the Arabs but all the Congressmen understood that that was the hidden message. So we got it across."

One very conservative and very honest Zionist leader, Nachum Goldman, spoke about this manipulation. He was the President of the World Zionist Organization and was detested towards the end of his life because he was much too honest—they even refused to send a delegation to his burial, I believe, or a message. He's one of the founders of the Jewish state and the Zionist movement and one of the elder statesmen. Just before his death in 1982 or so, he made a rather eloquent and unusual statement in which he said that it's—he used the Hebrew word for "sacrilege"—sacrilege to use the Holocaust as a justification for oppressing others. He was referring to something very real, exploitation of probably the world's most horrifying atrocity in order to justify oppression of others. That kind of manipulation is really sick.

DB: *That disturbs you and...*

Really sick. Many people find it deeply immoral but most people are afraid to say anything about it. Nachum Goldman is one of the few who was able to say anything about it and it was one of the reasons he was hated. Anyone who tries to say anything about it is going to be subjected to a very efficient defamation campaign of the sort that would have made the old communist party open-mouthed in awe. People don't talk about it.

DB: *I ask you this question because I know that you have been plagued and hounded around the United States specifically on this issue of the Holocaust. It's been said that Noam Chomsky is somehow agnostic on the issue of whether the Holocaust occurred or not.*

My "agnosticism" is in print. I described the Holocaust years ago as the most fantastic outburst of insanity in human history, so much so that if we even agree to discuss the matter we demean ourselves. Those statements and numerous others like them are in print, but they're basically irrelevant because you have to understand that this is part of a Stalinist-style technique to silence critics of the holy state and therefore the truth is entirely irrelevant, you just tell as many lies as you can and hope that some of the mud will stick. It's a standard technique used by the Stalinist parties, by the Nazis and by these guys.

DB: *There's tremendous support for Israel in the United States at least in elite groups. There's also on another level a very steady, virulent anti-Semitism that goes on. Can you talk about that?*

Anti-Semitism has changed, during my lifetime at least. Where I grew up we were virtually the only Jewish family, I think there was one other. Of course being the only Jewish family in a largely Irish-Catholic and German-Catholic community—

DB: *In Philadelphia?*

In Philadelphia. And the anti-Semitism was very real. There were certain paths I could take to walk to the store without getting beaten up. It was the late 1930s and the area was openly pro-Nazi. I remember beer parties when Paris fell and things like that. It was not like living under Hitler, but it was a very unpleasant thing. There was a really rabid anti-Semitism in that neighborhood where I grew up as a kid and it continued. By the time I got to Harvard in the early 1950s there was still very detectable anti-Semitism. It wasn't that they beat you up on the way to school or something, but other ways, kind of Waspish anti-Semitism. There were very few Jewish professors on the faculty at that time. There was beginning to be a scattering of them, but still very few. This was the tail end of a long time of Waspish anti-Semitism at the elite institutions.

Over the last thirty years that's changed very radically. Anti-Semitism undoubtedly exists, but it's now on a par, in my view, with other kinds of prejudice of all sorts. I don't think it's more than anti-Italianism or anti-Irishism, and that's been a very significant change in the last generation, one that I've experienced myself in my own life, and it's very visible throughout the society.

DB: *How would you account for that?*

How would I account for it? I think partly that the Holocaust did have an effect. It brought out the horrifying consequences of anti-Semitism in a way that certainly is striking. I presume, I can't prove this, but there must be, at least I hope there is, a kind of guilt feeling involved, because the role of the United States during the Holocaust was awful, before and during. They didn't act to save Jews, and they could have in many respects. The role of the Zionist Organization is not very pretty either. In the late 1940s there were plenty of displaced persons (DP) in the Jewish DP camps, some survived. It remained awful. They stayed in the DP camps. For a while they were dying at almost the same rate they were under the Nazis.

Many of those people, if they had been given a chance, surely would have wanted to come to the United States. There are debates about how many, but it's just unimaginable that if they'd been given a chance they wouldn't have wanted to come here. They didn't. Only a tiny scattering came. There was an immigration bill, the Stratton bill, which I think admitted about 400,000 people, if I remember, to the United States, very few Jews among them.

Plenty of Nazis were admitted, incidentally, straight out of their SS uniforms. The reason that bill passed, I think it was 1947, was that it was the beginning of the Cold War and priority was being given to the Nazis, because we were resurrecting them all over the world. A lot of them were brought in, a lot of Nazi war criminals, and others, but very few Jews. That's not a very pretty sight. You say, during the war you could have given some argument, not an acceptable argument, but you could have argued that you had to fight the war and not worry about the people being sent to the gas chambers. But after the war you couldn't give any argument. It was a matter of saving the survivors, and we didn't do it.

I should say the Zionist Organization didn't support it either. They didn't even lobby for the bill. The only Jewish organizations that lobbied for the admission of Jewish refugees to the United States were the non-Zionist or the anti-Zionist organizations. The reason was that the Zionist Organization wanted to send them off to Palestine.

Whether they wanted to go there or not is another story, the same matter being relived today, incidentally, with the Russian emigres. The Zionist Organization wants to force them to go to Israel. Most of them, especially from the European parts of Russia, want to come to the United States, and all sorts of pressures are being brought to bear to prevent that. It's kind of a reenactment at a less hideous level of the same story.

I suppose there's some element of guilt, certainly over the Holocaust and maybe over the post-war matter. Besides that, the Jewish community has changed socially and economically. It's now become substantial, not huge in numbers, but given its numbers it's a substantial part of the dominant privileged elite groups in every part of the society—professional, economic, political, etc. It's not like the anti-Semitic stereotype, they don't own the corporations, but relative to the numbers they're very influential, particularly in the ideological system, lots of writers, editors, etc. and that has an effect.

Furthermore, I think it's changed because of what's happened since 1967. In 1967 Israel won a dramatic military victory, demonstrated its military power, in fact smashed up the entire Arab world, and that won great respect. A lot of Americans, especially privileged Americans, love violence and want to be on the side of the guy with the gun. And here was a powerful, violent state that smashed up its enemies and demonstrated that it was the dominant military power in the Middle East, put those Third World upstarts in their place. This was particularly dramatic because that was 1967, a time when the United States was having only minimal success in carrying out its invasion of by then all of Indochina, and it's well worth remembering that elite opinion, including liberal opinion, overwhelmingly supported the war in Vietnam and was quite disturbed by the incapacity of the United States to win it, at least at the level they wanted. Israel came along and showed them how to do it, and that had a symbolic effect. Since then it has been presenting itself, with some justice, as the Sparta of the Middle East, a militarily advanced, technologically competent, powerful society. That's the kind of thing we like.

It also became a strategic asset of the United States. One of the reasons why the United States maintains the military confrontation is to assure that it's a dependable, reliable ally that will do what we want, like, say, support genocide in Guatemala or whatever, and that also increases the respect for Israel and with it tends to diminish anti-Semitism. I suppose that's a factor.

DB: *But you've pointed out that as long as U.S. state interests are being served and preserved, Israel will be favored, but the moment that those interests…*

That's right, it'll be finished, in fact, anti-Semitism will shoot up. Apart from the moral level, it's a very fragile alliance on tactical grounds.

DB: *So what happens to the moral commitment, the concern for justice in the Jewish state and all that   out the window?*

On the part of whom?

DB: *The United States.*

There's no concern for justice and there never was. States don't have a concern for justice. States don't act on moral grounds.

DB: *Except on a rhetorical level.*

On a rhetorical level they all do, even Nazi Germany. On the actual level they never do. They are instruments of power and violence, that's true of all states. They act in the interests of the groups that dominate them. They spout the nice rhetorical line, but these are just givens of the international system.

DB: *You've been very critical of the American liberal community and in fact you've said that they're contributing to Israel's destruction.*

The American liberal community since 1967 has been mobilized at an almost fanatic level in support of an expansionist Israel, and they have been consistently opposed to any political settlement. They have been in favor of the aggrandizement of Israeli power. They have used their position of quite considerable influence in the media and the political system to defeat and overcome any challenge to the system of military confrontation using all the standard techniques of vilification, defamation, imposing control over expression, etc. and it's certainly had an effect. I don't know if it was a decisive effect, but it had some noticeable effect on bringing about U.S. government support for the persistent military confrontation and U.S. government opposition to political settlement. For Israel that's destructive. In fact, Israeli doves constantly deplore it. They constantly refer to it as Stalinism. They refer to the Stalinist character of the support for Israel on the part of what they call the "Jewish community," but that's because they don't understand enough about the United States. It's not just the Jewish community, which is what they see; it's basically the intellectual community at large.

DB: *Edward Said, for example, has pointed out that there is much more pluralism in terms of the discussion, the debate, in Israel itself than inside the United States.*

There's no question about that. For example, the editor of the Labor Party journal, the main newspaper of the Labor Party, has asked me to write regular columns. I won't do it because I'm concerned with things here. But to be asked that is totally inconceivable in the United States. That's quite typical. The positions that I maintain, which are essentially in terms of the international consensus, are not a majority position in Israel, but they're part of the political spectrum and they're respectable positions. Here, they're considered outlandish.

DB: *In what ways, if any, has your work in linguistics and grammar informed your political analyses and perspectives?*

I suspect very little. Maybe, I don't know, I'm probably not the person to ask, but I think working in a science is useful because you somehow learn, you get to understand what evidence and argument and rationality are and you come to be able to apply these to other domains where they're very much lacking and very much opposed, so there's probably some help in that respect.

There' probably at some very deep and abstract level some sort of common core conception of human nature and the human drive for freedom and the right to be free of external coercion and control, that kind of picture animates my own social and political concerns. My own anarchist interests, which go way back to early childhood, enter here in a clear and relatively precise way into my work on language and thought and so on, but it's a pretty loose connection, not a kind of connection where you can deduce one connection from another or anything like that.

DB: *You have an international reputation for your work in linguistics and philosophy and obviously you weren't content with that, you wanted to go out into the social and political world—*

Quite the contrary. It's one of the many examples that show that people often do things that they don't want to do because they have to. I made a very conscious decision about this. Actually, my political views haven't changed much since I was about 12 or 13. I've learned more, I suppose they're more sophisticated, but fundamentally they haven't changed. However, I was not an activist. I was, until the early 1960s, working in my own garden, basically, doing the kind of work I liked. It's intellectually exciting, rewarding, satisfying; you make progress. I would have been very happy to stick to it. It would have been from a narrow personal point of view much better for me in every imaginable respect.

I remember I knew as soon as I got involved in political activism that there was going to be no end, the demands would increase forever, there would be unpleasant personal consequences—and they are unpleasant. I mean there are less unpleasant things than being maced, for example, or spending a day in a Washington jail cell or being up for a five-year jail sentence or being subjected to the endless lies of the Anti-Defamation League and its friends, etc. I didn't know in detail, but I knew it was going to be much less pleasant than just working in the fields where I felt I was good and I could make progress and so on. And I knew I had to cut back on things I really wanted to do and that I enjoyed doing, many things in personal life, and I knew personal life was going to contract enormously. Something has to give, and in many ways I knew there would be negative consequences. I really thought about it pretty hard and I finally took the plunge, but not with any great joy, I must say.

DB: *I think a lot of people are grateful that you did.*

Thanks.

State Power
and the Domestic Enemy

January 24, 1988

DB: *In your 1978 book* Human Rights and American Foreign Policy *you write: "If we hope to understand anything about the foreign policy of any state, it is a good idea to begin by investigating the domestic social structure." Would you talk about that?*

Foreign policy, like all state policy, flows from domestic institutions. It reflects the interests and concerns of those who have the capacity to organize the resources to either control the state directly or to influence what the state does. In the case of foreign policy, it's those segments of the domestic society that are particularly concerned with international affairs who will naturally have the major voice. So if you want to understand foreign policy you begin by looking at domestic structures.

In the case of our society, the answers to those questions are rather straightforward. Domestic power is highly concentrated in the corporate system, and those segments of the corporate system that are particularly concerned with international affairs typically exert an overwhelming influence on the design and execution of foreign policy. You can see that simply enough by just who staffs the executive and the top decision-making positions. They're overwhelmingly drawn from major corporations with international interests, investment firms, half-a-dozen law firms that cater primarily to corporate interests and therefore have a kind of overarching conception of the needs of the corporate sector rather than a parochial concern for one or another segment of it.

Occasionally you are allowed into the crowd if you are an "expert" in the sense in which Henry Kissinger explained the concept. Pretty frankly, he pointed out that an "expert" is someone who is able to articulate the consensus of people with power, and if you have that capacity, which in fact he had, then you can come in as an expert and be a state manager in the interests of external power. That's the core of it. Beyond that there are other influences, there are domestic lobbies and so on, but I think that's the essential core.

DB: *This analysis is characterized as a "radical critique."*

I think it's a very conservative critique. In fact, it's just plain common sense and there's nothing there that would have been surprising to 18th-century figures of the kind who founded this country. It's merely an extension of conventional doctrine of the kind they articulated to the specific structure of our own society. It's called "radical," but you have to recall that "radical" is just one of several terms of abuse which have no meaning, like "marxist." There's a whole array of terms of abuse which are used to protect ourselves from understanding of the world in which we live.

DB: *In* The Culture of Terrorism *you discuss two trends, the "right turn" and "crisis of democracy." What are they, and are they connected?*

They are very closely connected. The "crisis of democracy," which is not my term, happens to be the title of an important book published by the Trilateral Commission in 1975, their one major book-length publication. The Trilateral Commission was established by David Rockefeller. It includes more or less liberal elite elements from the three major centers of industrial capitalism, the United States, Japan and Western Europe. Hence Trilateral Commission. This book reflects the results of an extensive study they did of the phenomenon that they referred to as the crisis of democracy. The crisis, as they outline it, has to do with the fact that during the 1960's and the early 70's substantial sectors of the population which are usually apathetic and passive became organized and began to enter the political arena and began to press for their own interests and concerns. That created a crisis because that's not the way democracy is supposed to work. The chief American contributor, Harvard professor Samuel Huntington, stated that, back in the days of Truman, before there was a crisis of democracy, policy could be executed simply by a handful of Wall Street lawyers and financiers. That's a bit of an exaggeration, but it expresses the conception of the Commission as to the way democracy ought to function.

That was threatened in the 1960's as minorities, youth, women, aged people, all sorts of groups began to be organized and enter into the political system. That worldwide crisis, the participants agreed, had to be overcome, and the population had to be returned to its proper state of apathy and ignorance, returned to its task. Namely, that of ratifying decisions made by elites.

Various mechanisms were proposed for doing this. One of the mechanisms, in fact, constitutes the "right turn," which is a phenomenon among elites. It hasn't taken place among the general population. But among elites there has been a very notable right turn, meaning a turn towards a kind of reactionary jingoism, mislabeled conservatism very often. It has nothing to do with conservatism. That reflects the recognition that something has to be done to restore the earlier order of privilege and overcome threats to privilege. That has a domestic aspect and an international aspect. The international aspect is the Reagan Doctrine, which is just a phrase referring to international terrorism, the use of violence, subversion, and other methods to overcome the crisis of democracy that was beginning to arise elsewhere in the world. For example, in Central America there was a serious threat of meaningful democracy, meaning real rather than nominal democracy, actual participation of usually dispossessed segments of the population.

Domestically, there was a rising threat of social reform that had to be countered, and the Reagan Doctrine is an effort to counter that by the usual methods of violence and repression. At home, you can't just call out the death squads, so other, more subtle methods are necessary. So there have been major efforts at indoctrination. At an extreme level we find such interesting institutions as the Office of Public Diplomacy at the State Department, which is dedicated to controlling what they quite openly called "enemy territory," the domestic population.

Since this right turn represents a general elite consensus, it also includes the doves, the establishment liberals. The goal, only partially achieved, was to create a reactionary consensus which will support the right of U.S. power to exercise violence in the world for domestic interests and will also at home weaken the labor movement, break up the growing popular movements, restore the population to apathy, bring them to accept the policies of domestic austerity required for large parts of the population if American business is to recover its competitive advantages in the world, and so on. All of that constitutes the elite right turn.

DB: *You contend that elite groups view the domestic population as an enemy.*

Typically, yes. It's true of all states and all elites. Usually the enemy can be disregarded because it's sufficiently passive and apathetic. But if the domestic enemy begins to make unpleasant noises, then something has to be done about it. As I say, the methods are different abroad and at home. The conception of the population as an enemy is often rather clearly articulated. For example, on the right wing it's articulated when high administration officials use the phrase. When the Office of Public Diplomacy was first exposed by Alfonso Chardy of the *Miami Herald* in July 1987, he inquired among administration officials as to what it was up to, and they described it as the most spectacular achievement of the Reagan administration. One high administration official, whom he quoted, referred to it as the kind of program that you would carry out in "enemy territory," which is exactly right.

At the liberal end, you have the viewpoint expressed in the Trilateral Commission study, which is concerned quite explicitly with restoring apathy, passivity and obedience so that democracy in the preferred sense can survive, and that again reflects a conception of the population as an enemy which has to be controlled or suppressed or somehow marginalized. I might mention in this connection that the rise of clandestine operations is a reflection of the strength of the domestic enemy. If the enemy, the population, can't be controlled by force, can't be indoctrinated and can't be marginalized, it will in fact drive the state underground. The government will have to carry out its actions in secret because the domestic enemy won't tolerate them. The scale of clandestine operations is often a very good measure of domestic dissidence.

DB: *I'd like for you to clarify your views about elite groups, and let me make a point of argument here. Can you completely discount their necessity? For example, the mechanic who repairs the brakes on your car—you want him to be a member of an elite group, don't you?*

You want people to have specialized skills. The question is whether those specialized skills should confer power. Should the ability of a mechanic to fix your car lead to a system in which he can determine what car you buy?

The answer is no. Let's say—I'm not sure that this is true—but suppose that there are skills required for management. That's a dubious assumption, but let's assume it. Then we might want people who have those alleged skills to be able to exercise them. In a real democracy they would exercise them under public control, just as a doctor would or a mechanic or anyone else. No sane person would want a society without skilled people. The question is how power is distributed. Does power reside in the population? Or does it reside in elite elements in our society, elements that gain their effective decision-making power ultimately by their ownership of the central parts of the society, the domestic economy, typically?

DB: *You frequently mention the fact that in 1962 the Kennedy administration attacked South Vietnam and that this information is not known, not discussed, "down the memory hole." Why is that?*

It's not quite true that the information was not discussed. In fact it was on the front page of the *New York Times*. It's just that in a well-indoctrinated society the information doesn't have any meaning. So the *New York Times* can report, as it did, I think it was October 1962, that the Kennedy administration has committed U.S. planes and U.S. pilots to undertake direct participation, not just control, in the bombing and defoliation operations in South Vietnam directed against the large majority of the population, about 80 percent, in rural areas. Now that's aggression, but it wasn't understood as that. As the facts became filtered through our very effective indoctrination system, it became defense. It became defense against what Adlai Stevenson, our U.N. ambassador at the time, referred to as "internal aggression," namely the aggression of the Vietnamese, and particularly the Vietnamese peasants, against the United States in South Vietnam. A society that can use phrases such as "internal aggression" and can perceive the bombing of peasant villages as a defense of either us or our clients, has gone a long way towards a kind of operative totalitarianism.

DB: *Using the example of the Indochina war, can you talk about how dissident groups in the United States affected U.S. public policy?*

They certainly did affect it. It was an indirect kind of effect. Plainly it was not through the electoral system. In 1964, the population voted 2 to 1 in favor of Lyndon Johnson, who put himself forth as the "peace candidate," and to a large measure that vote was because Johnson stated openly and repeatedly that "we do not want a wider war." That was a vote against expansion of the war. As we now know, at that very moment Lyndon Johnson's advisors were planning the escalation of the war, the escalation of the attack against South Vietnam, and the expansion of the war to North Vietnam, which took place as soon as they had won the election. Plainly, the effect was not through the electoral system.

However, over a long period, a difficult period of education, organization, demonstration, protest and so on, the population became sufficiently disaffected by the war that the Johnson administration was unable to declare a national mobilization. As the war became a really major one, that raised serious domestic problems. It was necessary to fight the war on deficit financing, to fight a "guns and butter" war, as it was called. The reason was that the population was simply too disaffected to go along. It wasn't like World War II when people were quite willing to accept domestic austerity because of a commitment to the war. That was not true during the Vietnam war, in part, as a result of the continual activities of the peace movement. There were other factors too, but it was a large part of it.

The effects of that were quite significant. By the time

of the Tet offensive, in 1968, when it became evident that this was going to be a long, protracted war for the United States to attain its objectives of subjugating and controlling at least South Vietnam, at that point elite elements began to become disaffected, and the reason was, very explicitly, that the war was becoming too costly.

DB: *In economic terms.*

Yes, in terms of relations between the United States and its major rivals, Europe and Japan. The effects of fighting a guns and butter war were harming the U.S. economy. While stagflation was setting in here, our rivals were enriching themselves through the destruction of Indochina. For example, Canada became the largest per capita war exporter in the world—to us. That was its participation in the destruction of Indochina. The war gave a huge shot in the arm to Japan. Japan was not a serious rival to the United States in the early 1960's. In 1965 the balance of trade shifted and after that Japan became a very serious rival. The industrial takeoff of South Korea dates from the same time, largely as an off-shore producer for the American war and from the remittances of ultimately about 300,000 mercenaries that they sent to fight the war with us in South Vietnam. All of this was beneficial to our rivals but harmful to the United States. Since it was impossible to create a national mobilization here, the war had to be fought in a way which was quite harmful to the U.S. economy.

That became evident by early 1968. It led elite groups to urge, in fact to demand and require, significant change in policy. That's an indirect effect of the domestic dissidence. Powerful but indirect, a large part of which can be traced to the activism of people associated in one way or another with the peace movement.

The effects were actually more than that. The secret records tell us more. They tell us that by about May 1967 or earlier, the Pentagon was beginning to be concerned about domestic dissidence. Robert McNamara warned the President in a memo in May 1967 that things could get out of hand in the United States. After the Tet offensive, the Joint Chiefs were concerned about the danger of a real uprising. They wanted to make sure they had enough troops for "civil disorder control," as they put it. They were particularly concerned about massive civil disobedience involving many sectors of the population, including particularly women, youth, segments of the intelligentsia.

The ethnic minorities were beginning to blow up, and the army was beginning to collapse, a reflection of the youth culture at home. It was a citizens' army, not a mercenary army, so it's not dissociated from developments at home. All of these factors were beginning to create a serious internal crisis, and in these respects too the state managers, who were carrying out what was a simple war of aggression, were compelled to face costs that they ultimately decided they could not tolerate. In all of these indirect ways, domestic dissidence played a very significant, I think a decisive role in slowly, very, very slowly, with agonizing slowness, in forcing the United States to abandon its effort to literally conquer South Vietnam.

DB: *Thus provoking a "crisis of democracy."*

That was the crisis of democracy which then had to be faced. The crisis was rather broad. It was not only the crisis of democracy, the fact that segments of the population that are usually apathetic were beginning to participate in the political system or to demand that the state respond to their interests. There was also a serious threat to the profitability of American business as a result of the consequences of the war and the way it was fought. Stagflation was the fundamental phenomenon, and that required an attack on unions, lowering of real wages, breakup of the unions, and in general dismantling of the popular structures in the United States that would enable ordinary citizens to fight for their rights in opposition to those of the owners and managers of the society.

We've seen that strikingly during the Reagan period with an elite consensus behind it. The attack on the social welfare system and the transfer of resources from the poor to the rich, which was a very notable feature of the 1980's. All of these are part of the same effort of the dominant social groups in the United States, the owners and managers of the corporate system, to ensure their own privilege and to defend themselves against the rising domestic enemy.

DB: *You were very active in those years in the resistance against the war in Indochina, and that's why I want to explore this with you, because you are a historical source and record as well. There has been a lot of "historical engineering" that has occurred since that period. Two things come to mind: one is the popular notion that somehow it was the media in the 1960's that galvanized popular dissent against the war in Vietnam. You take exception to that.*

That's totally false, every study of the media completely refutes that really quite absurd view. I've just finished with Edward Herman, a colleague of mine, a book on the mass media [*Manufacturing Consent*], a large segment of which is devoted to the media coverage of the Indochina war, beginning around 1950 and up to today. There's simply no question that the media were very, very supportive of the war. Up until the late 60's there isn't even any debate over this. Everyone agrees on all sides that through about 1966 or 1967 the media were highly supportive of the war, very hawkish. A number of studies have shown that the effect of television in particular was to make the population more hawkish.

It's easy to demonstrate that on every major issue

the media simply went along with state policy. The only respect in which this was not true is that sometimes journalists on the scene had a different perception. They were basically seeing the war from the point of view of the American military command on the scene. They never reported the war from the point of view of the Vietnamese resistance, as they do, say, in Afghanistan.

Rather, the war was seen by correspondents from the point of view of American military commanders in the field, often junior officers, and they did to some extent reflect the perception on the part of officers and soldiers on the scene that things were different from the way they were being portrayed in Washington. So for example at the time of the formation of the strategic hamlets everyone on the ground could see that this method of trying to control the population, by violence, was simply not working. Washington was claiming that it was, the military on the scene knew much better, and the correspondents, reflecting the officers and sometimes men who they were with, did, to some extent, reflect their attitudes. Only in this very narrow and limited respect did the media diverge from state policy.

By January 1968, when the Tet offensive took place, there was one significant change. For the first time the journalists were able to see the war not under the control of the U.S. military. They weren't simply flown somewhere in a military helicopter and shown what the military wanted them to see. They could look out their window and see the war going on. As a result, there was some very graphic reporting, but within the framework of U.S. government propaganda, contrary to what is claimed.

For example, the media described the destruction of cities in the Mekong Delta south of Saigon graphically and vividly and they knew, as everyone knew, including the American command, that the cities were being destroyed to "rescue" them, as it was being put, from their own populations. It was understood that there were virtually no North Vietnamese there. The people who were doing the fighting were South Vietnamese, who we called Viet Cong, the National Liberation Front troops. The only foreign force in the Delta was the United States and the Thai and Korean and other mercenaries that the United States brought in. Nevertheless, the media described all of this as defense. We were "rescuing" Ben Tre when we conquered it from its own population. One famous phrase was we had to "destroy the town in order to save it," and that was the conception of the media: the United States was engaged in defense when it was destroying and murdering and attacking South Vietnamese. There was no departure from that.

Again contrary to many claims, the media portrayed the Tet offensive as essentially an American military victory. If you compare the media portrayal with the internal record of U.S. intelligence, the media were considerably more optimistic about U.S. successes than U.S. intelligence was. The reason was that the media were largely reflecting public statements. They didn't know what was being reported by the CIA. If you make that comparison it's dramatically the case. After that, the media simply continued to portray the war largely as perceived by Washington.

So as Washington began its attempt at a negotiated settlement that would leave it in control of South Vietnam, the media shifted attention away from the fighting in the south to the negotiations. This is particularly striking because this was the period of the greatest mass murder operations carried out by the U.S. military in South Vietnam, what was called the "post-Tet accelerated pacification campaign," which completely devastated the South Vietnamese resistance and prepared the way for the ultimate North Vietnamese takeover. That was sometimes described. There were some reporters on the scene who wrote about it, and there were even some very good analyses of it, in particular by Kevin Buckley of *News-*

week. He investigated one of these mass murder operations in depth, although his report was delayed for several
years before it was published, and then only in part. But
by and large the media shifted public attention away,
television almost completely, and these mass murder operations proceeded with minimal coverage and virtually
no understanding.

And that continued. At the time of the Paris peace
treaty, for example, the media went along totally with the
immediate U.S. efforts to unravel and undermine them
which succeeded, and to this day that's barely known.
There's simply no point at which the media diverged from
this framework, apart from very limited exceptions.

DB: *There's another little anecdote which involved you and
Tip O'Neill. In 1987 he wrote his autobiography* (Man of the
House). *It was reviewed by John Kenneth Galbraith. Can you talk
about that?*

Tip O'Neill was described by Galbraith, and describes himself, as one of the early leaders of the anti-war
movement in Congress. The facts are a little bit different.
The personal anecdote you have in mind, I suppose, was
April 8th or 9th 1965, the day after a major speech by
Johnson, when a group of New England professors, of
whom I was one, Howard Zinn was another, and there
were a few others, went to Washington to lobby, to try to
talk to Tip O'Neill. He was the representative from Cambridge, where I teach and others of us lived and worked.
We went to see the Massachusetts delegation just to talk
to them about the war. The position we were taking was
extremely narrow, embarrassingly narrow.

You have to remember that this was 1965. It was
impossible then to talk about the American war in South
Vietnam, nobody could even hear the words when you
talked about that. So we limited ourselves pretty much to
the bombing of North Vietnam. The reactions were differ-

ent among different people. Tip O'Neill's reaction was extreme. He didn't even let us into his office. He wasn't even going to listen to constituents who opposed the bombing of North Vietnam. Others were willing to let us into their offices. Some of the Republican Congressmen from Massachusetts were more or less sympathetic, but that was about it. Tip O'Neill was the most extreme example. This went on through about 1967. There was virtually no congressional opposition to the war.

As elite groups, as the U.S. corporate elite began to become disaffected with the war, segments of Congress went along, in particular by early 1968, when there was real, very extensive corporate disaffection. A famous meeting took place of a group of "wise men," as they were called—Dean Acheson, McGeorge Bundy, John McCloy, I believe—the usual people who staff the executive and represent the corporate and the military systems.

They actually went to Washington to give an evaluation of the war and told the President that he had to change course. In fact, that's when Johnson resigned and the process called "Vietnamization" began taking place. It was then that you began to get some very limited Congressional opposition. It's very similar to current Congressional opposition to contra aid. Violence is not succeeding, so we had better turn to something else to achieve our objectives. At that point you began to get the people who are the famous "anti-war leaders" appearing, for example, Gene McCarthy. He was invisible during the hard period of opposition to the war. Opposition to the war was extremely unpopular in 1966-67, and then you heard nothing from Gene McCarthy. McCarthy is a particularly interesting example. Galbraith has identified him as the "real hero" of the anti-war movement.

You get an understanding of a liberal elite political culture thinking that through. There was some early congressional opposition to the war: Wayne Morse and Ernst Gruening were the only people to vote against the

Tonkin Gulf resolution, and there were a handful of others who spoke up, but not Gene McCarthy. He joined the opposition to the war in an extremely vague way. If you look back at his speeches it's completely unclear what he was saying. But he was willing to put himself forth as the leader at the point when he thought that he could exploit the mass popular movement that he had done nothing to help organize. He thought that he could exploit it for personal political power. When he saw that he couldn't, he dropped from sight. That's extremely clear in McCarthy's case. He appeared, briefly. For a few months until the Democratic Convention of August 1968 he was willing to let himself be represented as an anti-war leader, because he needed the troops. When he didn't win the nomination, he effectively disappeared.

We can tell exactly how seriously he took the war issue by looking at what he did at that point. He had a lot of completely undeserved prestige, he was a public figure; he could have used that if he had cared a bit about ending the attack against Indochina, or the war however he would have conceived of it, the defense of South Vietnam or whatever phrase he would have used. If he'd even cared minimally about it, he could have used the prestige he had obtained without any right, but he had obtained it, to act as a public spokesman against the war. All we have to do is check and find out what he did. Answer: Virtually nothing. He disappeared. He had lost his bid for political power, he therefore disappeared, and he is now constituted among the highest-ranking liberal pantheon of anti-war heroes. That tells you something about the political culture.

DB: *Talking about American political culture, you've often pointed out that the U.S. lacks political parties, lacks an opposition press and is essentially depoliticized. Might that be an explanation for the fact that tens of millions of Americans don't vote, don't participate in the political process?*

I think there's very little doubt of that. There have been a number of studies of non-voters. Walter Dean Burnham, a political scientist, is one of those who's done some of the best work on this, and the facts are pretty clear. If you do a socio-economic analysis, a profile of the non-voters, it turns out that they're very similar to the groups that in some European industrial democracies vote for one of the labor-based parties. Almost every other industrial democracy has some political party with roots in the working class, the poor, the dispossessed, and so on. The party has various names. It's called sometimes labor or communist or socialist or one thing or another, but such a political formation has in the past existed.

They're now beginning to decline elsewhere, but they have in the past existed in the other industrial democracies. The one major exception is Japan, and even there it exists to a limited extent. Of course we created the Japanese political system. But the glaring exception is the United States, where the only two parties are the business-based parties. If you look at the non-voters, they are the people who would vote labor, communist, socialist, one of those groupings in the other industrial democracies. Voting in the United States is heavily class-based. It's skewed towards skilled rather than unskilled workers, towards white-collar rather than blue-collar, employed rather than unemployed, the rich rather than the poor, the professionals rather than the homeless, and so on. That reflects the same fact.

Large parts of the population, half roughly in presidential elections, two-thirds roughly in congressional elections, simply don't participate. There are a number of reasons for that, some technical reasons like difficulty of registering, but the main reason appears to be that they don't feel part of the political system. That also shows up in other ways. There were some very striking polls taken after the last two elections, which were very revealing. After the 1984 election, voters were asked whether they hoped that Reagan's legislative agenda would be enacted, and voters, by 3 to 2, hoped that it would not. That is, the people who voted for Reagan hoped that his legislative program would not be enacted. That means they were voting against their own interest, and that indicates a complete cynicism with regard to the political system. They were voting for some other reason, not because they thought they were influencing policy. Other polls help explain what those reasons were.

At the same time, about half the population, when asked, "Who runs the government?" answered "yes" to the question "Is the government run by a few big interests looking out for themselves?" That was the opinion of about half the population, and presumably that's correlated with the half that didn't vote, or the segments who voted for Reagan while hoping that his legislative program will not be enacted. That does reflect in my view a kind of understanding of the political system, or to put it more neutrally, a kind of cynicism about the political system, that's very widespread, particularly among the less educated, who typically tend to be more sophisticated and perceptive about these matters. The reason for this sophistication is that education is a form of indoctrination, and the less educated are less indoctrinated.

Furthermore, the educated tend to be the privileged and they tend to have a stake in the indoctrinal system, so they naturally tend to internalize and believe it. As a result, not uncommonly and not only in the United States, you find a good deal more sophistication among people who learn about the world from their experience rather than those who learn about the world from the doctrinal framework that they are exposed to and that they are expected as part of their professional obligation to propagate.

DB: *In the 1980's one hears much talk on a social level of "co-dependency relationships." You've suggested that there is such* *a relationship between the United States and the USSR.*

There is an interesting relationship that's developed since the late 1940's. Without going into the details of how the Cold War got started, the fact is that the Cold War has had a kind of functional utility for both superpowers. I'm convinced that that's one of the reasons why it persisted. It's in a way in their interests, the interests of the elite groups that run the two superpowers. This is true in spite of the enormous cost that it entails and the great dangers that it poses, including the danger of terminal disaster. You can see this very clearly if you look over the actual events of the Cold War. On the Russian side, what are the events of the Cold War? The events are such actions as the sending of tanks to East Berlin in 1953, or the invasion of Hungary in 1956, the invasion of Czechoslovakia, now the invasion of Afghanistan, and so on. Those are the events of the Cold War.

In every one of those cases, the Soviet Union was attacking someone in its domains, actually in the area conquered by the Red Army, or in the case of Afghanistan, in an area in which it had already attained substantial, in fact dominant influence. It was effectively attacking a client state and it had to mobilize its own population. You have to do that; any state, whether it's a democracy or totalitarian or whatever, has to organize and mobilize its own population for costly and violent actions. And it did it by appealing to the threat of the Great Satan. All of these actions were defensive. They were taken in defense against the threat posed by the United States, which threatens to attack and overwhelm and destroy the Soviet Union. That's the way you mobilize people, by convincing them that they have to defend their homes against some great enemy. For popular mobilization, the Cold War was very functional for Soviet elites. Exactly the same has been true here.

On our side, the events of the Cold War have been

regular interventions, subversion and aggression. When we overthrew the democratic capitalist government of Guatemala in 1954, for example, we were defending ourselves from Soviet attack. When we invaded South Vietnam, we were defending ourselves from an agent of the Russians or the Chinese. And so on up till today. When we attack Nicaragua today we're defending ourselves from Soviet expansionism. That's the way you mobilize a domestic population, and it must be done. There's essentially no other method.

It can be done up to levels of extraordinary absurdity. For example, the conquest of Grenada was actually presented in the United States as a defense of the United States against a threat. This speck in the Caribbean which you could barely find on a map, which has 100,000 people, was a threat to the existence of the United States. They could never convince the American population of that. But if you could pretend that somehow it was an outpost of the Soviet Union, a dangerous power with an ample record of brutality and bristling with missiles and so forth, then it becomes more plausible. So we defended ourselves by conquering this invisible speck in the Caribbean.

That kind of functional utility is required for imposing domestic controls. That's the main method. Typically, any state will try to defend itself against its domestic enemy by inducing fear to get the domestic enemy, the population, to accept policies to which they are opposed, policies under which they suffer. There is only one way that has ever been thought of to do that, and that is to induce fear. To induce fear, you need an enemy. If you look back at our history there have been a number of enemies. In the 19th century we were defending ourselves from the British and the Spanish. During the First World War, President Woodrow Wilson sent his troops to Haiti and the Dominican Republic, where they carried out brutal and murderous counterinsurgency operations, destroyed the constitutional system, reinstated slavery, and so on. At that time there was no Soviet Union; it was before the Bolshevik Revolution. So we were defending ourselves against the Huns. After the Bolshevik Revolution, we've been defending ourselves against them. We need an enemy to defend ourselves against.

There's an interesting little twist to this during the Reagan period. The population was strongly opposed to the major thrust of the Reagan program, the polls show that very dramatically, so we had a lot of "evil empire" rhetoric, we have to defend ourselves against the Russians, and so on. However, a confrontation with the Russians is a little bit too dangerous, so it was necessary to find an enemy which is weak enough so that we can attack them and destroy them and kill them without any cost to ourselves but yet strong enough so that you can use it to frighten the domestic population.

The public relations agents of the Reagan administration very quickly found the solution to this dilemma: international terrorism. They concocted an array of "little Satans"—Qaddafi, the PLO, the Sandinistas, Grenada, and so on—countries and even individuals who are sufficiently weak so that we can attack them without any cost to ourselves. We can bomb Tripoli and Benghazi and kill a hundred people at no cost to us. But nevertheless they are threatening because they are identified as agents of the evil empire. That was a brilliant public relations coup. It's now becoming difficult because of the enormous costs of the Reaganite follies, which have seriously damaged the domestic economy. It's becoming extremely difficult to conduct this aggressive foreign policy. As a result we discover that the Russians are less threatening, international terrorism is declining, now there's a need for statesmanlike poses, and so on. Nothing much has changed in the world, but something has changed at home. A general point throughout this whole period is that the Soviet Union and its alleged clients have been a very convenient device to induce fear to mobilize the domestic population. Something of the same sort has been true on their side. That's the functional utility of the Cold War.

DB: *How do you view Gorbachev's glasnost and perestroika policies and might they be unwelcome in certain U.S. circles given what you said about the need to maintain fear?*

I think they're very frightening in elite circles in the United States. That's why there's been a continual effort to downgrade and downplay them. It's already been harmful to the United States in Europe. A lot of Gorbachev's policies are quite welcome in Europe, not to the European elites, who are just as frightened of them as U.S. elites are. But there's undoubtedly a general popular major mass movement which would prefer to see a reduction in tensions, a reduction of the dungeon-like character of the Soviet Union and Eastern Europe, and who therefore welcome these policies. Gorbachev is a very popular figure in Western Europe, as indeed he's even becoming here. After the Reykjavik summit, the U.S. Information Agency carried out a secret study of the reaction in Europe to the summit. It was leaked and published in Europe. As far as I know, it was never published in any American newspaper. It was mentioned in columns occasionally but never published as news, to my knowledge. It was published as news in Europe, and what it showed was that the European population in every country outside of France was overwhelmingly supportive of Gorbachev against Reagan by figures of 4 to 1 and 7 to 1 and so on. Of course that's frightening. The United States has to ensure control over its clients, Western Europe in particular, that's the most important one, and the threat of detente has to be taken quite seriously.

At the same time there's conflict here. It's important to recognize how seriously Reaganite policies have harmed the American economy. It's extremely serious, and there's going to be a real cost to pay. As a result, the United States is not going to be able to throw its weight around in world affairs to the extent that the right wing would like, and hence it's necessary for the United States to move towards a less confrontational stance. In this respect there are factors here driving the country towards a kind of detente. At the same time, the loss of this mode of control over the domestic population and control over the client states and the allies, that's serious. It'll be interesting to see how these conflicting needs play themselves out in the coming years.

DB: *You have advanced the notion that the managers of the U.S. security state are not really interested in national security.*

I think it's not only true in the United States, it's generally true. Here you have to be a little cautious. If you look at the public, or for that matter even secret documents of just about any state, quite typically although not always, they describe what they are doing in terms of security. I say not always because often there's frank discussion in secret documents, occasionally even publicly. But in general, state managers see themselves as defending security. But you have to do a little bit of decoding here—security of what? For example, is the United States protecting itself from attack? Let's say in 1950, when we carried out the first major military buildup, approximately quadrupled the Pentagon system, were we defending ourselves against the threat of attack? That's ludicrous.

The United States was in a position of security that had never been attained by any country in history. We had no enemies nearby. We controlled both oceans. We controlled the opposite sides of both oceans. There was no conceivable threat of attack. We were overwhelmingly the most powerful state in the world, far more powerful than the Soviet Union. In fact Western Europe was roughly comparable to the Soviet Union economically and could have been militarily if it had wanted to be, and it was much more advanced in its institutional structure and the cohesion of its population. So it was plain we weren't defending ourselves against attack. The conventional explanation was that this was a reaction to the Korean War, which was perceived as Soviet expansionism. But there are two problems with that: There wasn't a particle of evidence that the Russians had anything to do with the North Korean attack, nor is there today. More significantly, we know perfectly well that the decision to increase the military budget preceded the Korean War.

The crucial planning document is National Security Council Memorandum 68, declassified in 1975. It's a very interesting document. It was two months before the Korean War when it called for a huge expansion in the military budget because of the threat of destruction at the hands of the Soviet Union. If you look carefully at the document, you'll discover that it estimated that the United States was vastly more powerful than the Soviet Union, even excluding Europe and Canada. Nevertheless, we were faced with destruction. They even have an explanation. Their explanation was that the Soviet Union was so backward that they can do "more with less," so their weakness is their strength, and therefore we have to defend ourselves from them.

There was also a breath of reality in it. NSC 68 pointed out that the United States might be heading into a depression, that there was an economic decline. It pointed out that military spending would be a stimulus to the economy, as it had been during the Second World War. Furthermore, there was a need to protect the very far-flung domains of the United States, which requires a deterrent posture. We have to deter any resistance to U.S. intervention, an idea very clearly articulated in the secret record. As a result, we had to build up U.S. military power, both for domestic and international reasons, but defense was not among them.

The same thing is true if you look at the other periods of big military buildup, say the Kennedy period. In the early Kennedy years there was a big military buildup, in fact, that set off the current stage of the arms race. The excuse at that time was the missile gap, but we know that the missile gap was a fraud, and the Kennedy people and managers knew that it was a fraud. They probably knew even before they came into office, but when they came into office they certainly knew. The internal documents are interesting.

McGeorge Bundy, for example, recommended that the administration keep the phrase "missile gap" even though there was none because, he said, it's a "useful shorthand to express our basic military posture," or words to that effect. To be precise, there *was* a missile gap at that time, vastly in our favor, about 10 to 1. The Russians had four operational missiles which were exposed somewhere on some airstrip. But it was necessary to carry out a big military spending program for the usual reasons: for stimulation of the domestic economy and for carrying out an aggressive interventionist foreign policy. There was nothing here about security.

Exactly the same is true in the Reagan period when, you recall, the pretext for the big military spending was the "window of vulnerability" so that the Russians could rampage all over the world. We don't have to debate this because the president's own Scowcroft Commission pointed out that there was not and never had been a "window of vulnerability." By now it's conceded across the board that it was certainly false, in fact just a fraud. The military buildup went on nevertheless. Whenever you find that the pretext is not the reason, you know that something else is going on. If you look at the details of U.S. security policy, you will see that security in the sense of defense of the country or defense of client states or defense of others, is almost *never* a concern. The actual concerns are quite different.

The concerns are using the power of the state to organize a public subsidy for advanced technology to the military system, or creating an international system in which we can intimidate others sufficiently so that we can intervene directly without threat or simply conduct direct intervention. A huge part of the military budget is simply for intervention costs. Nevertheless, all this is perceived as security.

I don't say that they're lying. The more intelligent people are just lying, but the less intelligent believe it, and they believe it by a very simple and very familiar psychological mechanism. Everybody knows it from their personal life, and it also works in political life. In your personal life, you want to do something. You know it's not the right thing to do, but you want it because it's in your interest, so you do it, and you find a system of justification that explains exactly why it was the right and proper thing to do. Anyone who is sufficiently honest knows that they do this all the time.

It's a very typical phenomenon of political life. You decide that you're going to overthrow the government of Guatemala because we can't tolerate social reform and democracy, but you can't put it that way, so therefore you create a threat. If you look carefully at the secret documents you can see just what the threat was. The secret documents, which are now declassified, are full of all sorts of raving about "Guatemalan aggression," in fact the operative policy was a National Security document called something like "Actions in the event of Guatemalan aggression in the hemisphere." Guatemalan aggression in the hemisphere is about as threatening as Grenadan or Nicaraguan aggression, but they believed it and they even gave examples. The example they gave was a strike in Honduras where they said there might have been some support from Guatemala. That's the kind of aggression they were concerned about. Guatemalan reformist, capitalist democracy might have an effect elsewhere in inspiring things like strikes against American corporations, and of course that's aggression, so therefore we have to defend ourselves against it by military action that overthrows the regime. That's very typical, when you look closely.

It's in this sense that while security managers may perfectly well believe that they are defending the security of the nation, the facts very clearly are that they're defending something totally different. They're defending domestic privilege and power. Just to mention one other example where it's less contentious and perfectly obvious, there are repeatedly surveys of businessmen in which corporate managers are asked to explain what they're doing. Typically, what they say is that they are deeply committed humanitarians who are dedicated to bringing people the best possible goods at the cheapest price out of their overflowing human kindness. The fact of the matter is that they're maximizing profit and market share, and they're doing that not because they're either good or bad, but because that's the way the institutions work. If they didn't do it they wouldn't be managers of the board any more. Insofar as maximizing profit and market share can be rationalized, justified in terms of these lofty objectives, they'll believe the lofty objectives. But if the lofty objectives ever happen to conflict with maximizing profit and market share, they're going to do the latter. We all understand this, and nobody is or should be deluded. Very much the same is true of political life where people sometimes are deluded, even people who should know better.

DB: *There's a paradox here that bewilders me. You're talking about the state managers, whose function is to preserve power and privilege. If that indeed is the case, how could they create this apparatus of extinction.*

The reason is that in a competitive system you do short-term planning only. Exactly the same is true in the business world. Let's take corporate managers, where there's no real confusion about what they're doing. They are maximizing profit and market share in the short term. In fact, if they were not to do that, they would no longer exist. Let's be concrete. Suppose that some automobile company, say General Motors, decides to devote their resources to planning for something that will be profitable ten years from now. Suppose that's where they divert their resources, they want to think in some long-term conception of market dominance. Their rivals are going to be maximizing profit and power in the short term, and they're going to take over the markets, and General Motors won't be in business. That's true for the owners and also for the managers. The managers want to stay managers. They can fight off hostile takeover bids, they can keep from being replaced, as long as they contribute to short-term profitability. As a result, long-term considerations are rarely considered in competitive systems. Exactly the same attitudes take over when the same managers move over into the state planning system. Which is also, to an extent, a competitive system. What you find specifically is short-term maximization of gain and very little concern for the longer term. This shows up all over the place.

Let's take another example, one which is more remote than nuclear destruction, say, depletion of American energy resources. Back in the 1940's and early 50's it was pretty well known where the world's energy reserves were, there haven't been many surprises. It was known that U.S. reserves would be depleted if they were extensively used, and that the major reserves in the world would remain in the Middle East. If anybody was concerned with long-term U.S. security, what they would have done would be to protect northern hemisphere reserves, the Gulf of Mexico and so on, save those and exploit Middle Eastern reserves. They did the exact opposite. They depleted American reserves, for reasons of short-term profitability. We're now in a situation where Louisiana and Texas are producing very little oil. We've got to import oil from abroad to fill holes in the ground as a strategic reserve. This was all completely predictable. It's just that basically nobody cared. They're making calculations in terms of short-term profitability. If in the long term it means that you destroy your own corporation, or you destroy the world, that's somebody else's business.

We saw the same short-term view in the Reagan administration. It was transparent that Reaganomics was going to lead to a massive debt and a massive trade deficit, it was going to really harm the country very seriously. But they were interested in short-term gain for the privileged. The longer term would somehow take care of itself. That is absolutely typical of corporate capitalism, state capitalism, to the extent that it's competitive, and it's very typical of state managers.

DB: *You occasionally appear on radio interviews, talk shows, call-ins and the like. Do you have any observations about the time constraints within which you are allowed to express your views?*

That depends on where it is. Let me just compare it with others. In Europe, Canada, Latin America, in fact just about everywhere I know outside the United States, the situation's dramatically different from what it is here in essentially two respects. For one thing, there's fairly easy access to the media for dissident opinion. Just to keep it personal, but others have the same experience, when I go to Canada or Europe or virtually anywhere, I spend a lot of time on major media, national television, national radio and so on, whereas here it's listener-supported radio, particularly, and virtually nothing else. That's one difference.

The second difference is an interesting structural one. Outside the United States, it is typically the case that discussion of issues can be the way we're doing it, long, extended discussion. In the United States there's a different system. The only other country I know that works like this is Japan. In the United States, if you do get on commercial radio or television you're allowed a minute or two, you can have a few words between commercials, that's what it comes down to, or you're asked to express an opinion. Pretty much the same is true of op-eds. It's not too difficult, in the national press it's almost impossible, but in the local quality press it's possible for dissidents to write an op-ed of seven hundred words, short. To get into one of the major journals of opinion, however, is extremely difficult.

There's a logic to this. In two minutes, between two commercials, or in a few hundred words, you can say some conventional things. For example, if I'm given two minutes on the radio and I want to condemn the Russians for invading Afghanistan, that's easy. I don't need any evidence, I don't need any facts, I can make any claim that I want, anything goes because that's conventional thought, that's what everybody believes anyway, so if I say it it's not surprising, and I don't have to back it up.

On the other hand, suppose I were to try in two minutes to condemn the U.S. invasion of South Vietnam, or the U.S. attack against Nicaragua. That sounds crazy. The U.S. isn't attacking people! So within two minutes between two commercials it sounds absurd, in fact any unconventional opinion sounds absurd. The reason is that if you say anything in the least way unconventional you naturally, and rightly, are expected to give a reason, to give evidence, to build up an argument, to say why you believe that unconventional thing. The very structure of the media in the United States prevents that, makes it impossible. The result is that what's expressible are conventional thoughts and conventional doctrine. That's a very effective technique for blocking thought and criticism.

Of course life is always much easier when you just express conventional doctrine. You don't have to do any work. But you're not allowed to do the work, even those who are willing to do it. They're not given the opportunity to back up their unconventional ideas, even on the rare occasions when they do get access to the media. That's a brilliant feature of the American mass media system.

DB: *In an interview in* The Chomsky Reader, *you comment that sometimes when you're driving you listen to radio talk shows on sports and you're struck by the enormous detail and concentration of analysis that callers bring to sports issues, but they can't bring it to social and political issues, which indeed have a greater impact on their lives.*

I don't follow sports, but apparently you can find out quite a lot about the details of the New England Patriots, the Red Sox or whoever's around. What's very striking is that the people who call in not only seem to know an awful lot, and judging by the reaction of the experts on the radio, they seem to talk like equals, but also they are perfectly free to give advice. They tell what the coach did wrong yesterday and what he ought to do tomorrow. The people who are running the talk show, the experts that they have, interact with the callers at a reasonable intellectual level.

On the other hand, people do not feel that they have the capacity to talk about affairs that affect their lives in international and domestic policy, and so on, and they don't. They don't have the information, they can't get the information. They are taught from childhood that they're not allowed to know about those things and that they're too stupid to think about them, and that they have to be put into the hands of experts. And unless you're pretty much of a fanatic, that's true. It takes real fanaticism to get enough information. There is in the public domain enough information to gain an understanding of what's happening in the world, but it takes an almost fanatic level of devotion to do so, whereas apparently it doesn't take that much effort to find out about the local sports team. I don't think that international affairs are harder. I don't think the national security policy is intellectually more challenging.

In fact that's a pretense of the social sciences, that they're dealing with deeply complex issues that are beyond the level of the ordinary person. That's mostly fraud. Outside the natural sciences and mathematics, there are very few things that ordinary people can't understand if they put their minds to it. They're simply not given an opportunity to.

You want to find out what's happening in Central America, you're really going to have to work. You're going to have to read exotic newspapers, you're going to have to compare today's lies with yesterday's lies and see if you can construct some rational story out of them. It's a major effort, and normal people, quite naturally, can't dedicate that effort to it. It's one of the techniques of marginalization. What you mentioned before about the encapsulation of expression, that's another technique. You never hear anything except conventional views. If you do hear them, they sound lunatic, rightly, because there's no opportunity to back them up.

DB: *I'd like you to talk about something I call "rotten apples vs. rotten barrels." It seems to be one of the techniques of the state managers to focus, let's say, during the Watergate or the Iran-Contra scandals, on individuals, to personalize the evil and to deflect attention from institutions.*

You're exactly correct. When something goes wrong and can't be suppressed any longer, when some scandal breaks out into the open, it's necessary somehow to prevent people from understanding what's really going on. In the Iran-Contra hearings, for example, it's very interesting to look at what was investigated. What was investigated were the alleged wrongdoings of particular individuals. Let's take sending arms to Iran. That's supposed to be the wrong thing to do, there seems to be an agreement about that. What was the focus of attention? It was on the so-called "transaction," with Ollie North and William Casey and so on, that took place from mid-1985 until it was exposed by the courageous press in the fall of 1986. An obvious question comes up: What was the U.S. government doing *before* 1985 with regard to arms to Iran? The answer is very simple: it was sending arms to Iran via Israel, exactly what it was doing during the "transaction." That has been public knowledge since 1980. The first notice I saw of it was in *Business Week,* I think it was in December 1980. In the early 1980's, it was reported widely.

In February 1982 it was completely public. In March or April 1982 Leslie Gelb of the *New York Times* had a front-page story in which he described the arms flow to Iran. He said that about 50 percent of it is coming from Israel with much of the rest from private arms merchants with Israeli connections. Arms from Israel means arms from the United States. Israel is a client state. They don't send arms to anyone unless we agree. In fact, it's mainly American arms. And that continued, publicly. Furthermore, absolutely in public, the Israeli officials involved explained why they were doing it.

On the BBC, for example, in February 1982, the very same Israeli officials who came up in the Iran-Contra hearings were interviewed. They explained that they were selling arms to Iran with the intent of finding military officers who would be sufficiently murderous that they would carry out a military coup. On the same program were high American officials, Richard Helms, former CIA director, who is also a former ambassador to Iran, and Robert Komer of the Defense Department. They said, yeah, that was a good idea, they thought that's probably what we ought to do. The Israeli ambassador to the United

States said openly in 1982 that Israel was supplying arms to Iran in coordination with the U.S. government at "almost the highest of levels," in his words, and the purpose again was to try to carry out a military coup. That's the way you do it. You send arms in order to establish relations with elements in the military. None of this was discussed in the hearings. Certainly what was not discussed is that this was *typical* U.S. policy, typical systematic policy. For example, when we were trying to overthrow the Allende government of Chile in the early 1970's—it's no secret that the United States was doing everything to overthrow that government—we were also sending arms, and we were rewarded, namely with the Pinochet coup.

The way you find internal elements to overthrow a government is to arm the military. We did exactly the same thing in Indonesia in the early 1960's. We were very hostile to the government. We sent arms to the military and we were rewarded with a coup and a huge massacre of 700,000 or 800,000 people killed and the destruction of the only mass-based party. The coup was very warmly welcomed in the West. And there are many other cases.

To look into these issues would focus on institutional facts. Therefore they are out. You can talk about "juntas" and "rogue elements out of control," "loose cannons," "patriots who have gone berserk," or something like that. All of that's safe because it doesn't lead to any understanding of the way the institutions work.

I should say that dissidents also contribute to this. This talk about "secret teams" and all that kind of business is highly misleading. The secret teams and the clandestine operations are normal government policy when the state is driven underground by its own population. When the population will not tolerate certain actions the state will be driven underground and will carry out clandestine actions. That's what happened in the 1980's; it's happened often before.

There's very little indication in my view that there are any "loose cannons" around. Maybe occasionally somebody gets out of control briefly, but it's a very marginal phenomenon. What happens is systematic behavior, very well intelligible in terms of the fundamental institutions. But you can't look at that. The Iran-Contra hearings were just a cover-up. Let's take the fact that the United States was illegally supplying arms to the contras during the period of the Boland Amendment. The claim that that was a secret is ludicrous. I discussed it in *Turning the Tide* which came out in 1985. I don't have any secret records, I was using the public record. I even identified Oliver North as the person involved, because it was all public. Again, I was writing about the U.S. arms sales to Iran through Israel in 1983, I discussed it in *The Fateful Triangle,* which came out in 1983. It was all public. But to deal with the public record and to show what's continually happening, that's going to lead you to an institutional critique, and that's no good. What you have to do is personalize it.

The same was true during Watergate. It was very dramatic, during the Watergate hearings. In fact, just think what Watergate was about? What was the big crime of Watergate? The crime was that the Republican Party had hired a bunch of kind of Keystone Cops to break into the Democratic Party headquarters for reasons which remain obscure to this day. That was the crime. There were some ancillary things.

At exactly the time of the Watergate hearings it was exposed in court cases and through the Freedom of Information Act that the FBI, at that point for 12 or 13 years, had been regularly carrying out burglaries of the Socialist Workers Party, which is a legal political party, for the purpose of disrupting their activities, stealing their membership lists, using the membership lists to intimidate people who joined the party, get them to lose their jobs, etc. That's vastly more serious than Watergate. This isn't a bunch of petty crooks. This is the national political police. It wasn't being done by some loose cannon, it was being done systematically by every administration. It was seriously disrupting a legal political party, whereas Watergate did nothing to the Democratic Party. Did that come up at the Watergate hearings? Not a mention.

What's the difference? The difference is that the Democratic Party represents domestic power, the Socialist Workers Party doesn't. So what the Watergate hearings showed, the great principle that was being defended, was "people with power are going to defend themselves." That's what it is. But you can't say that. If you were to say that, you begin to understand how the legal system works, how the state repression system works, therefore it's out. Watergate was framed and designed so that it could focus on the misdeeds of a particular individual, Richard Nixon, who made the serious tactical error of attacking people with power. Just to take another example, Nixon's "enemies list" was a great scandal.

DB: *People like Tom Watson of IBM were on the list.*

Yes. Actually, I was on the enemies list, too. I know perfectly well from my own experience that absolutely nothing happened to anybody on the enemies list. They didn't even audit our income tax returns, and that was particularly striking in my case because I was publicly organizing tax resistance. Nothing happened to anybody on the enemies list. Nevertheless it was a scandal. Why? Not because I was on it, but because people like Tom Watson were on it, and McGeorge Bundy and James Reston. In other words, it's a scandal to call powerful people bad names in private.

But at the very same time that the enemies list came out, it was revealed in court hearings that the FBI had been involved in an outright political assassination of a Black Panther organizer, Fred Hampton. Did that show up in the Watergate hearings? No, although it happened during the Nixon administration. Why? Because if the state is involved in a gestapo-style assassination of a Black Panther organizer, that's OK. He has no power, and he's an enemy anyway. On the other hand, calling powerful people bad names in private, that shakes the foundations of the republic. Again, powerful people are going to defend themselves, and that's all that Watergate amounted to.

The whole thing was crafted to focus on a particular individual, who incidentally was very unpopular in elite circles and who had been since he more or less tore apart the international economic system during the Nixon shock a couple of years earlier, and they were going to get rid of him. Of course, once that one bad apple was thrown out of the body politic, we were right back to our traditional purity. The institutional crimes just continue. Even the bombing of Cambodia was not part of the indictment.

It entered into the hearings. This was not a small thing, a bombing of another country in which several hundred thousand people were killed, a neutral country that was supposed to be friendly. Pretty serious business. It entered the hearings, but only in one respect. They didn't inform Congress, and that was considered so insignificant it didn't even enter the bill of indictment. Again, it means it's OK to attack another country, aggression is fine, but just notify powerful people about it. Don't encroach upon their prerogatives. To bring out any of these things would be to give some light as to how the system functions, and that's intolerable. Obviously, any powerful system is going to defend itself against understanding on the part of others. It's not obscure why.

Elite Power
and the
Responsibility of Intellectuals

February 15, 1988

DB: *You frequently use the term "elite." I think a working definition would be useful.*

There are various segments of the groups that we ought to call "elites." In the first place, there are those who are in the position to make decisions which affect crucially what happens in the general society. That would include political decisions, decisions over investment, production, distribution, and so on. Then there are the groups that are in managerial positions with regard to the political and economic institutions, the state managers, the corporate managers, and so on. There are also elites with regard to the ideological institutions, the top editorial positions and other positions of control within the media, the journals, etc. These groups, which are not only closely interconnected and interlocked, but also share a common set of values and associations, belong to the highly privileged class and are generally quite wealthy. They determine the basic framework of what happens in the society based on their power, which ultimately is rooted in economic power, in simple ownership of the basic facilities out of which the society is constituted.

DB: *And what of the role of the control of information and the decision-making processes?*

As far as control of information is concerned, it's largely dominated by a fairly small number of major sources of information. There are a number of good studies of this, but without going into the details, it's pretty narrow. This essentially is a set of major corporations: news or information corporations, including the major television networks, which themselves are part of broader industrial and financial conglomerates; the major newspapers, half a dozen or so of which are also substantial corporations; the wire services which are interconnected with them etc. These are major corporations which sell a product to other businesses.

As we've covered in another discussion, the product that they sell is audiences and readers. Newspapers and journals typically don't finance themselves through sales. They often lose money through subscribers, and obviously if you watch a television set you are not paying the channel. But the product that is sold is readers, and what's more, elite readers. Your advertising profile rises with the audience that you can offer to the advertiser. If it's a high-quality audience in terms of privilege and buying capacity your advertising rates go up.

The information system, from an economic point of view at least, is fundamentally a system of major corporations trying to sell their product, namely relatively privileged and influential elite audiences, to other corporations. Hence it's all deeply embedded within the same system of domination and control that organizes the economy and largely runs the state.

DB: *Is there a collective unspoken understanding of shared interests? Or are there backroom meetings with men smoking cigars and deciding what's going to happen?*

Of course that happens. There's nothing particularly conspiratorial about it. The same goes on in the business world, so it's not surprising to find the head of a corporation taking a business associate out to some fancy country club where they can have drinks and play golf and make business deals in the backroom. In fact we all know that there's no sharp break between the personal and cultural interactions in business practices.

There's nothing in the least conspiratorial. These are very small groups relative to the population that are very narrowly concentrated in high privilege. The values are shared, often articulated, often unspoken, and the inter-actions apply at every level, from Washington dinner parties to meetings of the Council of Foreign Relations to delegations from corporate law firms to state officials or simply the staffing of top executive positions in the gov-ernment by representatives of the major investment firms, corporations, information corporations. There's a lot of flow between the top levels of media and the govern-ment. There's a natural interpenetration due to shared interests, shared privilege, and simply the desire to wield power effectively in the interest of the institutions one represents.

DB: *In this "procedural democracy," as you've termed it in the past, do the elite view the role of the public as essentially one of ratification at the polls?*

That's a very conscious view. It's consciously re-garded to be the duty of the public. I think it was Maxwell Taylor, Kennedy's *eminence grise,* who once said that the role of the public is to know just enough to be able to do their duty, which is to ratify decisions at the polls. They don't have to know any more than that. The general attitude of any system of authority towards the public is as of an enemy, because they've got to be kept under control. If they get out of control they might do all sorts of dangerous things, and typically a state regards its domes-tic population as a potential enemy. That's been notori-ously true in the United States for a long time.

You can trace this issue of the roles of the public and the elite all the way back to the origins of the Republic.

John Jay's favorite maxim, according to his biographer, was that "the people who own the country ought to govern it." That's in fact exactly the way the Constitutional system was established. It was a system in which propertied white males, who were regarded as more or less equal, inaccurately but not absurdly, they were to govern the country. They had the franchise. As things have changed over the years with the rise of corporate power on the one hand, which restricted the possibilities of democracy, and the extension of the franchise, which theoretically extended it, this struggle between narrowly concentrated power and the enemy public has of course continued.

DB: *Is your societal vision outside the current state paradigm?*

I think the state paradigm is a very unnatural one. If you look at history, you can see that easily. To establish the state system in Europe required hundreds of years of murderous and brutal warfare and the only reason it stopped is that when it reached its latest stage in the early 1940's it was plain that the next stage would be total annihilation of human civilization. At that point the internal conflicts in Europe terminated, at least for a time. It was centuries of brutal warfare, murder, destruction, and that reflects the unnaturalness of the system. Everywhere where Europe has spread throughout the world we find what we would call, if we were honest, the "plague of European civilization." Everywhere it spread over the world it has led to exactly the same thing. In the colonial areas, where the European invasion imposed a version of the state system, it has also led to interminable and brutal conflict.

The problems are that this system has very little to do with people's perceived interests and needs and that it therefore has to be imposed by violence and force. It happens to be the governing world system at the moment, thanks to the European conquest of most of the world. But in the long term I would think it ought to be replaced by forms of association more related to actual human needs and concerns. That's a long term, however.

DB: *In the United States, what kind of ingredients, what kind of conditions would be necessary for the development of an alternative or, for want of a better term, a "progressive culture"?*

Talk about erosion of the state system is so far off that I don't think it's useful to even think about what would be needed. What's needed in the shorter term is exactly what elite groups fear. Anything they fear is probably good, and what they fear is what they call the "crisis of democracy," that is simply the engagement of the population in the political arena. The political arena is not enough, but even the engagement of the population in the political arena would be useful progress towards democracy in the United States. By that I mean not just watching the candidates on television and clapping for them, but actual participation, real participation in formation of programs, in meaningful selection and recall of representatives, etc. That, which virtually doesn't exist in the United States, would be a large step towards functioning democracy. But then, even if it were to be achieved in some measure, it would still be limited.

The fact is that what can happen in the political system altogether, the range of decisions open in the political system, is very sharply constrained by private power. This is not a problem that arises in the United States because the political system is so narrow and so much under business control that there are virtually never any major policy options offered. But in countries that function in a more democratic fashion, where there really are policy options, say in Latin America, you see it all the time.

If a reform candidate comes into office with real

policy alternatives, there may be a military coup, but if not there will be capital strike, capital flight, other pressures by the owners of the society to ensure that these policies can't be pursued. Again, that doesn't really arise in the United States because there are basically no major policy issues in the public domain. But it would happen if the political system ever opened up. What that reflects is the fact that in a system of private enterprise, with private control over the means of production and distribution and decisions over investment and so on, the range of political choices is restricted. It's heavily influenced by the resources available to those who own the basic institutions of the society, but it's also restricted simply by their capacity to control whether the society survives, how it survives, how people live, etc. That means that meaningful democracy will involve actual popular takeover of decision-making in the essential institutions, and that includes crucially the economic institutions. They are what determine basically what our lives are.

DB: *What do you mean by "fascism"? I'm particularly intrigued by a comment you made: "Fascism is deeply rooted in everyone's mind in the United States."*

When we talk about fascism, first of all, we're talking about a system of political, economic, social and cultural organization. If we want to talk about it reasonably we have to dissociate it from concentration camps and gas chambers. There was fascism before there were extermination camps, and it was bad enough then. Fascism meant from a socio-cultural point of view an attack on the ideals of the Enlightenment, an attack on the conceptions of what was in those days called "brotherhood of man." We would now put it in a perhaps more civilized form. But an attack on the idea that people had natural rights, that they were fundamentally equal, that it was an infringement of essential human rights if systems of authority subordinated some to others, the insistence that there were real bonds of unity and solidarity among people across cultures, etc. All of that was under attack. The ideas of solidarity were under attack under the principle of "purity of race and blood," typically in the Nazi version of fascism. The economic system was to be one of class collaboration between owners and workers, all working for the common cause, the cause of the nation and the state, under the control of a powerful state which would coordinate and intervene significantly in economic life to maintain authority, structures of power, etc. This is connected with control by the coordinated state-private monopolies over information, extensive censorship, permission for the state to determine what's true, historical truth, to enforce those decisions, etc.

That whole range of ideas, loosely interconnected, revealed itself in fascist movements which spread over much of the industrial world in the 1920's and 1930's. They took various forms in different societies, but elements of them could be perceived virtually everywhere. A lot of these principles unfortunately are very deeply rooted. For example, there's a very far-reaching willingness to allow the state, in coordination with private power, to control very substantial aspects of life. There's very little objection to this, whether it's cultural life, information flow, political organizations, etc. At the grass roots level in the United States there's a lot of opposition to it. You find a lot of independence and fierce individualism among the population, but it doesn't show up much in the dominant culture, that is, the culture that actually makes decisions and controls.

DB: *We've touched upon the question that I'm about to ask you: You've said that the non-educated classes in American society are not as indoctrinated with the state ideology as are the educated classes. Isn't that a bit romantic, and what kind of evidence do you have to substantiate that?*

It's not only not romantic, but it's pretty close to tautological. Education is a form of indoctrination, therefore we typically find in any society that the educated classes are more indoctrinated. They're the ones who are subjected to the constant flow of propaganda which is largely directed to them because they're more important, so they have to be more controlled. Furthermore, the educated classes become the instruments of propaganda. Their function in the society is to promulgate and develop the ideological principles. As a result they inculcate them, if they don't they're usually weeded out and are no longer part of the privileged elite. It's not at all unusual to discover the basic principles of the ideological system in any society most deeply entrenched and least critically accepted by the educated classes.

It would be romantic to suppose that the lesser level of indoctrination on the part of the less educated part of the population leads to some sort of revolutionary spirit or progressive impulse or whatever. It doesn't at all. It can lead to almost anything. For example, this can help create the mass base for a fascist movement. In many respects, fascist ideals are inconsistent with the demands of the elite culture and system of power and privilege. That's why in the United States you typically find the attack on real fascist tendencies led by business interests. The American Civil Liberties Union, for example, is basically a very conservative organization. It's a very valuable organization and I'm glad to be part of it, but we shouldn't delude ourselves as to what it's about. It's basically defending rights which are demanded by the wealthy and the privileged. They don't want a state which is able to infringe with their privilege, and as a result these rights are defended.

You could see it in the summer of 1987 in the Ollie North phenomenon. There was a kind of brief whiff of fascism there. It was detected, and you could see it in the editorials in the *New York Times*. Even the *Wall Street*

Journal ran a column by its Washington correspondent, lecturing to North et al. about the dangers of fascism. The business classes are quick to pick up the scent of fascism and they don't like it. They might turn to it in a time of crisis, but typically they want the state to be powerful enough to work for their interests, but not powerful enough to infringe upon their privileges. We find right at the roots of power some of the defenses against fascism. But among the general population, the less educated, less articulate and typically the most depressed part of the population, you can find at times an appeal by charismatic figures who promise to lead them out of their problems and to attack either the powerful or some other bogeyman, the Jews or the homosexuals, or the communists, or whoever is identified as responsible for their troubles. That kind of appeal is often vivid and powerful. We've seen it plenty of times in modern times.

In the United States, which is a highly depoliticized society, it's a very dangerous possibility. In particular the growth of religious fanaticism is a very threatening phenomenon. Fortunately the leading figures in this movement have been extremely corrupt, which is a very good thing. Every time I find that one of them wants nothing but gold Cadillacs or free sex, etc., I applaud. As long as they're corrupt they're not very dangerous. They'll just rip off their partisans. But if one of them wants power, they could be very dangerous. If someone comes along out of those movements who can combine religious fanaticism with the lust for power, not privilege and corruption, then it could be extremely dangerous in a country like this, particularly in a period in which much of the population may be compelled to accept a degree of austerity. Right now, to pay off the lunacies of Reaganite economic management, but more generally, or in periods in which the relative decline in power of the state, its decline in capacity to control the world, leads to all sorts of paranoid concerns about knives in the back and enemies outside and within.

That kind of combination does make it possible for the less indoctrinated segments of the population to deviate from the official ideology and off towards fascism. At the same time, these same groups have been and continue to be the basis for a very impressive resistance to state and corporate power and its violence. Take Central America. The sources of the substantial public opposition to U.S. atrocities in Central America are not in elite circles, by any means. They're out in the general population, in the churches, in the Mid-West, in sectors of the population that were not engaged much, and may even have been hostile towards the movements of the 1960's. So it's a complex affair, less indoctrination is not necessarily a hopeful phenomenon. It may be the basis for more hopeful developments, but it doesn't provide them.

DB: *In your essay, "The Responsibility of Intellectuals," originally published in* American Power and the New Mandarins *and reprinted in the* Chomsky Reader, *you discuss the role of intellectuals and the need to speak the truth. Steve Wasserman, in an August 1987 L.A. Times book review of the* Reader, *accuses you of not following your own advice in relation to Nicaragua. Have you muted your criticisms of the Sandinistas?*

Have I muted my criticism of the Sandinistas? No, I don't think so. What exactly did you have in mind? I read the review, but I don't remember that comment.

DB: *He suggested that you were very reluctant to criticize revolutionary liberation movements in the Third World.*

Actually, that was one of the innumerable misquotations in the review. There was a section to which he took exception, as many people do, in which I pointed out that an intellectual, like any human being, has the moral responsibility to consider the human consequences of what they do. That's just a truism. If you write you have a moral responsibility to consider the consequences of what you write, what are the consequences going to be for human beings. Then I gave a number of examples, which he excluded because they didn't help with his political aims.

So I said, for example, imagine a Russian intellectual now. Should that person write accurate criticism of the terror and atrocities of the Afghan resistance in the Soviet press, knowing that that accurate criticism will enable the Soviet Union to mobilize its own population for further atrocities and aggression? Would that be a morally responsible thing to do? I didn't answer that question, but if you want my answer I would say no, it's not a morally responsible thing to do. That example was not mentioned in his review. But I also pointed out that we face exactly the same problem. We have to ask whether we want to act in such a way as to enhance the atrocities and violence of our own state.

To take another example, suppose that I was a German citizen in 1938. Would it have been morally responsible for me to write an article in the Nazi press about the atrocities carried out by Jewish terrorists in Palestine, or about the crimes of Jewish businessmen, even if it was all accurate? Would it have been morally responsible for me to write those truths in the Nazi press? Well, again, I didn't answer the question there, but my own answer would be no, it would not. These are just truisms. If we are capable of recognizing truisms about others, then we're just cowardly and dishonest if we refuse to apply the truisms to ourselves. This leads to moral dilemmas. It leads to moral dilemmas in the case of the Russian intellectual and Afghanistan and it leads to the same moral dilemmas in the case of the American intellectuals in the United States. How one resolves moral dilemmas is a problem that individuals have to face.

DB: *In the United States today there is a good deal of* *awareness of and interest in Central America. There are solidarity groups, sister cities projects, delegations travel to the region. There are conferences, symposia, lectures and a plethora of books and articles. Alexander Cockburn has called it a "very sophisticated and mature movement." But it seems that that sophistication and maturity does not extend to the Israeli/Palestinian issue. Why not?*

First of all, this sophistication and maturity extends to virtually nothing. The typical phenomenon is exactly contrary to what is always claimed. What history shows is that even the peace movement is very much controlled by the official agenda. It has definite illusions and moral blind spots, namely about atrocities for which the United States is responsible. That's the typical phenomenon. Now that's not what you read, because the purpose of what you read is to undermine and destroy the peace movement and anyone else, so there's a flood of propaganda, most of it fabricated, about how the peace movement has illusions and blind spots with respect to our enemies and the Third World dictators.

Exactly the opposite is very easily demonstrable. Timor is a perfect example. During the entire Timor atrocity, which still continues and which was comparable to Pol Pot and, relative to the population, greater, there's been almost total peace movement silence. The reason is that the Timor slaughter does not conform to the state agenda, since the U.S. is responsible for it. The issue is removed from attention, and the peace movement has a blind spot too.

There are numerous other examples. With regard to Central America things have been different, and it's very striking. Take an indicator, like letters to the editor. You look around the country and it's dramatic that letters to the editor are more sophisticated, more knowledgeable, more penetrating, more balanced and far more accurate than the material that appears in the opinion columns, op-eds, news reports, etc. I assume that the newspapers are not specifically picking letters that undermine their own position. They are obviously flooded by them. That does reflect a difference of consciousness. But that happens to be focused on this issue, for particular reasons. The Israeli/Arab conflict, like most issues, is just outside this. There are special reasons for that. They have to do largely with what happened in 1967, as we've talked about.

At the same time there was a very interesting reaction to the Israeli victory among the intellectual elites that control the information system, liberal to right-wing, in this case. There was tremendous euphoria over the Israeli victory, and Israel really endeared itself to liberal and other intellectuals at that time because of its success in using the mailed fist. That's a phenomenon that has to be explained. It's obvious why it should be true with the ultra right, but it's particularly interesting with regard to left-liberal American intellectuals. I think there you have to look back at American society to understand the phenomenon. It was at that point that Israel became the object of awe and love. You find that until that time, even among the New York Jewish intellectuals, Israel and Zionism were pretty minor phenomena. You check back over journals like *Dissent* in earlier years and there's nothing about the topic, and the editors regarded themselves as non-Zionists at the time. All this changed in 1967.

I think the reason it changed largely had to do with domestic events. You have to understand what was happening in the United States at that time. In the first place, this was 1967. The United States was not succeeding in destroying the indigenous resistance in Indochina. We weren't able to "defend South Vietnam," as it was put, namely destroy and attack South Vietnam. It's important to bear in mind that liberal opinion was very strongly in favor of the war. There was a lot of concern that the United States wasn't winning.

Here Israel came along and showed how to use

violence against Third-World upstarts, and that was impressive. Furthermore, the failure to win the war in Vietnam was combined with a growing threat to privilege at home. This came from many sectors of the society, the student movement—the students were not obeying authority, they were asking the wrong questions, there were signs of intellectual independence, independent moral judgment, etc. All of that is obviously going to be intolerable in the faculty club. You could see the women's movement coming, the ethnic minorities were pressing for their rights. There was a kind of a general sense of a threat to privilege coming from the Viet Cong, the Black Panthers, the students, the bearded Cuban revolutionaries, the Maoists, all sorts of partially paranoid fantasies, but partial recognition of the reality of popular ferment threatening authority and privilege. Again, Israel came along and showed how to use violence effectively in restoring order, and that was an impressive demonstration. It was particularly important for liberal humanists, because Israel was capable, with its very effective propaganda system, of portraying itself as being the victim, while it very efficiently used force and violence to crush its enemies.

This combination is absolutely irresistible. The liberal humanist is supposed to be in favor of the victim, and in this case he could shed tears for the alleged victim while secretly applauding the victim's successes in the effective use of violence. That's an irresistible combination. It stayed that way. That has swung debate in the United States to the point where sane discussion of this issue has become extremely difficult in educated circles, and in the organs of communication and information that they control. There are other factors. For example, there were people, Irving Howe [of *Dissent*] is the most notorious, who quite cynically exploited the passionate enthusiasm for Israel that developed in order to undermine and attack activist elements of the peace movement and the student movement. He wrote vicious articles in the *New York Times* and elsewhere claiming that unidentified elements of the peace movement wouldn't be satisfied until Israel was destroyed by bloodthirsty Arab terrorists and wanted fascism in Israel, etc., and that was an effective device at the time. I wouldn't call it McCarthyist, because it goes far beyond McCarthy, but that kind of device to try to undermine the organized and activist peace movement and dissident elements was a very popular position among elites. That's why he could write these things in the *New York Times*.

This was a period in which there was a general elite effort to try to beat back and control the population, to try to undermine the popular movements that had begun to develop. The use of Israel turned out to be one effective device. That again strengthened the natural association between the liberal intellectuals, who were the commissars who were supposed to carry this out, and Israel. For all these reasons, some of them quite objective, namely the role of Israel as an actual strategic asset for the United States, some of them more complex, having to do with American culture and internal society, the issues were simply driven off the agenda.

Here the difference between the general population and the elites is very dramatic. As I've indicated before, polls—and polls have to be regarded a bit cautiously, but they tell you something—have indicated regularly that about two-thirds of the population is in favor of a Palestinian state. That's just not part of American politics. You can't find an American politician who will call for it. It's not part of discussion and debate. What's striking is that even without virtually any articulate presentation, it's still the position held by a majority of the American public, conforming to the international consensus that's been blocked by the United States for at least 17 years.

DB: *One question about the American left, and I know*

you're not terribly comfortable using that term: you've spoken about its marginalization, its lack of resources, lack of continuity. What about this phenomenon on the left of internecine warfare and what I call left-left-bashing? Is that a product of this marginalization?

It's partly that, and it's partly, to an extent that we don't like to recognize, that external power and privilege set the agenda for the left. For example, take *New England Peacework,* which is a Quaker-based journal and a very good journal for the local peace movement. Right now it's devoting page after page to a debate which is essentially determined by the Office of Public Diplomacy and they don't recognize it. There's a debate going on every issue, with half the issue devoted to it, about whether the left, so-called, took exactly the right position with regard to Cambodia in the late 1970's. The fact of the matter is that the left, such as it is, barely existing, took approximately the position that was taken by virtually all competent authorities, State Department intelligence, Cambodia scholarship, etc. At the same time the left and the peace movement were avoiding major atrocities elsewhere. Nevertheless, there's no debate going on about, let's say, the failure to respond to East Timor, or the failure of the left to respond to the U.S. bombing of Cambodia in the early 1970's, which probably killed tens if not hundreds of thousands of people, or the failure of the left to respond to the growing and already quite horrifying crisis in Central America. There's no discussion about that. There's discussion about the alleged failure of the peace movement to respond to Pol Pot.

What you find on the one side is lies, fabrication and deceit requiring no evidence because they are the position of established power, which never requires any evidence. On the other side are apologies or responses that are largely a waste of time. In fact, any effort to respond to the lies is self-destructive because the response to the lies and exposure of the lies simply proves you're an apologist for atrocities, within the framework of official doctrine, which also controls dissident thought to a notable extent. It's a no-win situation, since the agenda is determined by established power.

I give this example to illustrate that even the most sophisticated elements of the peace movement are trapped by the indoctrination system and to a large extent follow its dictates, and that is another factor that leads to recrimination. In addition to that, there are just all sorts of power plays, personal, group, etc. Everybody who's been involved in the popular movements for years knows perfectly well that one or another sect has got their technique for trying to take control of any popular development that takes place. They're parasitic on it, and try to bring people in and mobilize them and bring them into their own organization or their own particular cult or whatever. This is all going to go on, and as long as there are no stable and healthy popular institutions you can anticipate that it will continue.

DB: *I remember you talking about the June 1982 peace demonstration in New York, where you were initially involved and then you chose not to participate.*

That was a different story. It's true, I didn't participate in that. That was the demonstration that brought hundreds of thousands, maybe a million people to New York at the time of the U.N. disarmament sessions. This happened to have taken place about a week after the Israeli invasion of Lebanon. The Israeli invasion of Lebanon, apart from tearing the country up and destroying it, also happened, at that very point, to be bringing the world very close to global war. There were hot-line communications. Israel had attacked Syria. Syria had not expected that attack, even after the war began they thought Israel was going after Palestinians. Israel attacked Syria, which was a Soviet ally. Russians were killed; the Russian fleet was in the Eastern Mediterranean and there was a real danger of global war since the United States was supporting the attack. You couldn't imagine a more urgent issue.

The organizers of the demonstration decided to exclude it. That's part of the way in which the movements on the left protect Israel. They, as I saw it, thereby expressed their position that nuclear war is less important than protecting Israel from criticism. That was so outrageous that I personally decided not to even show up. That's a special thing, again, it's a case in which the agenda established by external power determines to a very large extent what is thought and what is done even in the dissident movements.

DB: *This is a very different question on the nature of evil. You're an empiricist, a scientist working with objective material. You've discussed U.S. atrocities in Indochina in the 1960's and 1970's and atrocities in Central America in the 1980's. For example, you've written about soldiers who throw babies up in the air and then bayonet them. The question arises: Many of these soldiers are fathers and brothers who have held babies in their arms. How could they be reduced to that? Also, as an addendum, you've said that individuals are not evil but that institutions are. Isn't that a cop-out?*

First of all, I've very rarely talked about atrocities committed by soldiers. I've explained why. The reason is that soldiers, in a situation of conflict, are frightened. The options open to them are very few. They can be enraged. These are situations in which people can't use their normal human instincts. You can find a few sentences in which I've quoted things of this sort from human rights groups, but I don't harp on it and I almost never discuss it.

To take one case, I was asked by the *New York Review* to write an article about the My Lai incident when it broke, and I did write such an article, but I had about three sentences on My Lai in which I pointed out exactly these things, that the actions carried out by half-crazed GI's in the field don't tell you very much. The much more serious question, I think, is how people who are subject to no threat, who are comfortable, educated and if they don't know what's going on it's because of a conscious decision not to know what's going on, how such people can, in the quiet of their living rooms, tolerate and support and back horrifying atrocities, and plan them in their well-appointed offices. That's the real evil, far worse than what's done by soldiers in the field. As to how soldiers can do it: apart from the conditions of combat, which are never very pretty and are in fact life-threatening, apart from that, you're talking about young kids, teenagers, who in fact are easily indoctrinated and can be turned into killers.

Take this example you mentioned. It happened to be the Salvadoran army. This is an army which is press-ganged. It's not a drafted army. They're press-ganged from poor areas. You take kids from poor areas, give them guns, give them training, give them indoctrination, and you can turn them into professional killers. Imperial powers have been doing this for centuries, and we're doing it too. As regards the question of evil, we don't have to think of exotic examples. We can look at ourselves and ask the question about ourselves. You ask, is it a cop-out to say that it's a matter of institutions, not individuals. I don't think so. Individuals are certainly capable of evil. We don't have to look very far to see that. But individuals are capable of all sorts of things. Human nature has lots of ways of realizing itself, humans have lots of capacities and options. Which ones reveal themselves depends to a large extent on the institutional structures. If we had institutions which permitted pathological killers free rein, they'd be running the place. The only way to survive would be to let those elements of your nature manifest themselves.

If we have institutions which make greed the sole property of human beings and encourage pure greed at the expense of other human emotions and commitments, we're going to have a society based on greed, with all that follows. A different society might be organized in such a way that human feelings and emotions of other sorts, say solidarity, support, sympathy become dominant. Then you'll have different aspects of human nature and personality revealing themselves.

DB: *Who has inspired and influenced you intellectually?*

There are too many people to mention. I could mention personal examples, but that would mean going back into personal history. The thing that inspires me most is exactly what inspired Rousseau, namely the sight of—I wish I could quote his words exactly—half-naked savages, and other ordinary people, fighting for their liberty and independence with courage and integrity. That's more inspiring than the writings of the sages.

DB: *Do you recognize or acknowledge the spiritual life, and is it a factor in who you are?*

By the spiritual life, do you mean the life of thought and reflection and literature, or the life of religion? It's a different question.

DB: *The spiritual dimension in terms of religion. Is that at all a factor?*

For me, it's not. I am a child of the Enlightenment. I think irrational belief is a dangerous phenomenon, and I try consciously to avoid irrational belief. On the other hand, I certainly recognize that it's a major phenomenon for people in general, and you can understand why it would be. It does, apparently, provide personal sustenance, but also bonds of association and solidarity and a means for expressing elements of one's personality that are often very valuable elements. To many people it does that. In my view, there's nothing wrong with that. My view could be wrong, of course, but my position is that we should not succumb to irrational belief.

DB: *Do you derive any strength from the Jewish tradition?*

I'm obviously very much part of it. I grew up deeply immersed in it and still feel that, but whether it's a source of strength I'd find it hard to say. I couldn't identify any way in which that's true.

DB: *Who are some people today that you admire and that you learn from?*

There are too many such people. I can't say. Take my friend Rubén Zamora, for example, who is now with tremendous courage expressing his willingness to go back to the terror state that the United States has established in El Salvador, facing a high likelihood of assassination and trying to exploit some political opening for his basically left-Christian Democrat commitment. I find that pretty inspiring, and I could think of numerous other examples. I know that's not the question you're asking, but I'm purposely evading it. I know there are people who have said smart things, which is fine, it's not hard to say smart things.

DB: *You're in great demand as a public speaker, you're booked into the 1990's. I traveled with you in Colorado and California during the last week of January 1988, and everywhere you went you drew appreciative and capacity audiences, standing ovations were de rigueur. What do you attribute that to?*

As you know from having heard me speak, I'm not a particularly charismatic speaker, and if I had the capacity to do so I wouldn't use it. I'm really not interested in persuading people, I don't want to and I try to make this point obvious. What I'd like to do is help people persuade themselves. I tell them what I think, and obviously I hope they'll persuade themselves that that's true, but I'd rather have them persuade themselves of what they think is true. I think there are a lot of analytic perspectives, just straight information, that people are not presented with. The only thing I would like to be able to contribute is that. I think by and large audiences recognize that. I think the reason people come is because that's what they want to hear. There are many people around the country, all sorts of people, who feel that they simply do not have access to an awful lot of information, analysis, interpretation, that is relevant to understanding the world, and I think it's a very healthy reaction to try to gain such access.

DB: *I noticed a very different Noam Chomsky when you were speaking about linguistics and philosophy. You were much more relaxed, you were given to humor. Clearly when you were talking about political and social issues in the other talks it affects you.*

You can't talk about the tremendous suffering that we're inflicting upon people without having a good deal of emotion, either under control or actually expressed. I try to keep it under control, but it's certainly there.

DB: *You have a singular position in the intellectual life of the country today, whether you like it or not, it's there. You're a "life preserver" for many people, organizations, bookstores, and community radio stations. People depend upon you for information and analysis. You're a kind of intellectual "axis mundi." Is that a burden?*

First of all let me say that to the extent that that's true, it's not a particular comment about me. It's a comment about the intellectual class in general, which has simply abandoned this responsibility of honest inquiry and some degree of public service in favor of the pursuit of privilege and power and subordination to external power. To an overwhelming extent that's true. To put it as simply as possible, there just aren't enough speakers available. If a group around the country wants a speaker on such-and-such a topic, there are very few people they can turn to. The few people who do this are under incredible demands. That's a comment about the intellectual classes, including the left, which does not provide this kind of service to ordinary people, or only to a very limited extent. Any group around the country who tries to get speakers is aware of this. Is it a burden? It's both a burden and a kind of privilege. A burden in the sense that there are 24 hours in a day and only so many things you can do, so obviously it's a burden, but it's certainly one that I would choose and do choose.

DB: *In response to questions about your prodigious work productivity, you say you are a "fanatic." Do you like that about yourself?*

I neither like it nor dislike it. I recognize it. It does require a degree of fanaticism even to be able to break out of the constant drumbeat of ideology and indoctrination and to gain the relevant information and organize it. Even that limited commitment requires a degree of fanaticism, and to pursue it beyond that, the constant travel, speaking, etc., sure, that's another form of fanaticism.

DB: *Where do you see yourself and your work?*

In these areas, as far as I'm aware, I know what I'm trying to do. Others can judge how well it's done. What I'm trying to do is simply provide the kind of service to popular dissident movements and scattered individuals that any person who has the resources, the privilege, the training, etc. should perform, nothing beyond that.

State Economic Planning

December 13, 1989, KGNU radio call-in interview

DB: *I'd like to ask you a few questions and then open it up to our listeners. The post-war U.S. economy has been structured on what you call alternatively "the Pentagon system" or "military Keynesianism," that is, a state subsidy of high-technology industry. In light of the U.S./U.S.S.R. rapprochement, what moves, if any, do you see the state and corporate managers of the U.S. economy taking to preserve their power and privilege?*

I think they are concerned about it. You can read in the *Wall Street Journal,* for example, articles with headlines like "Unsettling Specter of Peace Concerns U.S. Analysts." And rightly so. This has been the major technique of state industrial management since about 1950, the technique by which the government policy essentially compels the public to subsidize research and development for high-technology industry. But also, beyond that, for the pharmaceutical companies and others. There's no obvious alternative available. For the moment, there is a kind of leveling of military expenditure. Actually, this year's military budget was the biggest ever. It's supposed to level off at about that for a while.

For the foreseeable future they're talking about cutbacks, but if you look they're really not cutbacks, they're just a lack of projected expansion. Even those modifications are generally going to hit outlays, they'll cut down the force level, for example, while keeping the procurement level the same. For the moment, at least, the plans are to maintain those parts of the military system which do in effect feed into advanced industry. There are some very serious problems coming up. The Reagan administration, which pushed this state intervention in the

163

economy well beyond the norm, also in the last year or so began to organize Pentagon-based consortia. Semetech is the main one. In order to keep the semiconductor industry viable, Silicon Valley, etc., there is no clear alternative on the horizon to more public funding, meaning in our system through the Pentagon.

Yesterday there was some testimony in Congress by former Secretary of Defense McNamara and others calling for a very substantial military cutback. McNamara proposed about 50 percent, arguing strictly on military grounds and doubtless on military grounds what he said was even highly conservative. But as far as I can see from the papers he didn't address these problems, which are the central ones.

DB: *You've said that if there were going to be a move toward conversion, that is, getting away from the Pentagon system, that it's going to involve something like a social revolution.*

It's hard to conceive of how it could be done. It's true that other industrial democracies do it. Germany and Japan, for example, have a much lower percentage of military expenditures and have devised other ways for government coordination and subsidy for the industrial system.

DB: *MITI, for example, in Japan is the state consortium that organizes the economy.*

Yes. In Japan, MITI, the Ministry of International Trade and Industry, serves as a kind of coordinating agency. The Japanese economy is very differently structured. There are big financial-industrial conglomerates and through the coordination of MITI they lay out the planning, distribute investments, etc. for the forthcoming period. That gives a pretty high level of planning. The culture is quite different. The population is very docile and they basically do what they're told. It's straightforward for the Japanese government and industry simply to say, look, here's the level of consumption for next year and here are the prices. I don't think that would wash in the United States. The population is too independent.

DB: *Have you noticed any hostility or traces of racism vis-à-vis Japan? I have, and that's why I'm asking you. You see it in cartoons and editorials and in a new Hollywood film out called Black Rain. There are comments such as: the Japanese work too hard, they save too much, they have unfair trade practices, etc.*

Of course there's a lot of that, and there's a good deal of concern about Japan. It's true that their level of saving is far higher. The quality of their goods is much better. They're buying in very heavily into central sectors of the American economy right now. For the first time there's major Japanese investment in the U.S. high-tech industry, which is one of the last things that still functions around here, mainly through Pentagon facilitation. More visible than that is buying Columbia Pictures and Rockefeller Center, but picking up the leading sectors of the high-tech industry is much more significant in the long run. The Japanese soon will be in a position to constrain U.S. military expenditures, since they control a good deal of the advanced technology that's required for fancy military production, and some Japanese have actually threatened it.

DB: *In your view, have the media played their traditional role of obscuring reality from the American public, in this case the fact that the Pentagon system of economics in the United States has seriously eroded and corroded this country's ability to manufacture consumer goods?*

That certainly hasn't been a very big topic. I doubt whether you'll see an article about it. It's a mixed story. Without the Pentagon system we'd need some other system of state capitalist industrial management. The fact of the matter is that although there's a lot of talk about capitalism and free enterprise and free markets, no one who's actually involved in the business world believes a word of it. It's fine for after dinner speeches and editorials, but when push comes to shove, the sectors of the economy that work and the industrial economies that are successful are those that have a substantial state coordinating and subsidizing component. The same businessman who will make a passionate speech about free trade in an after dinner speech will also go off to Washington and make sure that the subsidies keep flowing. The question is what alternative system is going to be set up.

DB: *Do you have something in mind?*

That's where I think there ought to be social revolution. It seems to me that these decisions should not be made by business and the representatives of business who we call government. These should be popular decisions. They should be made beginning from the plant floor and from the community, and that would mean social control over investment. That's a social revolution.

DB: *That leads into my next question: Do you think the outbreak of popular democracy in Eastern Europe might be viewed with some trepidation by U.S. elites? What if it were to spread to this country?*

As you notice, they're really dragging their feet for all kinds of reasons. For one thing, popular movements are always frightening, even when they're overthrowing some enemy, because there's a spreading effect. It's not the kind of thing that ought to happen. It leads to these "crises of democracy" that elites are always worried about. There is a possible contagious effect. Also, it's bringing about changes in Europe that U.S. elites are pretty wary about. Western Europe is moving towards greater integration and also greater independence, and it's looking to restore what are in effect quasi colonial relations with the East. Japan probably has the same idea with regard to exploitation of Siberia. That kind of integration of the Eurasian economies, with a large part of the current Soviet bloc becoming a kind of Third World to be exploited by Europe and Japan, would turn the United States into a second-class actor on the world scene. The United States is very concerned to make sure that the blocs are maintained, the Warsaw Pact, NATO. NATO functions to keep U.S. influence in Europe and a degree of control, and in fact the confrontation makes Europe to some extent reliant on the United States. The United States has been trying to block East-West trade and has been pretty isolated in that. In general, there's a good deal of conflict brewing.

DB: *It seems that so much of at least the promotion of the Pentagon system within the United States is predicated on the "Evil Empire" or some kind of enemy: the Russians are coming, the terrorists are coming, the Libyans, the Nicaraguans, right now it's the drug lords. Who is going to be the enemy to fuel this system?*

I think it's going to be very hard with the Russian threat becoming less and less credible. There was always a tremendous amount of exaggeration and hype about the Russian threat, but at least there was *some* substance behind it. It was, after all, an Evil Empire. That wasn't false. It was brutal and it had missiles and it did ugly things. That had very little relation to any of the alleged threats to us, but that much was real.

There was an attempt in the 1980s to try to find substitutes: international terrorism, crazed Arabs running around trying to kill us. Don't forget that that had a degree of success, enough to just about kill the tourist industry in Europe in 1986 because Americans were afraid to go to Europe because of Libyans, who weren't there. Right now, in this last fall, there was an effort to

manufacture hysteria about a drug war which was supposed to take the place of the Evil Empire. These things
have a short life span. They work for a while, but it's very
hard to keep them up. I don't think it's going to be so easy
to find a credible enemy. Maybe it'll be the Japanese.

DB: *Joel Brinkley, in the* New York Times *of Sunday,
December 10, 1989, in a long article on the intifada, begins his piece
with "24 months into the revolt, many Palestinians are beginning
to lose their buoyant mood." My question to you is, what kind of
measures are the Israeli military authorities taking that might be
contributing to a lessening of Palestinian buoyancy?*

There is, first of all, an increase in violence. They're
shooting much more freely. Casualties are going up. Killings of children are going up. The constraints on use of
live ammunition are being reduced. But that's the least of
it. What they're actually doing is extending over the
territories I think the world's most extensive system of
totalitarian control. The worst thing that's going on right
now is arbitrary acts. There's what's called, for example,
the "invisible transfer." In the last couple of months,
hundreds of people, almost all women and young children,
have been forcibly expelled from their villages and sent
across to Jordan. The troops come in the middle of the
night, 3 o'clock in the morning helicopters come into the
village, using collaborators, and go into particular homes,
wake the family up with loudspeakers, call for all the men
to go into the village square and congregate. Then the
troops come in, tell the women you've got five minutes to
pack up with your children and get on a taxi which you're
going to pay for and go to the Jordan River, where you will
pay for travel across the bridge. If you don't do it we'll do
it for you. We'll stick the kid in the cab and send him.
When the man comes back their families are gone. There's
a lot of things like that, either humiliation or arbitrary
acts of punishment or control of every aspect of life.

Right now, for example, they're reviving the old village leagues. That was an attempt made in 1982 to control the population through networks of corrupt collaborators called village leagues, local people. Most typically local populations are controlled by local collaborators, that's the way South Africa ran the black ghettos, in fact it's the way the Nazis ran the Warsaw ghetto. The village leagues didn't work at the time, but now they're trying to reinstitute them. It will mean that a number of corrupt officials collaborating with the Israelis will have control over every aspect of life. If you want a driver's license, if you want to cross the street, if you want to get married— you pay these guys off. All in all, there's a network of very tight controls, arbitrary harassment, daily humiliation, severe punishments, beatings, a whole network of actions to make the population understand that life is going to be totally unlivable unless they completely submit to Israeli authority and, as the expression goes, don't raise their heads.

DB: *You cover some of these issues in your January, 1990 article in Z magazine entitled "The Art of Evasion: Diplomacy in the Middle East." I was wondering if you could talk about the non-violent tax-resistance campaign that was going on in the West Bank Palestinian town of Beit Sahour, particularly a comment that you made to me a couple of weeks ago that the American peace movement really failed on this one.*

This was a completely non-violent protest in a Christian town on the West Bank, by West Bank standards a relatively well-off town. The protest was a tax resistance protest, refusal to pay taxes, which is a very legitimate act. The taxes are not used for the benefit of the local population. They're extortion, really, and are used for imprisoning them more effectively. They refused to pay their taxes. Yitzhak Rabin, the Defense Minister, stated very clearly that they're going to be severely punished for this. The town was placed under curfew. There were lots of arbitrary arrests and beatings. It ended up with confiscation of most of the property in the town, the robbery of most of the property in the town. They were very steadfast about it. They kept at it and they're still keeping at it.

To get back to the point you raised: There is a non-violent movement in the United States which exhorts people to undertake non-violent resistance and talks and lauds non-violent resistance. People who talk about non-violent resistance can be taken seriously, as the more serious advocates of non-violence have pointed out, A.J. Muste and others, if they don't just talk but if they in fact put themselves on the line, participate as best they can in supporting on-going non-violent resistance. Non-violent resistance activities *cannot* succeed against an enemy that is able freely to use violence. That's pretty obvious. You can't have non-violent resistance against the Nazis in a concentration camp, to take an extreme case, but the same holds generally.

Non-violent resistance can succeed if there's erosion of the capacity to oppress, and that means participation within the camp of the oppressor. We're directly involved in all of this. The United States funds it, pays for it, encourages it. There was no reaction here that I noticed, no detectable reaction in support of these non-violent resistance activities. This has been true for many years, long before the *intifada* there were efforts at non-violent resistance on the West Bank which were simply crushed by force. Merchant strikes, for example. When merchants struck in protest against the occupation, the Israeli Army would just come in and weld their shops closed or break in and force them to open or take them out and arrest them. Naturally, that breaks up any act of non-violent resistance. Since there was no reaction here and essentially no reaction in Israel, the oppression could continue. That tells us that the call upon people to resort to non-violent means is not being made seriously. Maybe it's the right thing to do or maybe it isn't the right thing to do, but you can't take seriously people who call on others to carry out non-violent resistance but who don't participate to help them when they do it.

DB: *In your article you state that the Baker plan is the Shamir plan.*

Actually the Shamir-Peres plan, because the two parties in Israel, contrary to what's reported here, are in consensus agreement. There's basically no difference between them on these issues.

DB: *Is there any room for Palestinian representation within that formula?*

No. They're very explicit about it. As far as I'm aware, the terms of the Baker-Shamir-Peres plan have never even been published here, at least anywhere near the mainstream, which is kind of interesting, since this is the only proposal on the table as far as the U.S. government is concerned and as far as the U.S. media are concerned. So here's the only proposal on the table, as they constantly drum into us, and they don't tell us what it is. The Baker-Shamir-Peres plan begins with what are called its basic premises, which are three: first, that there can be "no additional Palestinian state between Israel and Jordan." The point is, both parties in Israel will assert, there already is a Palestinian state, namely Jordan. If the Palestinians and the Jordanians don't agree, that's their problem, but Israel has determined that Jordan already *is* a Palestinian state and there can't be another one. That means that there's no issue of Palestinian self-determination. They've already got it. There can't be another one. That's the first premise.

The second premise is that there can be no negotiations with the PLO, which Israel agrees is the representative for the Palestinians in the territories. The reason why there can be no negotiations with the PLO has been made very clear and explicit. Prime Minister Shamir a couple of days ago said in the Knesset that he was willing to talk to Satan but not to the PLO. The reason is not that the PLO is a terrorist organization, he went on, but because if you talk to the PLO you're talking about a Palestinian state, and that we will never accept. So point number two in the basic premise is no negotiations with the political representatives of the Palestinians, the reason being that it would involve the question of a Palestinian state.

The third basic premise is that there will be no change in the status of Gaza, Samaria and Judea, the occupied territories, except in accord with the guidelines of the government, and those guidelines exclude the possibility of Palestinian self-determination. Those are the basic premises of the agreement.

Then it goes on about the modalities for reaching this result. That's not a serious proposal, which is why the United States is alone in the world in supporting it. The *Times* itself has pointed out that there's no other country apart from the United States which has endorsed this plan. But in this respect I should say that the subservience of the media is mind-boggling. Take the *New York Times*. They've never reported the terms of this plan. They've said, look, this is the only plan there is, there's nothing else on the table. They have pointed out explicitly that there isn't another country in the world that supports it outside the United States, but just yesterday there was an article in the *New York Times* headlined "Soviets Trying to Become Team Player in Mideast." They're trying to become a team player. What does that mean? They've moved away from their support for radical positions in their policy of confrontation with the United States and they now want to join with the United States. So to become a team player means to join with the United States off the spectrum of world opinion.

What were those "radical positions" that the Soviet Union was previously advocating? They were advocating a two-state settlement like just about everyone else in the world. You can't imagine what's in the minds of people who could write this sort of thing. They say that the United States is totally isolated but the Soviets are trying to become a "team player" by joining with us. In other words, if the world isn't on our side, the world's just wrong. And we're the team, even if the whole world's on the other side.

DB: *As you so often have pointed out, the peace process is by definition anything that the United States proposes.*

That is the way it works, but I must say that it's kind of astonishing to see the extreme levels of self-delusion and deception that are reached in a highly ideological society like ours. People can read that headline: "Soviets Trying to Become Team Player in Mideast," to join us in opposition to the rest of the world, and not laugh.

DB: *Let's talk about Central America. The Central American presidents in Costa Rica on December 12, 1989 issued a declaration in which they said, among other things, that they expressed their "decisive support of Salvadoran President Alfredo Cristiani and his government as a faithful demonstration of their unvarying policy of supporting governments that are the product of democratic, pluralistic and participatory processes...and they energetically demand...that the FMLN publicly renounce all types of violent actions that may directly or indirectly affect the civilian population." I'm interested to know why Daniel Ortega would sign such an agreement.*

His back's against the wall. They're desperate to try to get the United States to live up to the earlier agreements on disbanding the *contras,* and apparently they're willing to sign anything. This is a great victory for the United States, this accord yesterday. The only explicit thing that's said in the agreement is that the United States must immediately stop any kind of funding for the *contras* and must send funds through the United Nations, but of course everyone understands that the United States will disregard that, because the United States doesn't obey any international laws or agreements. That's a given. So though that's there, it's completely meaningless. Washington has already announced that it's meaningless. So we can put that aside.

However, the reason why it's a major victory for the United States is that for years the United States has been trying to draw a parallel between the FMLN guerrillas and the *contras*. The parallel is ludicrous on the face of it. The FMLN is an indigenous guerrilla force consisting mainly of people who were driven to the hills by U.S.-organized terror. They fight within their own country with essentially nothing in the way of support. The *contras,* on the other hand, are a foreign-organized mercenary army constructed by the United States, the superpower that runs the region, based in a foreign country, provided with armaments at a level that goes beyond that of many Latin American armies, unheard of by any guerrilla force. They have no political program. They don't even have the remotest resemblance to guerrillas. So for the United States to establish that parallel—the parallel has been regarded as ridiculous over the years.

But through the unremitting use of violence and terror the United States has succeeded in establishing that parallel, and it has also succeeded in establishing the legitimacy of this murderous terror state which its own population doesn't regard as having anything to do with democracy. El Salvador has polls. They're never published here because they have the wrong results, but over the years when the United States was raving about Salvadoran democracy the polls were showing that about 10 percent of the population saw a democratic process in operation. The point is nobody can look at that government or the conditions under which it was elected and say the word "democracy" without shuddering. But the United States, just by virtue of its monopoly over the means of violence and terror, has succeeded in establishing its conditions. And of course the requirements in the accords that the United States is supposed to live up to are immediately recognized as meaningless because the United States doesn't live up to agreements.

DB: *Given what you have just said, and also in light of the rather astonishing and sustained FMLN attack in November and early December of 1989 in the capital city of San Salvador, how are the media in the U.S. and the political leadership going to persuade the American public that on the one hand you have this parallel of the struggling, budding democracy in El Salvador vs. this horrible dictatorship in Nicaragua?*

How are they going to convince them? I think it's been done already. It's been done years ago. There's been virtual unanimity in the U.S. media—this goes back to the early 1980s—that El Salvador is a fledgling democracy and that Nicaragua is a totalitarian state that never had an election. Here the American media are basically unanimous. As you know, I've done a lot of detailed analysis of this, and departures from this party line are at the level of statistical error. In these matters the United States is as uniform as the best organized totalitarian state.

DB: *We're going to go to some phone calls now.*

Caller: *My question is this: Given everything that's going on, the total lack of responsiveness of the U.S. government to Central America, to the Middle East, to our own domestic problems as well, and given that these are both Democrats and Republicans doing it, that those that fund the death squads in El Salvador and the brutality on the West Bank, that's done with votes from the Democratic party, it seems to me that we really do need some kind of a social, if not revolution, then a very fast evolution. My question*

is how to build it. It seems to me that whatever we do has to end
up going through the political arena. I don't want to make this a
forced choice; if you see a third way I'd like to hear it. It seems to
me that we've really got a choice of either working within the
Democratic party or of trying what you could call either a third
party or truly a second party. Both of those ways have been tried
in the past and neither has succeeded. Do you have any comment
on which of these two ways is more likely to succeed?

I think it is a kind of forced choice. The fact is that I
have nothing against working through a two-party system
if one existed. The point is that political parties don't grow
out of a social vacuum. They reflect the social reality. The
social reality in the United States is that this is a busi-
ness-run society. Those who control investment decisions
and control resources also overwhelmingly control the
political system. We don't have a two-party system in the
United States. We have a one-party system, and we've had
it through most of American history. That one party
consists of two shifting factions of the business party, the
"property party," as C. Wright Mills called it. That's why,
as you said, the parties basically agree: because they
represent the same social sectors. They represent those
who fund them. They represent the interests of owners,
managers, relatively privileged sectors, etc. There are
exceptions to this, but again, it's kind of around the
margins.

There's very little political participation in the
United States. Incumbents in Congress almost always
win. In the last election I think it was something like 98
percent incumbency, which is less turnover than there
was in the Politburo in the pre-Gorbachev period, which
means that there's really no issues coming up. People
aren't shifting around because they reflect different sectors of the population or different issues. In presidential
elections, nobody even pretends that there are any issues.
In the 1988 election the only question was could Dukakis

figure out a way to duck the mud being thrown at him by Lee Atwater. That was the issue in the 1988 election. In earlier elections the issue was could Ronald Reagan remember the lines that he was told to read. But issues don't arise. And when they do the population doesn't care about them. So to talk about operating within the political system is a little misleading. We don't have a political system, except rather marginally.

If I could reframe your question: How can we create a functioning political system? That means, how can we create the social background out of which political issues can arise and the population can become actively involved in formulating political positions, in putting them on the agenda, clarifying them, determining which ones they want and which ones they don't want, and then struggling for them. *That* would be a social revolution. Then you could do it through the present formal system. That's the kind of change that's required.

That doesn't happen here because there just aren't ways for people to get together at a sufficient level to enter into this process. Maybe you can do it in local elections in Boulder because the scale is small enough so that it can be done. But to do it on a large community level or the state level or the national level requires organization and resources. In many industrial democracies it's done through the unions, but the United States basically doesn't have unions. We have a very class-conscious business class, and that's it. That's where class consciousness ends. They've seen to it that unions are very weak and even when they functioned, except for a brief period, they were basically business unions.

It's hard to remember now that there was a bitter decade-long struggle with a lot of heroism and a tremendous resistance and dedication to try to achieve a 40-hour week. The 40-hour week lasted a couple of years after it was achieved. By now it's an idle dream. For families now it's more like a 100-hour week, because one wage earner isn't enough for the family to survive. But workers don't expect to work a 40-hour week. The achievements of the union movement, which were not unreal, are being very rapidly eroded. There's been a steady decline in real wages in the United States since 1973. That's absolutely without any historical precedent. It's in part because of the success of the business classes and their class warfare, destroying any organized resistance. That's just one major aspect of the depoliticization of the society. The formal democratic system looks good on paper. I don't think that paper reforms are very important. The question is, does it function? The answer is: It functions as a reflection of the social reality, but that social reality happens to marginalize from decision-making all but a very small sector of highly privileged parts of the population.

Caller: *It seems that, Professor Chomsky, you are merely a critic of society and you don't have a definite program or political alternative or system that you are clearly advocating. In what you write and what you say you give only the barest and vaguest solutions. You talk vaguely of a social revolution or something of this nature, but you don't say concretely what you believe in. Another point I'd like to ask you about is the Pentagon budget, which is only about 6 percent of the GNP, and military procurement is only 2 percent or 3 percent of the GNP. If you think that exists to benefit high-tech industries, it seems like it would make more sense for the government to directly fund high-tech industries if they wanted to do that. Probably the public would be even more supportive of it, like they are in Japan. Number three: I've heard you criticize and criticize and go on and on about what you dislike about the United States' political and economic system. Is there anything, anything that you have ever said, or could you say something now, about the U.S. political and economic system that you approve of, that you think is an achievement, a success? I like to hear if you can say anything positive about the politics and economics of this country.*

On the first point: You say I haven't written about what I believe is an alternative. That's just not true. I've written a lot about it. You probably haven't read it, but then it's not easily accessible. I've written quite a lot about what I think a libertarian society should look like and what it would mean to take the radical democratic ideals of the Enlightenment, for example, and translate them into a form in which they would apply to a modern industrial society. I could go on to describe it. I'll be glad to give you references, but point number one is just not true.

Point number two: The figures about percentage of GNP are almost totally meaningless. The point is that the corporate managers in advanced industry—this is true of electronics, computers, pharmaceuticals, etc.—expect that the government, meaning the public, will pick up the costly parts of the production process, the parts that are not profitable—research and development. That's got to be paid for by the public. Furthermore, the public, through the Pentagon, provides a state-guaranteed market, which is available for waste production if commercial markets don't work. That is a gift to the corporate managers. It's a cushion for planning. When something can be sold on the market, you sell it. If not, the public purchases it and destroys it. Furthermore, the public pays the cost while the corporation makes the profit. If you take a look at particular industries you can see how this works.

Take, say, the computer industry, the core of the modern industrial economy. I'm kind of smoothing the edges here, but the story is essentially accurate. You can put in tenth-order effect, if you like. In the 1950s, computers were not marketable, so the public paid 100 percent of the cost of research, development and production through the Pentagon. By the 1960s, they were beginning to be marketable in the commercial market, so the public participation declined to about 50 percent. The idea is that the public pays the costs, the corporations make the profits. Public subsidy, private profit; that's what we call free enterprise. By the 1980s there were very substantial new expenditures required for advances in fifth-generation computers and new fancy parallel processing systems, etc. So the public's share in the costs went up very substantially through Star Wars and the Pentagon, etc. That's the way it works. Percentage of GNP doesn't tell you anything relevant to this process.

As to why the government doesn't just come to the population and play it the Japanese way, the answer is, in my view, and this has been the answer that business has given and I think they're right, that the public here wouldn't tolerate it. This is not a docile, submissive population like Japan. You can't come to the population here and tell them: Look, next year you're going to cut back on your consumption by this amount so that IBM can make more profits and then maybe ten years from now your son or your daughter will get a job. That wouldn't wash. What you tell people here is: The Russians are coming, so we better send up a lot of missiles into space and maybe out of that will come something useful for IBM and then maybe your son will get a job in ten years. Those last parts you don't bother saying.

Caller: *Who are you quoting? Are you quoting yourself or some analyst in the military or what?*

What I'm saying is what politicians in the United States say.

Caller: *I've never heard them say that.*

You've never heard a politician in the United States say, the Russians are coming, we have to have more missiles?

Caller: *I never heard them say that we need it because we have to fund some high-tech industries.*

You didn't hear what I just said. I said that the last two sentences I added were not what is publicly said. How you do it in the United States is you say, look, we've got to defend ourselves, we need Star Wars, we need the Pentagon system, and the effect of that is to achieve what I just described with regard to the computer industry, or the semiconductor industry, or whatever. That is because this is a relatively free society.

If politicians were to approach the public telling them, look, we've decided that next year you're going to cut back on your consumption so that IBM will make more profit, the reaction in the United States would be a healthy reaction: Who are you to tell me to cut back so that IBM will make more profit? If it's going to be a social decision of that kind, I want to take part in it. And that's precisely why business does not want to be put in those terms. They do not want social policy, which is going to organize people, to become involved in making decisions over investment. This issue has come up over the years, many times, in the business press. Go back to the 1940s. It was recognized, as any economist will tell you, that you can get the same priming effect for industry, maybe even more efficient, through other forms of government intervention besides military production.

Caller: *Right. That's my point.*

Sure you can do that, but it's irrelevant, and business understands exactly why it's irrelevant. You can read editorials in *Business Week* going back to the late 1940s where they point out there are two techniques: one technique is the military system, the other technique would be social spending, infrastructure development, hospitals, services, etc. or useful production. But the latter is no good. It will work from a technical, economic point of view, but it has all sorts of unwelcome side effects. For example, it tends to organize public constituencies. If the government gets involved in carrying out activities that affect the public existence directly, people will want to get involved in it.

Caller: *Professor Chomsky, it's a pleasure to ask you these questions. I'm from Canada, where your books are obtainable in virtually every bookstore. Your last book,* Necessary Illusions, *is on a paperback non-fiction bestseller list. I don't see the same availability of your thoughts in America. That's the first question: Why is that? The second question is: Do you have any comment on the elite media coverage of the situation in El Salvador regarding the [killing of] six Jesuit priests? The third question is, regarding the Middle East: A comment that I'm hearing again and again from people like Martin Peretz [of the* New Republic] *and others regarding the Palestinians is that these are Muslims, they're tribal savages, they're pre-Enlightenment and they pose a threat to Israel. Israel is a democracy. Why should we consider allowing another dagger to be pointed at Israel's existence? I'd appreciate your comments on those three questions.*

As for the availability of books, your description is correct, but that's only one part of it. For example, this book that you mentioned was based on lectures that were delivered over Canadian Broadcasting Corporation on problems of thought control in industrial societies. It would be next to impossible for anything comparable to happen in the United States on any major public outlet. The United States is different from most other societies in that respect. Most industrial societies, even ones that are very much like us, have a good deal more openness in their public media to dissident opinion. There are a lot of reasons for that.

The previous caller had asked whether I had ever said anything nice about the United States. The answer is, very often. One of the things that's extremely nice about the United States is the degree of freedom that it has. It is a free society, much more so than any other, and that very freedom has led to problems. If you can't control people by force, you have to figure out other ways to control them. Corresponding to American freedom, which is unusual, are very highly sophisticated measures of ensuring that that freedom doesn't work, and one of them is the one that you're describing. A whole array of devices have been developed to ensure that dissident opinion just isn't heard, although it isn't suppressed either, given American freedoms. So what you're describing is true, and I could elaborate the way it works if you like.

With regard to the second point, the coverage of the murder of the priests: The murder of the priests was considered an outrageous act here, and that particular action was covered reasonably well. It's always considered a mistake for a friendly government to commit atrocities essentially in front of television cameras. They should commit them when nobody's looking, and killing of priests, obviously by the military, is bad news. Therefore, there was some coverage of it. But the coverage will decline, and under U.S. pressure there may be a decision made. If the government of El Salvador is smart, they'll find some scapegoat, a lieutenant, and put him on trial and then put him away in some country house somewhere for the crime. But the chances that they'll go after the authorities who are responsible, say, the higher officers of the First Brigade, that's very unlikely. It's even more unlikely that the American press will point out what that means. What does it mean, for example, that the one witness had to be spirited out of the country to the United States so that she could survive? What does that tell us about the democratic society we're supporting if the one witness to the murder of six priests can't be kept in the country because she'll be murdered? Exactly what does that tell you? It's clear what it tells you, but that wasn't the lesson that was drawn from it in the editorials. So the event itself was covered, and after that the cover-up begins, and it will be continuing.

On the matter of the Palestinians, I'm sure that what you heard is what many people say, and the only thing that I can respond to, apart from the false statements, is the level of racism it reflects. That reflects the assumption that there are human beings, the Jews, the Israelis, who are human beings and have rights, and then there are these strange animals, the indigenous population, who aren't human beings and who don't have rights, and what right do those animals have to threaten the human beings? That's not something that's unique in European or American history. It was attitudes like that that made it possible for those who conquered the United States, the European settlers, to basically wipe out the indigenous population, who, as George Washington once put it, were not really humans; they were just wolves who looked like men. As long as that's true, you can do anything you like to them. I think those are the attitudes that you're reflecting, the same attitudes expressed by the worst sectors of white South Africans. There's no arguing with those positions, any more than you could argue with a Nazi who told you that the Jews weren't human.

Caller: *I have a couple of questions about Eastern Europe. The first one is: Are you concerned about some of the forces that may be unleashed, especially nationalism, with the recent democracy movements? Secondly, do you see any down side or any unanticipated consequences to German reunification?*

I think both of those are very serious concerns. The Soviet Empire, ugly and tyrannical as it was, did keep the lid on some extremely ugly manifestations. Eastern European nationalism has its very unpleasant aspects, to put it mildly. This is not something unique to Eastern Europe. It's been true all over the world. The history of Western Europe consists of centuries of murderous, barbarous violence while one ethnic group dedicated their existence to destroying some other one. That continued up until

1945. The only reason it stopped then was because the next step would have been to destroy the world. So the establishment of the state system in Europe, which is basically the imposition of a certain formal political system on a network of rival groups who often bitterly hate one another, was a bloody, murderous process. The process hasn't been consummated in the East. As the Russian imperial system begins to erode, it's going to be rearing its head, and it could be an extremely ugly one. We've already seen that in Armenia, Azerbaijan, and we'll see that elsewhere.

So yes, I think you're quite right in pointing to that as a very serious problem. It's similar in some respects to what happened when the Ottoman Empire was removed from large parts of western Asia. The Ottoman Empire was a pretty ugly affair, but it did reflect the realities of the region in a way in which the European imposed state system does not. So it did allow some degree of local community control and it didn't impose sharp borders. You could travel from one end of the Ottoman Empire to the other without passing through customs barriers and troops. The European-imposed state system didn't correspond to the realities of the region at all, and it's been a violent and brutal affair. The same in Africa. The same everywhere. Chances are that will happen in Eastern Europe.

With regard to German unification, that's something that worries everybody. A Frenchman quipped that he loves Germany, loves it so much that he's glad there are two of them. The history of Germany is not so pretty, and a reunified Germany frightens a lot of people. The story of German partition is a pretty complicated one. Right after the war, the United States and Britain were influential—whether they were decisive you could argue, but they were certainly influential—in bringing about partition in the first place. The reason was that there was concern about a unified labor movement in Germany, and influences from the Eastern zone, primarily ideological influences, which would strengthen socialist elements, working-class elements in Western Germany and undermine the British and American project of restoring the old conservative order. That's why people like George Kennan, early on, in 1946, called for "walling off" West Germany from the Eastern zone, that was Kennan's phrase, and stopping what the British Foreign Office called "Russian political aggression," meaning ideological and political influences from the East. That was one factor in the partition of Germany.

In 1952, Stalin made an interesting offer—we don't know if it was serious or not because it was immediately rejected—calling for reunification of Germany under Four-Power control with free elections, the only condition being that a reunified Germany not join a hostile Western military alliance. Any Russian leader, no matter who it is, is going to insist upon that, for obvious historical reasons. The United States rebuffed that out of hand. In fact it was barely reported, just dismissed, so we don't know if he was serious. The United States much preferred a Europe split into two military pacts: NATO, which was being established at the time, and the Warsaw Pact, which came a couple of years later. There have been several other Russian proposals of this kind over the years, always rejected. Right now you'll notice that the United States is still very ambivalent about it. If you read James Baker's speech in Berlin, which appears in today's papers, you'll notice he was all effusive about democracy in Europe, reunification of Germany, etc. But the bottom line was the same: a reunified Germany has to be part of NATO, he said, meaning it has to be part of a Western military alliance in which the United States will dominate. It's highly unlikely that any Soviet leadership or any East European public would accept that, given the history. It's not so likely that the rest of the West would accept it either, but that's the bottom line. So far, at least, we have not been willing to conceive of the possibility of a neutralized Germany, and that's the only sane possibility for unification.

U.S. Intervention and the Demise of the Soviet Threat

February 1, 1990

DB: *Let's talk about what Henry Stimson called "our little region over here which has never bothered anybody," Central America, Latin America. You trace the origins of the crisis in Central America to the Alliance for Progress, Kennedy's program in the early 1960s, and you term it as "one of the most fateful decisions in modern history." Why was the Alliance for Progress so pivotal?*

I wouldn't quite trace it to that. I think the Alliance for Progress intensified a system of exploitation and oppression that had been in existence for a long period. If the Alliance for Progress hadn't happened things wouldn't be much different. It simply accelerated a process that was ongoing. The Alliance for Progress was only part of the Kennedy program. That was the carrot part. The stick part was the shift of the mission of the Latin American military, which is essentially dominated by the United States, a shift in their mission from hemispheric defense to internal security. The Eisenhower administration had toyed with that idea but hadn't been able to put it through. The Kennedy administration did in 1962, right after the failure of the Bay of Pigs.

Internal security means essentially war against your own population. It was understood by the Kennedy administration that the programs that they were instituting, the classical programs that the United States had supported, would require an ultimate reliance on force. They were not going to be acceptable to the general population. The Alliance imposed a certain development model. But it was development essentially oriented towards the needs of U.S. investors. It came to solidify and entrench and extend the already existing agro-export model which is a strong inducement to Latin Americans to produce for export and to cut back on subsistence crops. So for example, that means produce beef for export to American markets instead of crops for local consumption. The idea in general is to turn Latin America, Central America in particular, into an area which will serve the function of providing resources and markets and cheap labor and other Third World amenities to primarily U.S. investors. That's a classic position. The Alliance for Progress gave it a new form and a push forward. Where the population doesn't accept it, you have the police in reserve. If they don't work, you've got the army in reserve. If that doesn't work, you have American force in reserve. That's been the structure of American policy towards Latin America very explicitly for a large part of U.S. history, but crucially since the Second World War. The fateful decision of the Kennedy administration, in my view, was this combination of the shift to internal security, that is, to much tighter control of the domestic population by force, alongside entrenchment of an agro-export model that yields a rise in GNP, statistical growth, but also increasing misery and subservience for substantial parts of the population. Displacement and impoverishment of peasants in Central America, for example, which is what immediately led to the critical situation in the late 1970s and early 1980s, was to a large extent a result of the Alliance for Progress. The same is true of drug production, for rather obvious reasons.

When you undermine Peruvian agriculture by subsidized American agricultural exports and other pressures to drive Peruvian peasants towards export production, and you try to get them to play the capitalist game, they'll do it. They'll produce the kind of export crops that are profitable. And the export crop that happens to be by far the most profitable is coca, so naturally they shift to coca production. That's exactly what we drive them to do. Then we come in, of course, and destroy it. That leaves them with nothing.

DB: *You've described the dual, interlocking U.S. interests in the region as one being "keeping the area safe for U.S. investments," and two being "preventing independent development." Is that going to continue into the 1990s?*

Of course. U.S. policy, any policy, is based on institutional structures. There's some fluctuations as individuals change, but it pretty much reflects the institutions. The institutions are very stable, therefore the policies have been very stable. There's very little internal challenge to them. There's no serious external challenge because of the extraordinary power and security of the United States. So you have stable policies running over long periods. The policy towards Latin America was articulated clearly in the highest level of planning documents after the Second World War. There's no reason to expect that to change. That policy is, as repeated in document after document, the threat to our interests is nationalist regimes which are responsive to pressures from the masses of the population for improvement in low living standards and diversification of production for domestic needs. We have to block that. That's the major thrust of our policy, to block that in favor of an environment conducive to private investment of domestic and foreign capital and repatriation of profits and production for export.

That's the major theme repeated over and over again, so obvious that it's subject to no challenge and in public discourse not even discussed. It's sort of like the air you breathe. It's what's called "freedom." Since we're in favor of freedom, we're obviously in favor of that.

It's also understood all the way through that that will not be accepted willingly by the domestic population.

So if you read State Department studies on what's called the U.S. A.I.D. program, they point out that the police forces that they train are critical because they can detect discontent among the population early. The police are a major mechanism by which the government can demand, impose acceptance on the part of the population. The studies use wording approximately like that. The police can move in in order to suppress dissent early before what's called "major surgery" is necessary. They can avoid the need for major surgery. If you need major surgery, then you use the army, which is, by the Kennedy period, dedicated to internal security.

If the army doesn't work, you send in U.S. force. Where the army in the Latin American countries, and in particular in Central America, can't be controlled by the United States, then you basically have to overthrow the government. That's one of the problems in Nicaragua. The Carter administration tried very hard to keep the National Guard intact when they couldn't hang on to Somoza any longer. That's the classic device: if you can't control the government, you control the army, because they'll control the government by force. The Sandinistas refused to permit U.S. control of the army, and that's one factor that critically led to the break with the United States.

In the case of Panama, although the Panamanian Defense Forces were an instrument of U.S. power, Noriega got too independent and was not under control, so he had to be replaced and the Defense Forces reconstructed with essentially the same officers, the same drug-running, the same everything else, now under U.S. control. That's classic, and there's just no reason to expect that to change. There are new factors, undoubtedly, and they'll change the way in which these commitments are implemented, but the commitments remain the same, because they just grow out of institutional structures, and there's no challenge to them.

DB: *Beginning in 1964 with the military coup in Brazil that launched a series of national security states, as you call them...*

It's not my term, but a standard one.

DB: *Those states, particularly in the southern cone, have now evolved into more traditional models. What do you attribute that to?*

The Kennedy administration strongly supported the planning for the military coup in Brazil, which instituted a neo-Nazi style national security state with torture, repression, etc. in order to destroy Brazilian democracy, which was just becoming too independent. That, as you say, led to a rash of these developments over the hemisphere in an extremely bloody period. The military destroyed the economy. There was social dissolution, economic disaster, at a certain point the military decided that the best idea would be to place civilians in power to try to administer the chaos and take responsibility for it. Other devices were available to ensure control by the traditional elites, the oligarchy, the business classes and the military, that's essentially the dominant ruling group and the group that the U.S. supports.

Other devices now include things that weren't available earlier, for example, the IMF and the debt crisis. The IMF constraints, which impose free-market demands, no food subsidies, no protection for domestic industries, those devices suffice to ensure that the wealthy and the privileged run the show and it maintains the two-tiered societies that are regarded as necessary: a super-rich elite and a relatively privileged professional class that serves them, on the one hand, and an enormous mass of impoverished, starving people on the other. The IMF system suffices to maintain that, and the indebtedness and the economic chaos left by the military pretty much ensures that the IMF rules will be followed, short of major revolution, at which point the military steps in again. That's why I'm talking about tactical changes, that reflect changes in the global situation and the domestic economic scene.

Take a place like Brazil, potentially an extremely wealthy country, enormous resources, big population, high industrial development, lots of wealth and incredible poverty. For much of the population the situation is probably on a par with Ethiopia, maybe most of the population, vastly worse than in Eastern Europe, for example. The same is true pretty much throughout the continent. From the point of view of the military and the groups they serve, largely the traditional elites, oligarchy and business, it's not efficient to have military rule to maintain that system. It's just a focus for popular discontent. It gives a bad international image, and besides, the military then would have the responsibility of running the economy, which is not anything that any sane person would want to accept. They'd much rather have somebody else face those disasters in, say, Argentina today.

DB: *A propos of what you just said, I recall your saying that if a peasant in El Salvador were to fall asleep and wake up in Poland, he would think he were in heaven.*

Not much doubt about that.

DB: *How did the December 20, 1989 U.S. invasion of Panama differ from other interventions?*

Well, it did differ, and it differed in a way which reflects the changing situation. In fact, it was a historic event in one respect. It's a classic invasion in most respects, in fact, so classic that it's barely a footnote to history, but in one respect it was different, and that's in the propaganda framework. Up until now, for decades, in fact really since the Bolshevik Revolution, it's been possible to justify every U.S. use of violence as a defense against the Soviet threat. So for example, take the recent ones.

When the United States invaded Grenada in 1983, we were defending ourselves against the effort of the Russians to strangle us by conquering such powerful outposts as Grenada and South Yemen, etc. I remember hearing the Chairman of the Joint Chiefs of Staff on the radio explaining how in the event of a Soviet attack on Western Europe, Grenada could interdict oil supplies from Trinidad and Tobago to Western Europe and we wouldn't be able to defend our beleaguered allies. You know, this is comical, more than comical, but that kind of story was enough to develop public support for the invasion.

The attack against Nicaragua was justified by the claim that if we don't stop the Russians there they'll be pouring across the border at Harlingen, Texas, only two days drive away. You remember that stuff. For the educated classes, there were more sophisticated variants, which were approximately equally weighty. These examples go way back. The overthrow of the democratic capitalist government of Guatemala: we were defending ourselves against the Russians because our existence is threatened, etc.

By December 1989, not even the imagination of the State Department and the editorial writers could reach quite that far. So you needed another justification. The propaganda framework had to shift. You needed new pretexts. The pretexts had nothing to do with the reasons, ever, but now you couldn't use those old pretexts. Another framework was needed. This problem had been foreseen. It was clear a couple of years ago that it would be harder and harder to conjure up a Russian threat. In fact, through the 1980s an alternative was developed: international terrorism, crazed Arabs running around trying to murder us because they hate Americans. That worked to a limited extent. It certainly built up lots of hysteria and racism, as intended, but it's not too convincing. It will carry you through the one-day bombing of Libya, but not much more.

About 1986-87, for interesting reasons, the United States shifted its attitude towards Noriega. He had been on the CIA payroll for decades, but they decided he was getting too big for his britches and had to go. The press took the cue quickly. They understand these things, and they immediately started the project of demonizing Noriega and turning him into the worst monster since Attila the Hun. It's basically a replay of the Qaddafi project. In fact, Noriega remained a very minor thug, exactly what he had been when he was on the CIA payroll, but the U.S. government attitude toward him had changed. So therefore automatically the media attitude towards him changed. By the time the invasion took place, you could get Ted Koppel talking about how Noriega is one of that small group of monsters like Stalin and Hitler and Qaddafi and Khomeini who Americans just love to hate and so we have to destroy him. He was very happy about that. Dan Rather and Peter Jennings described him as one of most odious creatures of modern times. The mood was set, and it's true that Americans hated Noriega by 1989. They've been inundated with this totalitarian-style propaganda for several years, and yeah, they hate Noriega.

The drug war was used to help out. The drug war is a government-media hoax. It has little to do with drugs, but it has a lot to do with organizing and controlling the population and imposing the fear of a hated enemy now that the old one is harder to conjure up. All of that was manipulated very effectively elsewhere and it created the propaganda framework for the invasion. The difference between the reaction in the United States and elsewhere is remarkable. I was reading excerpts from the Honduran press the other day. Honduras is, of course, an ally, in fact a client. The press is not bad, but hardly radical or dissident. Their bitterness about the invasion is enormous. They describe how it's "international totalitarianism" under the guise of democracy, a day of shame and despair for Latin America, "Latin America is in pain" at its incapacity to protect its independence from the tyrant from the North, on and on.

That's going on while Congress is giving Bush a rousing ovation and the press is off in a kind of jingoistic ecstasy. An article in the *Toronto Globe and Mail* pointed out quite accurately that in the United States if you want to hear the kind of opinion that dominates in most of the world you've got to go way out to the fringes of discussion, fringes so far out that it's not considered part of the political spectrum. And it also commented on the jingoistic hysteria that is so dramatic and obvious in the United States. That's all true, and that was the framework in which the invasion was carried out and justified.

DB: *So in your view was there a successful manufacturing of consent on Panama? By the way, when you talk about manufacturing of consent, you say that the population is marginalized and they don't really matter, they don't participate in political processes in any way. Whose consent is being manufactured?*

Well, if you look at it more closely, to start with there are two different groups. At the first level of approximation there are two targets for propaganda. One is what's sometimes called the "political class." There's maybe 20 percent of the population which is relatively educated and more or less articulate and plays some kind of role in decision-making. They're supposed to participate in social life, as political or economic or cultural managers, like teachers and writers and so on, and they're supposed to vote. They're supposed to play some role, not a determinate role, but some kind of an active role in the way economic, political and cultural life goes on. Their consent is crucial, because they have to carry out the policies. They're the administrators. They have to make decisions with some relatively coherent grasp of the world, so that's one group that has to be deeply indoctrinated.

Then there's maybe 80 percent of the population

whose main function is to follow orders and not to think or pay attention to anything. They have to be marginalized. But they also have to accept. They're the ones who usually pay the costs.

For example, Bush gave this magnanimous aid to Panama. We're going to give a billion dollars to Panama after we destroyed the economy and then wiped the place out. That's the headline. Then you go down and look at what the newspapers didn't report. You look at what is this billion dollars of aid. Four hundred million of it, forty percent, is incentives for U.S. business to export to Panama, so it's purchase of U.S goods. What that means is 40 percent of it is a gift from the American taxpayer to American business, and about another hundred million is export-import bank guarantees and other kinds of subsidies which are another form of subsidy from the taxpayer to American business. Most of the rest is payoffs to banks. It's called "stabilizing the economy," but if you take it apart, it's paying off to the banks loans taken by the Panamanian government during the period when the United States was crushing and destroying the economy.

So the American taxpayer is supposed to pay that back, exactly the way the taxpayer is supposed to pay back the hundreds of billions of dollars in the savings and loan fraud. That's the aid program. This is typical. That's the 80 percent. They're paying the costs, and they have to more or less accept it, too. However, their acceptance doesn't have to be based on any real understanding—they don't even have to know where Panama is. They can think it's in Africa, as long as they accept that this is somehow necessary, so therefore we're willing to pay the burden. That large majority of the population, that's where the real mass media work. By the mass media, I mean the tabloids and the Super Bowl and the sitcoms, etc. They just have to divert people, just get them to be isolated, separated, accept the basic values of the society: greed, personal gain, not caring about other people, etc. Any real understanding about what's going on in the world is superfluous, even negative.

But for the more educated sectors, the sectors that make a difference, the people who are reading the *New York Times* and the *Washington Post,* they have to have some relatively informed grasp of the world or they will just make bad decisions that will harm people with real power. So to begin with, there's at least a two-tiered system of indoctrination, and then if we look in more detail we can find more nuances. But manufacturing consent is not a uniform process, it's a diversified process.

In the case of the Panama invasion, the general population just has to be roused to jingoist hysteria, because finally we're getting this bad guy, cops and robbers, that's enough. You don't need any more than that. The more educated sectors have a different role to play, and that's been interesting to look at. A typical example was David Broder, who is a highly respected liberal commentator for the *Washington Post,* one of the main national reporters. He had an interesting nationally syndicated column in which he very much praised the invasion but in a judicious way, not like columnist George Will's style about how this is an exercise in good neighborliness, etc. He started off by saying that there has been some carping from "the left" over "the prudence of Bush's actions." That statement very nicely typifies the liberal ideology. By the "left" he means the center right: the National Council of Churches, etc. Anything farther to the left than that is unthinkable, just off the spectrum of discussion. It's equally beyond the thinkable that there should be any objection other than about the "prudence" of the action. So that's liberal ideology. The spectrum is bounded by the center and the far right. You've got to make sure there's no dissidence in the society. And secondly, the only questions that can be asked are about success. So what he called the "leftist" criticism is whether the actions were prudent, are they going to work, are they going to cost too much, etc.

DB: *The very issues that were raised in Indochina, the pragmatic questions.*

Exactly. Then he says, well, this carping from the left, we have to eliminate it, get rid of it. It's just total nonsense. He then says that the historic importance of the invasion is that it has helped establish what he calls a "new national consensus" on intervention. He then describes the new consensus on intervention. He says it was outlined first by Casper Weinberger, who provided six criteria. They were, as he puts it, "well phrased," very proper. Of the six criteria, four of them say that intervention should be carried out only when it's going to work. The fifth says it should be carried out when we regard it as vital to our interests. The sixth says we should try other means first and if they don't work, then use intervention. Those are the criteria. Those are criteria that Hitler could have invoked. In fact, anybody could have invoked them. Carry out intervention when it's going to work, and when you want it, and obviously don't use force unless you have to. Then he claims that Dukakis accepted those criteria and that's the new consensus on intervention. That's important.

What that means is that for the sectors of the educated elite that Broder speaks for, which is a large part of the liberal, educated population, from their point of view, they finally succeeded in overcoming what's been called the "Vietnam syndrome." That is, the opposition to the use of force and violence to achieve our ends.

I think they're wrong about that. So far we've been talking about the political class, the educated, articulate, decision-making sector of the general population, but in fact there's a lot of the population that's just not part of this. I've been reading letters to the editor in newspapers around the country, the ones I can get hold of, the national press, and the local press in various places where people send me things. It's been kind of interesting. I haven't done a scientific sample, but my strong impression is that the letters to the editor are largely quite hostile to the invasion, and furthermore very informed. They provide analysis and information that the professionals are careful to exclude and express a lot of shame and distress. It reads kind of like the Latin American press. I assume that editors are not purposely picking letters which make the editors look like fools. So I imagine this does represent what they're getting, and that reflects a substantial sector of the population which simply hasn't been controlled by the indoctrination system. Those are people who are not the commissars. They're not articulate in the sense that they write columns for newspapers. They are not the top decision makers, but they're out there. That's where the solidarity movement comes from. That's where the dissident movements come from, and I don't see any reason to believe that the "Vietnam syndrome" has been overcome among probably a large majority of the population, any more than it had been by the quite spectacular propaganda triumphs of earlier years. This looks like a hardcore resistance. So Broder, as others before him, may applaud the fact that finally we've tamed the beast, but I don't think he's right.

DB: *The media, in their traditional adversarial role on these issues, for example have been very reluctant to talk about or compare Noriega's Panama human rights record to the "fledgling democracies."*

His record is quite clear and doesn't take much work to write about it. If there were any journalists writing about this topic, the first thing they would do is to turn to the latest human rights reports on Panama. In 1988 Americas Watch published a report on human rights in Panama, and it gives an unpleasant picture. There are a handful of people who were killed of whom one could plausibly say that Noriega had something to do with it. Some people were beaten up. There's a range of abuses which certainly require censure. Let's compare it to Honduras, which is not just a murderous terrorist state like El Salvador and Guatemala. Panama looks much better than Honduras. There's one U.S.-trained battalion in Honduras, the 316, I think, which alone has carried out far more atrocities than Noriega. In fact, Noriega is a very minor thug. Americas Watch doesn't go into the drug business much, but the same is true there.

Take a look at the indictment of Noriega in the Miami court. I think there is only one charge after 1984. That's kind of interesting, because up until 1986 he was our boy. Since then he's become a devil. But the charges against him are overwhelmingly during the period when he was palling around with George Bush. In fact, certainly Panama has been a major center for narco-trafficking, but that's been primarily the banks. Those are the people we're putting back in power. Panama had a free and open banking system which was the basis for its highly artificial economy. No regulations, etc. That immediately attracts criminal money and other forms of capital flight from Brazil, etc. That's the basis for the Panamanian economy. Back in 1983 a congressional committee investigating banking and drugs identified Panama as probably the main center in the Western Hemisphere for laundering of drug funds and other forms of narco-trafficking. Those are the people we're putting back in power. Noriega was certainly involved in that. He's a criminal. He's taken his cut, in a pretty heady manner. But with regard to atrocities, he cannot be compared with Guatemala and El Salvador. That's absurd.

There's another aspect of the invasion that the media handled in an interesting way. The Bush administration almost flaunted its contempt for human rights right at the time of the invasion of Panama. It's almost as if they were daring the media, trying to humble or humiliate them by making them eat crow. Exactly at the time they invaded Panama because of their deep commitment to human rights, they selected that moment to announce that they were eliminating the trade sanctions against China and were selling China $300 million worth of high-technology equipment, which of course, has military and other uses. There were some questions about this, and Marlin Fitzwater, the White House spokesman, said, "Well, this is $300 million worth of business for American businesses." It's good for business, so you've got to shut up. And they shut up. In addition to that, the Agriculture Department announced that it was resuming subsidized food sales to China. I don't even know if that got reported, I didn't see it. The White House then announced that they were blocking the entry into the United States of Chinese scholars now in Europe who had been invited by American universities, in deference to the wishes of the nice guys who carried out the Tiananmen square massacre. They also announced, this had already been announced before, that contacts with China had been resumed immediately after the massacre. In addition to that, they announced, and this was kept silent, as far as I know, that they were eliminating sanctions against loans to Iraq. All of this is around December 22, December 23. I didn't see a word about most of this.

What does that mean? In comparison with Bush's buddies in Baghdad and Beijing, Noriega looks like Mother Teresa. The newspapers are expected to take all of this and accept it and go on with their jingoist hysteria about our love of human rights. And what's amazing is they did. Comparing Noriega to El Salvador or Guatemala or Saddam Hussein or Deng Xiao Peng is ridiculous, they're not in the same world. He is a minor crook, just as he was when we supported him.

DB: *As late as 1987, John Lawn, the Director of the Drug*

Enforcement administration, was writing letters of commendation to Noriega.

I have a copy of a letter from May 1986. In May 1986 John Lawn wrote a letter praising Noriega for his vigorous struggle against drugs and his enthusiastic participation in the drug war. Another one has been reported in 1987. In May 1987, Edwin Meese, then Attorney General, intervened to quash investigations of Noriega in Florida. Later than that, August 1987, after the Esquipulas treaty, about two weeks after that, in Central America, Elliott Abrams was quoted in the *New York Times*. Congress had passed a resolution calling on Noriega to step aside until an inquiry was conducted into his criminal activities. Elliott Abrams opposed that, said it would be counterproductive to try to pressure Noriega in this way. They were still protecting him in August 1987. In fact, Lawn's comments on Noriega's cooperation in the drug war were probably perfectly accurate. He probably did cooperate. Why not? Why not cooperate in U.S. efforts while you're also raking off money from selling cocaine? There's no contradiction there. All of this reflects the ambivalence in U.S. policy.

Incidentally, this is so typical that again it's hard to see how the media can't see what's happening. This is exactly what happens with every thug and gangster that the United States supports. Go through the list: Trujillo, Somoza, Marcos, Duvalier—the United States supports them enthusiastically. They were all much worse than Noriega. Again, they were not in the same league as this minor thug. They're real gangsters. The United States supported them enthusiastically right through the worst terror as long as everything was in order and profits were flowing.

But there comes a point in the trajectory, typically, when they just overshoot the mark. Instead of just robbing the poor, like they're supposed to, they start interfering with the rich. At that point a domestic business opposition

develops, and they begin even interfering with U.S. prerogatives. They start getting too independent or interfere
with U.S. investors. That happens often. At that point we
suddenly start hearing about human rights violations and
our yearning for democracy immediately becomes dominant and all sorts of elevated remarks about American
ideals, etc. Then there's a period of some ambivalence.
After all, you can't flip instantaneously. There's a period
in which you try to decide what to do about this. In the
case of Trujillo, after supporting him for decades through
horrifying atrocities, the CIA tried to assassinate him. In
the case of Somoza, the Carter administration tried to
save him, and when it was clear that he could not be saved,
they tried to ease him out somehow, and did. They got him
out to Miami, but tried until the end to keep the National
Guard in power so the whole system would remain. With
Marcos, they waited until the army had turned against
him, and then Washington turned against him. In the case
of Duvalier, when the business community really turned
against him, the White House did, too.

That's what happened with Noriega. By 1987 a civic
opposition was developing in Panama which was white,
European businessmen. There's a big race-class issue in
Panama. There's a traditional white elite, a couple of
dozen families that have run the country forever. That
was changed in 1968 when General Torrijos, a populist
dictator, had a coup, and there was a shift of power there
with the black mestizo poor population getting at least a
share, maybe symbolic, but sometimes a real share in
power. The civic opposition that developed in 1987 was
rich, white folk in Mercedes cars meeting in plush hotels.
That was already an indication that for Noriega the hand-
writing was on the wall. They are the U.S. allies. It took
a year or two while the U.S. adjusted its policy. You get
signs of this vacillation as late as August 1987 with
Abrams. There are other factors involved. This is just
standard. This is predictable with every gangster we

support, big ones like Marcos and Somoza or minor ones like Noriega. It's a natural progression, you can see why it's going to happen. The only question is the timing.

That was one factor in the change of U.S. attitude towards him, but there were others. One crucial factor was that January 1, 1990 was the day on which most of the administration of the Panama Canal goes over to Panama. In the next couple of years, the rest goes. Furthermore, there's an oil pipeline through Panama which is 60 percent owned by the Panamanian government and which I think carries about 10 percent of U.S. oil. It's significant, in other words. You had to make sure that by January 1, 1990 Panama was in the hands of a compliant, reliable government run by rich white people. The rich white minority had to be placed back in power, and there wasn't much time. You could adjust a little, but not much time.

Secondly, as I mentioned before, Noriega was just getting too independent. For a long time, he had been doing the U.S.'s job. Panama was a base for the war against Nicaragua, but he was getting out of line. For one thing, Panama was supporting the Contadora Treaty. The United States was strongly opposed to the diplomatic efforts of the Latin American democracies, preferring to keep to the arena of violence, where the United States is dominant. Panama was strongly supporting the Contadora efforts, which led finally to the peace treaty. That was a big black mark against him. He was also apparently dragging his feet on the *contra* war, playing both sides of the street in the intelligence game, etc. And just not reliable, too independent. These various factors meant that he had to go.

The only question was the timing. You can see what happened. In July 1987, there was a big repression of the civic opposition, this basically white, upper-class opposition. A demonstration was repressed with gassings and beatings and torture, etc. That was carried out by a

Noriega sidekick named Colonel Eduardo Herrera Hassan, who is a favorite of the United States. In fact, he was just placed in command of the Panamanian Defense Forces, just to illustrate our love of human rights. He's the guy who's now in charge under U.S. military occupation. He's the guy who carried out the repression in 1987. Another event took place at the same time. Torrijos had died or was killed in 1981. How nobody knows. And there was still a Torrijista element in the military, kind of a populist element in the military which was regarded as left-leaning and unacceptable by the United States. The second in command after Noriega was a guy named Diaz Herrera, who was Torrijos' cousin and who was supposed to be the leader of this populist tendency. Getting rid of Noriega would be no use if you get a populist military officer, so as long as Diaz Herrera was second in command, you couldn't get rid of Noriega and maintain the Defense Forces.

In July 1987 Diaz Herrera was kicked out. That freed things up. At this point it was possible to move ahead with getting rid of Noriega but keeping the Defense Forces and restoring the white aristocracy back to power. That's the point at which U.S. policy dramatically changed, July 1987. It took a little time before it got solidified, but that seems to be the point of the sharp change, as John Weeks and Andrew Zimbalist have pointed out. Then come the economic sanctions, which essentially destroyed the economy. They were carefully designed. They were designed to try to avoid penalties to U.S. companies but to place the burden on the poor and black population. The assumption was that this would erode Noriega's support. That's his natural constituency. It did, over a year or two. Noriega's support as a nationalist with some populist gestures had eroded. By the end of 1989 he was hated because he was the person who everybody could see as responsible for the fact that your children are starving. That's why the United States is strangling us. That was a well designed project. They began to support military coups. Finally, when that didn't work, came the invasion, basically just in time to ensure the establishment of a compliant government run by the United States and the white rich elite in Panama prior to January 1.

There's a lot of ironies in this, if anybody wants to look closely at things that aren't being reported. The President whom we put in power, Guillermo Endara, did, in fact, undoubtedly win the election in May 1989. He was kicked out because Noriega stole the election, with a certain amount of violence and a few people were beaten up. The previous election was in 1984.

DB: *George Shultz went to Panama at the time.*

Reagan sent a telegram of congratulations seven hours before the electoral council even came out with the certification of who won. George Shultz went down there for the inauguration to praise Panamanian democracy. What happened in 1984? Noriega stole the election. That was good at the time, because he stole the election to prevent Endara and his boss, Arnulfo Arias, from taking power. The problem was that Arias, who was an old Panamanian politician, was a right-wing Panamanian nationalist. But nationalism is what's bad. It doesn't matter whether it's right or left. Arias was a nationalist, and the United States didn't want to have him in. He's the man who's Endara's saint. Endara was his spokesman and minister. The violence was more severe than in stealing the election of 1989; they killed a number of people. So in 1984 we endorsed Noriega's rip-off of the election enthusiastically. Our candidate was put in with violence and thuggery and vote stealing and our enthusiastic endorsement.

In 1989, the same guy does the same thing, and we are appalled because he's kept out by less violence and thuggery. In fact, Endara himself—and nobody bothered to quote him much during this invasion, because he's just a figurehead—around the end of December 1989, gave a talk in which he denounced the "fraud of 1984." That didn't get reported because that begins to give too much insight into reality. But if our sensibilities are so offended by Noriega in 1989 keeping out Endara, how come it was all fine when the same thing and worse happened in 1984 keeping Endara out? Actually there was a review of media coverage of the 1984 election by Ken Silverstein published in 1988 in the *Columbia Journalism Review*. He went through the major newspapers, the *Times,* the *Post,* the *Miami Herald,* the *L.A. Times,* etc. Nobody had a word to say about the fraud. It was fine.

DB: *I recall at the time Shultz chastising the Sandinistas in Nicaragua saying they should emulate Panamanian democracy.*

That's right. He went down to the inauguration and challenged the Sandinistas to do the same. Of course, they did have an election, a free election, and of course that was delegitimized. It's just amazing what the propaganda system can tolerate and not respond to. None of this stuff is reported. You can sort of put it together if you look at a sentence here and a sentence there. These are not obscure things. The obvious question that would come to mind when the U.S. government expresses its outrage over the stealing of the election in 1989 is, What happened in the previous election when Noriega was still our thug? That's not a complicated question. Immediately you find out it was stolen worse, and we liked it. The president who was put in, incidentally, was a former student of George Shultz, a right-wing banker named Ardito Barletta, who's been called "Fraudito" in Panama ever since then.

DB: *In a January 29, 1990 article in* The Nation, *you contrast what the Soviet Union has done in its realm in Eastern Europe over the last year compared to what the United States does* *in its domain.*

It's a pretty dramatic contrast, and again it's kind of surprising that north of the Rio Grande no one seems to see it. What's going on in our domains is just the traditional Cold War. You suppress independence and democracy and social reform and you do it by violence because there's no other way. That's just getting worse. That's what the Soviet Union had also been doing in its half of the Cold War for a long time. Its domains are much narrower, because we're a global power, and they use force right on their periphery, but the Cold War for the Soviet Union has been tanks in East Berlin and Budapest and Prague. In the United States it's been overthrowing governments all over the world and torturing union leaders, etc., in too many cases to mention. That continues to go on in our domains, strikingly in Central America, which is just a charnel house.

What's remarkable about Eastern Europe is that the imperial power has backed off. Not only is it permitting popular movements to function, it's actually encouraging them. That's historically without precedent. It's not happening because the Russians are nice guys. It's happening for internal reasons, but it's happening. So therefore big popular movements in Eastern Europe are actually able to make gains. They don't have to face anything remotely like the terror that anyone like that would face in the American domains. Havel, for example, wouldn't be in a jail in El Salvador, he'd be mutilated and left dead by a roadside somewhere. I'm not denigrating East European movements; they're quite impressive. But they don't have to face violence like what happens here. State force has eroded and collapsed. It's backed off and dissolved. It's very hard to think of an analog for that historically. Furthermore, the Soviet Union has actually, and this again is unprecedented, apologized for the past use of violence. Big headlines on the front pages of the newspapers here proclaim that finally the Russians are joining the civilized world because they said that the invasion of Afghanistan violated international law and was illegitimate.

That's astonishing. You have to look pretty far to find anyone suggesting that maybe the United States ought to try to rise to the moral level of the Kremlin and say that the attack against South Vietnam violated international law and was immoral. In fact, we couldn't say that, because that would admit that it took place. We can't even say that it took place. Or an apology for the invasion of the Dominican Republic, or of Grenada, or for that matter the invasion of Panama. Let's not go back too far. Or a dozen other cases you can imagine. That's just not in the cards.

I think the whole Cold War has been misinterpreted by the left and the right from the beginning. If you look at the actual events of the Cold War, you find, in my view, a kind of tacit compact between the Soviet Union and the United States to allow them to share in world management. The official line is not totally false, and that's worth going into, but a large part of the Cold War was a mechanism by which the United States could fight a war against the Third World and control its allies in Europe and the Soviet Union could maintain its own internal empire and its satellites, each appealing to the threat of the other. That's a large part of the function of the Cold War. There were other functions, but that's a large part of it. From that point of view, half the Cold War continues. In fact, it's intensified. The United States is still playing the game. The other half of the game has been called off. That's a change. It's not an end to the Cold War. What you have is that one side has called off the game, while the other side is going ahead as before.

Interestingly, people like Elliott Abrams are very aware of this and very happy about it and they draw the obvious conclusion: Abrams, after the Panama invasion, was naturally ecstatic, and he pointed out quite accurately that there is a difference now from before. Now we don't have to worry about the Soviet deterrent. He says now the United States is much more free to use force because we don't have to be concerned that it's going to explode into a superpower conflict, because the Russians have backed off. The line all along has been: We contain the Russians and we deter them. The reality has been: They contain our global designs and they deter us, and that's natural because we're a global power, our global designs are everywhere, not just in the historic invasion routes. Russian intervention, except for Afghanistan, has been in historic invasion routes from the West against the Russians. There's nothing like that in our interventions. Abrams understands correctly that the deterrent has been removed, or at least reduced, so now we're more free to use force. We can play the Cold War game even more effectively.

You asked before, what's the significance of the Panama invasion? I think we now see two aspects, both related to the changes in the international environment. One is that a new propaganda framework is needed. A second is we're more free to use force. Both of these facts result from the same phenomenon: the collapse of the Soviet system. This has been perceived for some time. You may remember I was writing about this about a year ago and talked about it on British television quoting U.S. commentators over a year ago, saying that the big advantage of the collapse of the Soviet system is that it's going to free us up to use military force. That's true. That's exactly what happened. We don't have to be concerned as much with the deterrent effect of the Soviet Union.

DB: *Adding to what you said about Eastern Europe and the events there, the one country where there was violence was the very country where the Soviet Union had the least amount of influence: Romania.*

And where we had the most influence. Romania had been our ally. Not just ours, but the British as well. Back in 1980 or so Ceausescu came to England and was given a real royal treatment, photo opportunities with the Queen, etc. One of the British newspapers reviewed some of the stuff recently. It was quite funny. He was treated as a great man. The United States also gave him favored nation treatment, trade advantages, etc. He was just as brutal and crazed then as he was in the next decade, but the point is that he was partially on our side in the international struggle. He had largely withdrawn from the Warsaw Pact, followed an independent course. We're in favor of independence in *other* people's empires, not in ours. So he was kind of a crazed independent nationalist inside the Soviet system, which was all to the good. He recognized Israel and was a conduit to China. There are all these good things, so therefore he was a wonderful guy. That's the only place where there was violence. The rest of the popular uprisings in Eastern Europe were just astonishingly peaceful. There was some repression, but by historical standards it's unique. I can't think of another case that comes close.

DB: *In that same* Nation *article you write very excitedly about the prospects for libertarian socialist ideals coming forth in Eastern Europe. Do you really see that happening?*

I wasn't thinking as much of Eastern Europe there as of the West, frankly. I don't know if I put it very clearly. I think the prospects for Eastern Europe are pretty dim. The West has a very clear plan for Eastern Europe. They want to turn it into a new, easily exploitable part of the Third World. You can see that in the U.S. budget, in the foreign aid program. "Foreign aid" is a kind of euphemism that means funds sent to enhance U.S. interests. So in places that are of strategic importance, which means can help us control the Third World or that are crucial for

American investment or regarded as so, then you'll get what's called "aid." And it's shifting from Central America to Eastern Europe. If you go to Europe it's even more so. Western Europe is enthusiastic about the new possibilities for exploitation. After all, the history of Europe is basically robbery and plunder and destruction all over the world. Now they've got this new place. Actually it's sort of an old place, because there were quasi-colonial relationships between Western and Eastern Europe and the Russians blocked it. That's part of the reason for the Cold War. Now it's being reestablished. In England and Germany and France they're ecstatic about these new opportunities. There's a lot of resources you can steal. You can set up assembly plants with very cheap labor. It's necessary for us to impose on them the capitalist model. We don't accept it for ourselves, but for the Third World we insist on it. That's the IMF system. If we can get them to accept that, they'll be very easily exploitable. There's a lot of opportunities for enrichment through exploitation of the Third World, and I expect that's what'll happen there. I doubt that most of the region can resist that. I hope they can.

The prospects for libertarian socialism, I think, are in the West. One of the most effective techniques of population control in the West has been through associating socialism and reform with the Soviet Union. That's supposed to be "really existing socialism." The left and the right collaborated in a colossal deceit. If these values, the values of solidarity and egalitarianism and social justice and other things traditionally associated with socialism, if they're typified by Eastern Europe, then we don't want any. Any sane person will say, "I don't want that." That's been a major technique by which popular movements have been contained and controlled and diverted and sometimes just destroyed in the West. That's a total hoax. The Bolshevik coup in October 1917 destroyed socialism, what there was of it, in the Soviet Union.

DB: *But it took its name.*

It took its name, sure, like we use "democracy" to refer to El Salvador, too. In fact, they call their satellites "People's Democracies." They're socialist. They're also democracies. They're as much socialist as they are democracies. We joke about the democracy part, but we play up the socialist part, because it's important to denigrate and undermine socialism.

Now, with the collapse of the Soviet system, that technique of population control is also, maybe, gone. There's going to be a big effort to maintain it. That's why there's all this flap about the victory of capitalism over socialism, etc. But it too could become harder. That means there are opportunities for reviving the libertarian socialist thinking and ideals that were largely crushed by the Bolshevik Revolution and were crushed in the West by associating them with the Bolshevik Revolution. That's where I think the hope lies. How big that hope is, I don't know. But at least one roadblock is eliminated.

DB: *How will planners and elite groups here prevent the rot from spreading, as it were? What if people in the United States wanted open political parties and access to the media, etc.?*

They recognize that as a problem. That's one of the reasons why the United States and Western European elites are not too happy with these moves towards detente. This is an old story. It goes back to the mid-1940s. The United States had a major part in the partition of Germany, because they were concerned that it was necessary to break up the German labor movement and to prevent what was called "ideological aggression" from the East. That was the kind of aggression that we were really concerned about. George Kennan back in 1946 already said it would be necessary to "wall off" western Germany from influences from the East if we wanted to restore the old traditional conservative order and make sure there were no social democratic tendencies or a powerful labor movement, etc. That was just a piece of what was going on all through the world. That's been going on ever since, and it remains true today.

For example, when Brzezinski [former National Security Council Adviser under Carter] recently made a big speech in Moscow talking about the wonderful triumph of capitalism, he ended up by saying, but let's not go too far. Let's keep the Warsaw Pact and NATO in existence, because that contributes to what he called "stability," which is one of those code words which means "rule by the right guys." There's always been a fear of what the Prime Minister of South Africa, Jan Christiaan Smuts, once called "letting politics loose among these peoples" in Europe, talking to his friend Winston Churchill in 1943.

DB: *Creating crises of democracy.*

Sure. You've got to make sure you don't let politics loose among these peoples, and the pact system helps prevent that. That's one reason why European elites are quite happy with it, and even want to keep American forces there. They want to keep some measure of confrontation going, because that keeps politics from getting loose among these peoples with all sorts of funny ideas. Here you're going to have to look for substitutes. That's in fact a major function of the drug war and of the international terrorism hysteria. Other things will have to be invented. How stable it's going to be is hard to say. I don't think any of this has the propaganda appeal of the Evil Empire, which, after all, was evil and was an empire and was brutal. No matter how insane the idea that they're strangling the West, it was true that they were ugly. I don't know if you can find a substitute for that very easily. Those are the kinds of conflicts that are now arising within the ideological system.

Substitutions for the "Evil Empire"

February 2, 1990

DB: *In the winter 1990* Daedalus *there's an article by "Z" entitled "To the Stalin Mausoleum." This has attracted much attention in the mainstream media. It's been excerpted in the* New York Times. *Do you have a take on this piece?*

First of all, there's a big conceptual framework which I think we can pretty well ignore. It is full of such insights as that the left regarded Stalin as a hero and that mainstream Anglo-American Sovietology, with its liberal to radical slant, described Stalinism as democratic and lauded the master, etc. That business we can forget about. When you cut away the fluff, the meat of the article, which is in the last couple of pages, the ones that were excerpted in the *Times,* consists of one general thesis and of one policy recommendation that follows from it. The general thesis is that there is no third way between Leninism and the market, between Bolshevism and constitutional government. So any effort to find anything in between those is impossible. That's the general thesis. The policy recommendation is that U.S. aid to the Soviet Union be restricted to what the author calls "parallel structures" based on private investment and the free market, and that around the periphery of Russia, in the Baltic States, etc., the United States should attempt to impose IMF restrictions, with free trade zones, and that that should gradually be extended into the interior of the Soviet Union. That's the policy recommendation.

Let's go back to the thesis, which has one minor defect. The first part rules out of existence virtually every society in the world. There is no society which adheres strictly to free-market principles and few that are Leninist in their state management style, especially as these command economies are eroding. It's certainly not true of the industrial democracies, obviously not the great success stories like South Korea and Taiwan. And as to the claim that there's no third ground between Bolshevism and constitutional government, the second of those two dichotomies, that rules out of existence most societies of the world, which are neither Bolshevik nor have constitutional governments. The major thesis is not just false, but too absurd to even merit discussion. You can understand why the author wants to remain anonymous, given the intellectual level of the discussion, both the part that I've indicated before and the thesis. However, all of this is really for show. What's significant is not the conceptual framework but the policy recommendation, so let's get back to that.

The policy recommendation says that the United States and the West generally should try to turn Eastern Europe and the Soviet Union into a new Third World. We, of course, do not accept free-market principles and capitalist structures for ourselves. No businessman would ever tolerate being subjected to the ravages of competitive capitalism and the free market without a government to protect him and a public subsidy, etc. But we do insist upon that for our victims. It makes them much easier to exploit. That's what IMF conditions amount to: no subsidies, no protection, no government stimulation of the economy or interference with foreign investment, etc. If you can impose such structures on Third World countries, that makes them much more easily exploitable. The policy proposal is very crass and simple: Let's try to turn the collapsing Soviet Empire into a new Latin America that can be robbed and exploited in the same fashion as our old Third World. That's what it amounts to. The rest is just intellectual games to make it look serious.

DB: *You are troubled by Gorbachev's reforms in the sense that they're top down. Does he have much of a choice?*

That's not a criticism of Gorbachev. It's a criticism of the Leninist system that destroyed civil society. There was very little in the way of popular structure. This goes way back in Russian history to before the Bolsheviks. People have compared it with Peter the Great and Alexander II. The system did require substantial changes, maybe total dissolution, and Gorbachev did it from above, initiated the moves from above. They're of course setting in motion all sorts of popular movements. That's a reflection of the nature of Soviet society, not a comment on Gorbachev.

DB: *The Pentagon system of industrial management in this country needs an enemy. Who is going to be a credible substitute for the Soviet Union? The media will present Medellín drug lords and the PLO and the Sandinistas and Libyan hit squads, but they don't quite sustain themselves.*

That's been a problem all throughout the 1980s. It's been obvious from the early 1980s that it's going to become very hard to keep the hysteria going about Soviet imperialism. The Reagan administration came into office committed to carry out quickly the huge expansion of the military and the cutback on social programs that had been proposed by the Carter administration. Now they were going to implement it and do it fast. That required a lot of jingoist hysteria and fear, etc. Of course, there was lots of talk about the Evil Empire stalking the world, but also other things. Alexander Haig, the Secretary of State, in one of his first statements said that international terrorism would be replacing human rights as the central feature of their foreign policy. There was a big campaign about the Kremlin-inspired international terrorism with Arab lunatics and Sandinistas, etc. A good deal of hysteria was worked up about that. For example, by 1985, Mideast and Mediterranean international terrorism was actually ranked as the top story of the year in a poll of editors by Associated Press.

That laid the basis for atrocities like the bombing of Libya. It was a very selective use of terrorism, and there's a lot to be said about that, and that was tried, but as you say, it didn't really stick. It's very hard to keep people mobilized over international terrorism, although there's plenty of effort to try and a lot of distortion and fabrication in the effort to do it. That's a big story in itself.

The next one, as again you said, is the drug war. So the Medellín cartel is a natural substitute for the Soviet Union, and that has at least temporarily worked. Like you, I think it's very temporary. I don't think that has the staying power of the Soviet threat. However, it's certainly worked. It's enough to look at the polls. For example, the big government-media blitz about the drug war actually dates from September 1989, and the effect on public opinion was immediate. I monitored the wires just for the fun of it, just to see what the distribution of stories was. This isn't a scientific analysis, but a pretty close sample. Over the AP wires there were more stories on drugs than on Latin America, Asia, the Middle East, and Africa combined. It just shot up. If you looked at television, every news program had a big section on how drugs were destroying our society, the greatest danger in history, etc. And the polls reflected it. So when Bush won the election in November 1988, when people were asked an open question: What's the main problem facing the country?, usually the top percentage you ever get on a question like that is about 10 percent, because people are free to suggest anything they want as the main problem. The top choice was the budget deficit. That was the biggest problem. Drugs were way down, I think about 3 percent of the population said that drugs were the main problem. After this September media blitz, drugs were at the level of about 40 percent or 45 percent, which is just unheard of in an open question, and the deficit was way down. That shift reflected the very effective media propaganda. Nothing new had happened about drugs that would account for the change in this period.

There were also some pretty remarkable ironies during this. For example, hard drugs are doubtless a serious problem. Alcohol and cigarettes are a much more serious problem, at least by any statistic that anyone knows. So the number of annual deaths from tobacco and alcohol is probably in the nature of half a million. Hard drugs, it's maybe 5,000, and from some drugs, like marijuana, it's essentially zero. In fact the drug war over the years has tended to shift drug use from relatively harmless drugs like marijuana to much more dangerous drugs like cocaine. That's sort of inherent in the methods of deterrence. But even with that, the federal figures, which are probably understated, are probably under 5,000 deaths a year from illegal substances and something on the order of half a million a year from alcohol and tobacco. Even if those numbers are off by a large factor, the discrepancy is substantial.

Right in the middle of this big media blitz about the drug war, the U.S. Trade Representative, a branch of the Executive of the government concerned with unfair trade practices, met to hear a complaint by the tobacco companies over the fact that Thailand was refusing to accept American tobacco shipments and was imposing various restrictions on tobacco and on advertising for tobacco in an effort to prevent substance abuse in Thailand. The plea was to ask the U.S. government to impose trade sanctions on Thailand to compel them to accept American tobacco and to compel them to accept cigarette company advertising. Similar trade sanctions had already been used under the Reagan administration to force Japan and South Korea to accept a flood of American tobacco. The Surgeon General, Everett Koop, testified. He condemned this as utterly scandalous, said it was a complete scandal to ask other countries to stop sending drugs to us while we force them to accept even more harmful drugs from us upon pain of trade sanctions. Witnesses compared it with the opium wars in the 1840s, when Britain forced China to accept opium because it couldn't sell them anything else and set off a huge opium epidemic there after they forced them to accept it through war. This went essentially unreported. I think the *Wall Street Journal* and the *Christian Science Monitor* had a notice about it. Nobody even covered the content of it. It was just unreported. That's a big story. The story is "U.S. Biggest Narco-Trafficker in the World," or "U.S. government forcing other countries to accept U.S. drugs." But that was just passed over in complete silence.

Anyway, the effect of all this was significant. Today's newspaper, for example, quotes Alfredo Cristiani, President of El Salvador, complaining that the U.S. government isn't sending them enough money. What he says is, if you cut back on the funds for us, it's going to make it harder for us to deal with the illegal drug problem. When Quayle was in Jamaica a couple days ago, [Prime Minister] Manley tells him, you've got to give us more money or we aren't going to be able to fight drugs. The line is, Well, how are you going to stop drugs? Everyone's got the line. If you want more bread, put it in this context. It used to be, how are you going to stop the Russians? Now it's how are you going to stop the drugs? This is a good cover. It has first the function of mobilizing the population in fear because the drug problem is very severe, although the part they're looking at is a very small part and the way they're dealing with it is not intended to deal with the problem. It will probably intensify it. It's nevertheless a problem, no doubt.

Secondly, this provides a very solid basis for intervention. It gives a basis for maintaining U.S. force in regions where there are counterinsurgency activities. The aid to Colombia, so-called, is going to the military, which is up to its neck in drug trafficking, as everybody knows, and the military will use it for its purposes, which are death squads, atrocities, killing peasant leaders, massacring the political leadership of the one independent party, which has lost about a thousand top leaders in the last couple of years through killings, counterinsurgency, etc. That's exactly what it'll be used for. When the U.S. wants to move in it will have a cover to do it. It's already begun. For example, when Colombia asked the United States for assistance in establishing a radar facility to monitor illegal drug flights from the Andean countries to their south, the United States in fact installed a facility, but it installed it at the point on Colombian territory which is farthest, most remote, from the area where the flights are coming. They installed it way up in the north on an island which happens to be off the coast of Nicaragua, and of course it's used for surveillance of Nicaragua.

When Costa Rica asked the United States for similar assistance, it did make a proposal. The Costa Ricans didn't have a way of checking it, so they checked it with the British government, who assessed it as a counterinsurgency operation which had nothing to do with drugs. That's exactly what's going to go on, the same in Peru and Bolivia and everywhere. It's a cover for intervention. It's a way of mobilizing the population. It's going to be a method to pump-prime either through what's called aid or through the domestic form of aid, through the Pentagon, etc.

Whether it will work is another question. Like you, I think it's pretty flimsy. It'll work for a while. It did work, for example, in the Panama invasion. One of the pretexts used to invade Panama was that we were somehow defending ourselves against drugs. It was ludicrous, but it certainly was used as propaganda with some degree of effectiveness.

DB: *Do you think decriminalization of drugs is a way out of this? Do you favor that?*

I think it's something that should be explored. You don't want to be too casual about it. It's a complicated issue. Some form of decriminalization would probably be very much in order. The experience of decriminalization is actually a complex one in other cases. Take the decriminalization of alcohol. It depends on what facet you look at to figure out how it works. Nobody advocates recriminalization of alcohol. I have yet to hear anyone say we ought to reinstate Prohibition. There are good reasons for that. I agree. I think we should not reinstate Prohibition. But those same arguments hold for hard drugs. There's no fundamental difference. The question is whether there can be some form of access combined with government regulation and other measures which will tend to increase the penalty for harmful drugs and decrease the penalty for benign drugs. That's the basic idea. That's been done in England over centuries with regard to alcohol. There are tax and other regulatory procedures with regard to alcohol. Their net effect is that they induce beer drinking and reduce hard liquor drinking. That's the effect that they have overall. That's in general sane social policy. Pretty much the same is true in the tobacco case. It would be a mistake to put people in jail for smoking cigarettes. But you can use controls on access, like six-year-olds can't buy a pack of cigarettes. Also, the tax structure, and educational programs, which are extremely important, can have an effect on this, where people are in a position to make choices.

Just to continue with this, the obvious effect of the government policies on drugs, which has been pointed out over and over again, has been exactly the opposite. Marijuana happens to be bulky, and marijuana imports are easy to interdict. The effect of the drug war has been to interdict marijuana and not to prevent but to restrict marijuana production domestically.

DB: *Which drives up the price.*

Not only drives up the price, but turns people to more high-tech drugs, like cocaine, which can be brought in very compactly and even constructed in laboratories and happen to be more lethal. The content of cocaine on the drug market has been increasing over the years just through market forces. You drive the price up, people are going to make it more lethal. So the net effect of the whole drug interdiction has been exactly the opposite of the sane regulatory procedures that have been used in England with regard to liquor: they've driven people away from the relatively harmless drugs towards the much more harmful and addictive ones. And that's going to continue. After crack will come something that people can make in a laboratory that will be even more addictive, like ice, which is now sweeping the West Coast, etc. Again, I don't think you can take the figures too literally, because there's a lot that's not known, but they mean something. The federal figures on drugs indicate not one known case of a marijuana death from overdose, and there have been an estimated 60 million users. If those figures are even in the ballpark, which I suppose they are, they would indicate that marijuana is much safer than alcohol and by far safer than tobacco. That's what's being interdicted. What's been driven up is dangerous drugs like cocaine and now crack and ice. That's inherent in the methods.

I think some sort of nuanced decriminalization is probably a sensible policy, but it doesn't get to the heart of the matter. You have to ask yourself, Why are peasants in Peru and Bolivia producing coca? Why are kids in the inner cities using it? The answers to that are not very obscure. In Peru and Bolivia, that's in part due to American foreign so-called aid. U.S. policies over the years have been designed to impose a kind of agro-export model on

Third World countries. There are a lot of ways of doing this. One way is Food for Peace, for example, which sends subsidized U.S. farm products, meaning a gift from the American taxpayer to American agribusiness. Subsidized American farm products are sent to Third World countries, where they undercut local agriculture and therefore drive the peasants to produce export crops. That's what happened in Peru and Bolivia. When peasants are compelled to function on the capitalist market, they do it just the way Milton Friedman says they should: they look for the most profitable crop per hour of labor input. By any measure, that's going to be coca. So we drive them to produce it. Then when we don't like it we go there and defoliate the farms. We don't defoliate the farms in North Carolina which are producing tobacco. It would be a lot easier than sending bombers out to Peru. Of course the point is not to attack rich and powerful people, it's to attack poor people. That's the whole point of social policy.

One factor is the production end, and that is complex, but deeply rooted in long-standing U.S. policies (including the CIA and counterinsurgency, another matter). If you want to deal with the production end, you've got to create a different development program for the Third World, which won't drive people to do this. On the consumption end, people in the inner cities have good reasons to get involved in drugs. You're a fifteen-year-old black kid in the inner city, and you take a look at the options available to you. You can be unemployed or maybe sweep the floors somewhere. Or you can do what that other kid is doing, walking around with a car, lots of cash, etc. He's playing the capitalist game. He's going where the money is and maximizing gain. That happens to be by working as a street peddler for the drug lords. Or if you've got a choice as to whether for the next hour to face this miserable, hopeless existence or get high on drugs, it's not an irrational choice to get high on drugs. As long as that's the set of choices that are available, you can expect people to make them.

In the white suburbs, where people have a range of choices available to them, drug use has been dropping fast, quite independent of any drug war, which has had no effect whatsoever. Usage of hard drugs, again by federal statistics, has been dropping quite rapidly, over the years. Of course, people have been seeing the effects, and they have choices. It's not that it's eliminated, it's serious, but there's a range of choices available and people can deal with it. As long as there's no range of choices, you can see what's going to happen: use will continue and grow in some areas.

If there were a serious attempt to deal with the drug problem instead of this fraudulent hoax, the first thing that they would go after would be money laundering. That's pretty easy to monitor. The laws require now that bank deposits over $10,000 be registered. So the Federal Reserve banks can actually monitor big increases in deposits, which usually mean criminal deposits. And they've done that. When you look at it, it's pretty obvious what's happening. So when the cocaine flow started, the deposits in Miami banks shot up, around 1980. There was at that time a small federal program, Operation Greenback, which was monitoring money laundering and prosecuting it, and they started going after the Miami banks. So the illegal funds in Miami banks went down and they shot up in Los Angeles. Meanwhile, drug lords like Milian Rodriguez, a launderer for the Medellín cartel, testified in Congress, described how he flew to Kennedy airport and was met with a limousine from a New York bank and went down to talk to the guy in charge of illegal drugs and they did whatever they do, and then he went back to Kennedy airport in the limousine and took off. Nobody's going after the New York banks.

In fact, George Bush was the drug czar back in the early 1980s, and one of his major contributions, actually his only known contribution to the drug war, was to terminate this small federal program that was going after banks. Even a small program going after money laundering was eliminated. Furthermore, the Reagan administration, as part of its shift of government activities—it was not a decrease but just a shift—included cutting down on bank regulation. So the number of people monitoring banks and illegal banking operations was sharply reduced, one reason for the Savings and Loan fiasco. One effect was that, although they have the figures on heavy deposits, including criminal deposits, they can't find them because they don't have the manpower to check it. In fact, the general effect of the Reagan drug war was to increase the problem. It increases the problem by increasing the consumption problem in the inner cities: increase poverty and desperation and you're going to increase drug use. It was carefully designed to avoid all the major issues like, obviously, rich tobacco farmers and alcohol, that's out of the question. In fact, they were ramming these lethal addictive drugs down the throats of other countries. Even going after the banks was ruled out. The policy had the effect of shifting drug use from relatively benign substances to much more harmful ones. And the new drug war is equally phony. It's largely a technique of population control, a way of imposing harsher constraints on the population. Look at the expenditures: They're going for jails, policemen, more ways of cooping up people in these concentration camps called the inner cities. They're just sticking them in jails directly. It calls for attacks on civil liberties, more death penalties, harsher police measures. It's exactly what you would expect of this kind of so-called conservatism—advocacy of a powerful and violent state. It has nothing to do with drugs except it probably made it worse.

DB: *Let's talk about Israel and the Middle East. About three years ago I was interviewing Edward Said and I asked him if he expected more from Israel because of the history of Jewish persecu-*

tion that Israelis should be more sensitive to the sufferings of others, obviously in this case the Palestinian question. He answered, "Yes," and I've always had trouble with that. I think that's a kind of racist notion. Do you expect more from Israelis?

No, of course not. I think that's completely wrong. There's no reason to expect more from them because they suffered in the past. Absolutely no reason. There's nothing in history or anything else that suggests that that would happen.

DB: *You said your intellectual and emotional roots are in the Middle East. I'm surprised that you said that they were not in Eastern Europe, from whence your parents came.*

My parents came from Eastern Europe. Of course, they fled from Eastern Europe. They maintained no connection with Eastern Europe. The Eastern European community that they were a part of by the time I was ten years old was being wiped out by the Nazis. Eastern Europe, from their point of view, is a place from which you flee in horror. My father fled to escape the Czarist draft, which was basically a death sentence for young Jewish men, and my mother's family left when she was a baby, so she doesn't even remember it.

DB: *When was that?*

My father came in 1913, my mother came somewhat earlier. But Eastern Europe was not a place where you had roots except in a shtetl, and the shtetl from their point of view had largely been transferred to places like Baltimore. By the time the Nazis came along there was nothing left. The Eastern European Jewish community which they knew wasn't *Fiddler on the Roof*. It was pretty unpleasant in many ways. It was something to escape from. People escaped in Eastern Europe in all sorts of ways. Many escaped in Poland, for example, which was the main center of Jewish settlement, by joining the Bund, which was socialist and trying to break out of this system. They were much stronger than the Zionists, for example. Although the traditional religious element was very powerful, it was collapsing. The shtetl was run by rabbis who were often harsh and authoritarian, with power coming from the state authorities. It was a very backward society. You weren't supposed to read, to know anything, no books. This *Fiddler on the Roof* version has not very much to do with it. That's not where people's roots were.

As far as my immediate environment was concerned, my father was a cultural Zionist, Ahad Ha'am-style. My parents' commitment was to the revivification of Jewish life in other parts of the Diaspora, the United States, where people could survive, and with a cultural homeland in what was then Palestine. So that was the immediate environment in which I grew up. I had my own understanding of it.

DB: *I remember you telling me, I can't recall the exact details, that this feudalism from Eastern Europe extended to the United States and your mother had to walk on one side of the street? What was that exactly?*

I've never seen a very good study of this, but according to what I can figure out, from what my parents themselves told me or what I've been able to read elsewhere, as the Eastern European community transferred itself to the United States it underwent many changes. One of the changes was a kind of regression. For example, my father described his family as moving back even more into the Eastern European mold in some ways after they came here. My mother, her family came over when she was one year old, but by the time she was a high-school student in New York she remembered and described to us how if she was walking down the street with friends and saw her father coming towards her, she would cross the street so as not to undergo the embarrassment of having him pass by without acknowledging her existence, because she was just a girl. As a child, I saw a bit of this, in the very orthodox Jewish environment that my parents had come out of.

My grandfather, for example, lived in the United States for fifty years, and I wonder whether he even knew that he wasn't in Eastern Europe. It sometimes seemed that he saw the place he lived as a kind of Eastern Europe where the peasants were black. He was living in a shtetl environment which may have regressed even back from what it had been in Eastern Europe. The attitude toward the blacks, in fact, was just a carry over from the attitude toward the Ukrainian peasants. You've got to be scared of them because they're pretty dangerous and you can also cheat them because they're really stupid. You can really cheat the schwarzes like you could cheat the Ukrainians, but you've got to watch out because you never know when they're going to strike back. They're dangerous. This kind of mood I can remember as a kid.

The orthodoxy was just crippling. These are called the people of the book, but that's just a joke. It was a very anti-intellectual society, authoritarian and rigid. You can see it in the religious right wing in Israel, which carries it over. People have been surprised that Menachem Begin was so welcomed by the Moroccan Jews. A lot of Moroccan Jews apparently think Begin was Moroccan, because he's obviously one of them. There's some truth to that. Begin and Shamir came out of an environment which was very similar to the semi-feudal environment of parts of the Jewish community in North Africa. Now the more educated sectors went to France, but many of the less educated and more traditional, who lived in a manner not unlike semi-feudal Poland, went to Israel. So the cultural similarities are in a sense real.

In communities in Israel they have religious leaders who are saints, who carry out miracles, and you go visit them and they get rid of your problems. Some of them even come back from the dead. They speak through their children. They call them up and give them orders as to who to vote for. During the last election there was one leading rabbi who's on television saying, Anybody who doesn't vote for our party is going to be cursed and go to hell, and then some other rabbi gets on and does a counter-curse and says, If you vote for our party we can take care of him. That's a part of the traditional culture. It's been very much prettified in all sorts of folklore, but it wasn't very pretty. When my father lived in the shtetl and wanted to learn something about the outside world, to learn Russian was heresy. Even to learn Hebrew was improper. You don't read the Bible, that's just too light. You start when you are three years old memorizing the Talmud and that's it. Of course you know Hebrew because you have the prayers and the Bible insofar as it's in the ritual, but to learn the modern Hebrew language was considered breaking out.

DB: *So learning was the property of the priesthood.*

There was no learning. What they called learning was rote memorization, largely, and under harsh control. In the European Jewish ghettoes I don't think they had any history or geography books until the nineteenth century, because the Bible didn't say it so it wasn't true. There was no America. The Bible didn't say anything about America. What kind of nonsense was this? It was a very anti-intellectual environment. There was an assimilationist strain of Jews. Basically that's what we all come out of. In Western Europe, Germany, Austria, the Jewish community became assimilated starting from the late eighteenth century. They joined Western European culture and felt part of it. That's where you get Freud and Einstein, etc. They came out of the assimilated part which was breaking away from the traditional culture and had total contempt for it.

There was also a Renaissance, a Jewish Enlightenment, in the areas of dense Jewish population in Poland,
the pale of settlement, the places where the Jews were
allowed to live in the Czarist Empire. That was early in
the nineteenth century, and out of that comes the revival
of Hebrew and the origins of modern Zionism. There was
also a big socialist movement. These were all break-away
things from the traditional society.

DB: *Were your parents fairly coercive with you?*

Not particularly. I went to a very progressive exper-
imental private school. They had their own life. Their life
was basically Jewish. Hebrew scholarship, Hebrew teaching, Jewish life, etc. But in their framework, American
society, which they saw as a genuinely pluralist society,
should have plenty of room for a community of people
whose main interest is Judaism. That's us.

DB: *What did they think of you hopping on a train and going
up to New York and hanging out at anarchist bookstores on Fourth
Avenue and talking to your working-class relatives there?*

They didn't mind, as far as I know. To the extent they
were aware of it, of which I'm not entirely sure. I don't
think they minded. After all, the family was split up. Like
a lot of Jewish families, they went in all sorts of directions.
There were sectors that were super-orthodox and other
sectors that were very radical and very assimilated and
working-class intellectuals. That's the sector that I naturally gravitated to. That's where I'd hang out when I'd go
to New York. This was all considered legitimate, the whole
range.

DB: *You've described the intellectual and cultural life you
experienced in New York in the thirties as the richest of your life.
What was some of the fabric of that? What contributed to that
richness?*

I began to be of an age where I could appreciate it around 1940, I guess, ten or eleven years old. It was a very lively intellectual culture. For one thing, it was a working-class culture with working-class values, solidarity, socialist values, etc. Within that it varied from communist party to radical semi-anarchist critique of Bolshevism. That whole range was there. That was not untypical. But that was only a part of it. People were having intensive debates about the Stekel's version of Freudian theory, a lot of discussions about literature and music, what did you think of the latest Budapest String Quartet concert, or Schnabel's version of a Beethoven sonata *vs.* somebody else's version. It was a very lively, rich intellectual life at every level. I was very much attracted to it. A lot of the people involved were more or less formally uneducated. The one uncle who was the main influence on me never got past fourth grade. After that he was a kind of street person in New York. Then he got himself together. Since he had a disability, he was given a newsstand to run. New York law favored the disabled, so he got a newsstand somewhere where everybody would hang out and have lively discussions, late into the night. It was a very exciting environment. I used to really look forward to helping in the newsstand.

DB: *He was your mother's brother?*

He was actually my aunt's husband, technically family by marriage. He later became a lay analyst. He got involved with some German emigré psychiatrists, a lot of German emigrés were coming over in the late 1930s, and this newsstand became kind of a magnet, a place for people to hang out and talk and argue. He himself was very deeply involved in psychoanalytic literature, a very impressive guy intellectually, and he became friendly with some of these people and finally ended up doing a didactic analysis under the supervision of one of them. He gradually started having more patients. Some of his patients went on to become big shots in the profession and referred patients to him, and finally, without going through the whole story, he ended up being a fairly wealthy lay analyst with a Riverside Drive apartment.

DB: *You used to go to that apartment, and I remember you telling me that when he had patients visiting you'd have to stay in the kitchen.*

That was when he still lived in a tiny apartment before he was able to get an office. If patients were knocking at his door we would all have to run into the kitchen and hide there while they came in and went into the bedroom, which was where the office was. Then we were able to come out and sit outside until the session was over and then go back into the kitchen again while the patient left.

DB: *There's not a trace of that culture left, is there?*

I doubt it. I doubt that there's anything left. It just disappeared and dissolved during the war and the postwar repression. After all, business was very aware of the ferment in the working class. You read the business literature back in the late 1930s, and although I don't think they had any sense of this kind of thing, business was concerned with what they called the rising power of "the masses." That literature sometimes tends to be kind of vulgar Marxist in its rhetoric and its conceptions. But they were concerned about that, and they felt it was necessary to combat it and make sure it didn't develop any further. It was considered a major threat to business dominance. Starting from the late 1930s, there was an understanding that you were going to have to go after this working-class culture at its roots and at the public support for it. One approach was what was called the "Johnstown Formula," a major public relations effort to break a big steel strike, which was successful. The war had its own effects.

In the post-war period, there's the phenomenon that we call McCarthyism, which is a misunderstanding. McCarthy was a latecomer. By the late 1940s there were intensive efforts using the Cold War framework and anti-communism and all sorts of other devices to undermine and destroy the incipient labor movements that had begun to develop during the 1930s, and the whole culture that went along with them. It was successful. By now you scarcely see a trace of that kind of consciousness. I should qualify that. There's the Pittston strike, Camp Solidarity of the Pittston strike. I haven't been there, but from what I've read, I suspect that you'll see a lot of that kind of consciousness. So when I say that it isn't there, it's maybe that we don't see it. At least in the sectors of the society that I have anything to do with, it was there and it's not there any more.

DB: *I'm interested in something you talked about at the Rowe Center in April of 1989, a change that you discerned in New York after World War II, and it sort of corresponds to some information that I have on New York. You said in the 1930s people were poor and had no money, but there was a sense of hope. Then after the war, something happened, something changed. I'm very curious about this, because you were rather imprecise about it, and you're usually so precise.*

I am imprecise about it, and I don't understand it, to tell you the truth. As far as I can see this has happened all over the world, in different parts of the world at different times. Anyone who knew New York in the 1930s can see this. My family was mostly unemployed, living in slums, but there was no sense of despair. There was a sense of hopefulness. A lot of the hopefulness was illusory.

Let me tell you another personal story which will illustrate. A couple of years ago I was talking to some friends about family doctors from childhood and I was trying to remember the name of the family doctor we had when I was a kid. This was a Jewish family, which means if a kid has a fever my mother figured the world was at an end. As a six-year-old, you feel that: my brother's got a fever, oh my God, he's going to die. Then the doctor would walk in with his mellifluous voice and calm and everybody would settle down and you'd feel better. That's the culture. I don't know if you recognize it. I was trying to think what was the name of that doctor, and the only name that came to mind was Roosevelt. I knew his name wasn't Roosevelt. So I was trying to figure out why was I thinking it was Roosevelt? I finally realized that it was because when Roosevelt started on those fireside chats, that was exactly the way my parents reacted: Yeah, OK, all these horrible things are happening, but the doctor's here, he's coming, he's going to take care of things, no big problem. I don't remember what he said, I was seven years old, but I remember the mood. You pick up your parents' mood, and the mood towards Roosevelt's talks was very much like the mood towards this miraculous saint coming in to take care of my brother's fever. I don't mean to suggest that the hope was necessarily well founded. A lot of it was illusory, but it was definitely there.

Furthermore, there was infrastructure. You'd go to the library. The library was there. It was open. It had books and they'd help you. There were unions. And you could walk around the streets. When I was a ten-year-old kid, I thought nothing of walking down by the Hudson River at night or walking through Central Park alone. Something might happen, but you could get hit by lightning too. There was no sense that you were in danger, even in the poorest parts of the city.

DB: *Now you say you need a platoon of Marines.*

Yes, you need a platoon of Marines. You take your

life in your hands anywhere, even if you take the subway. Furthermore, if you go through the inner cities now, occasionally I've walked through the slums of New York trying to remember. I don't want to rely too much on my childhood memories, obviously, but to me it looks totally different. These desperate, worse than Third World conditions that you see, I don't think were there. I've talked to people who have worked in New York over the years, teachers who have taught in New York schools, and their impression, from what I've heard, is pretty much the same. In the 1930s it was very poor, but you didn't have a grandmother sitting with a baseball bat all night over the kid's crib to keep the rats from biting. Or the sense that you were in a war and had to defend yourself. There was a sense somehow that things were going to get better. An institutional structure was around, a method of struggling, organizing, of doing things, you had some hope.

I don't think there's much hope in the inner cities now. I think there's despair and I think you sense it in the serious degeneration of urban life. Also, the extremes of wealth and poverty are so much more crass than they were. You walk down somewhere on the East Side of New York and the wealth is obscene. You go a couple of blocks away and you have poverty of the kind that's simply horrifying. I don't do it, but friends tell me you sit in a fancy restaurant in New York and there's homeless people leaning on the window panes outside; you just don't notice it after a while. That kind of thing was not true before. The tone of urban life got much harsher, not just in New York but everywhere. It became very ugly.

For example, when I was a kid there were big race riots all over the place and for a while during the war teenage kids were all under 7 p.m. curfew in Philadelphia, where I lived. So it wasn't pretty. But even in a period like that, it didn't feel as though you were living in a war zone. We happened to be the only Jewish family in a largely German and Irish-Catholic neighborhood which was passionately anti-Semitic and actually rather pro-Nazi in those days—this was the late 1930s—quite pro-Nazi in fact. My brother and I knew a couple of paths we could walk on without getting our heads bashed in, but even with that I didn't sense the danger and threat and hostility of walking down the streets of New York today. There was a sense that we kind of had it under control. Maybe when they came out of the Catholic school they'd be raving maniacs wanting to kill the Jews. I don't know what happened in that school. But a couple of hours later or over the weekend you could play baseball with them. You sort of felt there were ways of coming to terms with it. During the war, we sometimes had to have police escorts to get to Hebrew school. We took the subway to the subway stop and had a two-block walk to the Hebrew school, and we had a police escort for a while, because that was the only way you could make it. The police would hang around the school to keep it from being broken into. When you made it to the subway you were on your own. But even with that, I don't recall the feelings of fear and danger that you get in the urban environments today.

I think that that's spreading over the world. The reason I'm being imprecise is that I don't really have precise knowledge. It's a sense, a feeling you pick up when you visit places. My sense is that it's been spreading over much of the world ever since at a different rate. I think you find similar developments in London maybe forty years later and in European cities a generation later. There's a kind of element of barbarism creeping into social life which at least I don't remember from those days. Maybe I missed it as a ten-year-old, but I really don't think so. I think it was different.

DB: *You had a very instructive experience with your brother David that you still talk about today. There's one in particular where you cut your hand and blamed it on him.*

That was just kids fighting.

DB: *What about the fat kid in the schoolyard?*

That was a personal thing for me, I don't know why it should interest anyone else. I do remember it.

DB: *You drew certain conclusions from it.*

Yeah, it had an influence on me. I remember when I was about six, first grade. There was the standard fat kid everybody made fun of. I remember in this schoolyard he was standing outside the school classroom and a bunch of kids outside were taunting him. One of them brought over his older brother from third grade, a big kid, and we thought he was going to beat him up. I remember going up to stand next to him feeling somebody ought to help him, and I did for a while, then I got scared and ran away. I was very much ashamed of it. I felt, I'll never do that again. That's a feeling that's stuck with me: You should stick with the underdog. The shame remained. I should have stayed with him. I think everybody must have personal experiences of this kind that sort of stick with you and color your choices later on.

DB: *While your parents were still alive did you feel inhibited in talking about Israel?*

Yes. Consciously, in fact. I didn't want to say too much. It's not that they disagreed with me. In fact, we were in basic agreement.

DB: *Would he be called an anti-Zionist today?*

No. He wouldn't criticize Israel very harshly. He just loved it. When he went there he told us that the sun was always shining. It never rained. Everybody was always happy. It was very pollyannish.

DB: *He didn't see any Palestinians while he was there?*

He didn't think about it very much. He really saw it through rose-colored glasses. He was just in love with the place. The revival of Hebrew was very exciting to him. But still, his intellectual attitudes were pre-state in many respects. They were rooted in the critical cultural Zionism of Ahad Ha'am. But that was the real importance of Israel, not that it had big borders and big armies, but that it would be a center for a culturally rich, lively Diaspora Jewry. When I started writing about it, he basically didn't disagree. My mother, who was somewhat more leftish in her orientation, certainly didn't disagree. But they were hurt very much by the bitter attacks, which began instantaneously, as soon as I opened my mouth on the topic. They lived in that community, and when all the vilification and lies and hysteria started pouring out it naturally bothered them. And you couldn't say a word without this stuff coming. Just one move away from the party line, and the whole defamation apparatus, which is well organized, started pouring out in streams. For that reason I was inhibited to an extent in speaking and writing about it while they were alive.

DB: *Out of filial piety?*

I didn't say anything I didn't believe. I am not even conscious of having not written. But I'm sure it constrained things that I said and did at the time.

DB: *People are interested in your work process also: how you obtain documents, national security memoranda, are these easily obtainable?*

It's not a major effort. It's not like going to your corner grocery.

DB: *Are they mailed to you? How do you get them?*

You get them from libraries. Most good libraries will have reference departments where you can get the materials.

DB: *Are they on microfilm?*

Yes, you can get access to them. If you really want to do detailed archival work, you have to do things which I don't have the resources for. For example, you'd have to go down to the Johnson Library and work through the stored materials. I just don't have the resources and the time for that sort of thing. But whatever you can get through libraries, I can get and other people can get too. It's work.

First of all, you have to read a ton of stuff before you find anything good. Most of it's just junk. But if you want to do the work, there are enough guides, often in secondary sources, to give you a hint as to where you ought to look. Sometimes you'll find references in secondary sources which look intriguing. I often find that they're misinterpreted, but they suggest you may want to go back and find a nugget there. So it's no big mystery, really. It's not like science, which is intellectually difficult. It just requires work. It's intellectually pretty simple. That's why anybody can do enough to gain a fairly good understanding of the world as a spare-time job.

DB: *In a 1986 interview that we did, you were fairly negative about the possibilities of an alternative media developing. Since then, however, we have the establishment of Z magazine, the growth of community radio, cable TV, Fairness and Accuracy in Reporting, I understand a Canadian film crew is doing a documentary on you, there's been a lot of developments. Do you see that as a positive thing? Are you surprised by it?*

I don't remember what I said in that interview, but I've always felt it would be a very positive thing and it should be pushed as far as it can go. I think it's going to have a very hard time. There's such a concentration of resources and power that alternative media, while extremely important, are going to have quite a battle. It's true, there are things which are small successes, but it's because people have been willing to put in an incredible effort. Take *Z* magazine. That's a national magazine which literally has a staff of two and no resources, none, except for what some friends give. Putting out a magazine with no resources is backbreaking labor.

South End Press has sort of made it, that is, they're surviving. It's a small collective with again no resources, and they put out a lot of books, including quite a lot of good ones. But for a South End book to get reviewed is almost impossible. Take the *Boston Globe,* for example. By the standards of American journalism it's a very liberal newspaper. Their book review editor a couple of years ago said publicly that she would never allow a South End book to be reviewed. The reason that she gave was that I was a South End author, and as long as I was a South End author she'd never allow a South End book to be reviewed. My books are not only not reviewed in the *Boston Globe,* but they won't even list them. There's a section on Sunday where they list things by local authors. Like some local author wrote a chapter in a cookbook. They won't even list my books under listings by local authors.

In fact, sometimes it's kind of comical. For example, the National Council of Teachers of English every year gives out what they call an "Orwell Award" for exposure of doublespeak. It was awarded to me for *On Power and Ideology* two years ago. This year it was awarded to the book that Edward Herman and I did, *Manufacturing Consent.* Just at the time when that award was given, I think it was November, a *Boston Globe* columnist, a rather left-liberal columnist, incidentally, wrote a column interviewing the guy who is in charge of this award. It was a very upbeat column about what a terrific idea this is to give an award for exposure of doublespeak. She listed some of the people who had gotten it in the past, Ted Koppel, etc. There was a very striking omission: This year's award was not mentioned. It happened to go to a local person, which usually is mentioned. It also happened to be the first time, I think, that anybody had gotten it for the second time. Furthermore, both of the books in question were books about the media. It's not what Ted Koppel does. It was critique of the media. None of that could be mentioned. South End has a very hard time getting a book reviewed. It's been written up in *Publisher's Weekly,* in fact, which has discussed this.

If you don't have access to capital resources, advertisers, the powerful modes of public articulation, your outreach is going to be extremely limited. You can make up for it to some extent with just hard work. There are ways of compensating. Some of these ways are important. For example, dissidents in lots of societies cooperate. I spend an awful lot of time, for example, just xeroxing stuff, copying stuff for friends in other countries who are, in their countries, in roughly the situation I'm in here. They do the same for me. That means that although I don't get a research grant to work on this kind of stuff or time off or whatever, I do have access to resources that mainstream scholars or for that matter the CIA don't have. The CIA or mainstream scholars don't have a very smart and perceptive guy in Israel scanning the Hebrew journals for them picking out the things that are important, doing an interpretation and analysis of them and sending reams of this material to me.

DB: *You're talking about Israel Shahak.*

Yes. That is a big difference. That means I've got resources. Shahak is the main one and there are others. I've got other friends that do the same thing. I and others do the same for them. The same is true in Australia and England and other places. So there are kind of networks of cooperation developed. Here on my desk, for example, is a collection of stuff from a friend of mine who does careful monitoring of the whole press in Los Angeles and a lot of the British press, which he reads, a selection so I don't have to read the movie reviews and the gossip and the rest of it. I get the occasional nugget that sneaks through that you maybe find if you're carefully and intelligently and critically reviewing a wide range of press. There are a fair number of people that do this, and we exchange information. The end result is that you do have access to resources in a way I doubt that any national intelligence agency can duplicate.

So there are ways of compensating for the absence of resources. People can do things. This happens all over. A couple of years ago I gave a talk in Manhattan, Kansas, and they asked me to meet beforehand with the local Central America solidarity group, so I thought, OK, four people will be in somebody's living room. To my surprise it wasn't four people in a living room but a couple of hundred people in a church. It was a town of 30,000 or so. There was a lot of literature, including literature I'd never seen, information I'd never seen, and people who were up and back from Central America, who'd been living there doing solidarity work, dragging their congressional representatives down there. Very informed people. I'm sure they know more about Central America than you'd find at the Central America desk of an American newspaper or many Latin American departments. That's the kind of thing you can find all over the country. People have just found other ways of getting information and educating themselves and each other and figuring things out. There are ways of getting around the constraints, but it's not simple. To try to make it reach any scale that would have an impact is difficult.

DB: *I'm interested that you've said that commercial radio is less ideological than public radio.*

That's been my experience. Here I'd want to be a little more cautious. Public radio out in the sticks, in my experience, is pretty open. So when I go to Wyoming or Iowa I'm on public radio, for longer discussions. That would be very hard to imagine in Boston or Washington. Occasionally you might get on with somebody else to balance you for three minutes, in which there are three sentences for each person. But anything that would be more in depth would be very difficult. It's worth bearing in mind that the U.S. communications system has devised a very effective structural technique to prevent dissidence. This comes out very clearly sometimes. The United States is about the only country I know where anywhere near the mainstream you've got to be extremely concise in what you say, because if you ever get access, it's two minutes between commercials. That's not true in other countries. It's not true outside of the mainstream either. You can get maybe ten or fifteen minutes, you can develop a thought. If you can get on a U.S. mainstream program, NPR, Ted Koppel, it's a couple of sentences. They're very well aware of it. Do you know Jeff Hansen?

DB: *He's at WORT, Madison.*

Last time I was out there, he wanted to arrange an interview when I was in the area giving some talks on the media. He started by playing a tape that he had that you've probably heard where he had interviewed Jeff Greenfield, some mucky-muck with *Nightline*. He asked Greenfield, How come you never have Chomsky on? Greenfield starts with a kind of tirade about how this guy's a wacko from Neptune. After he calmed down and stopped foaming at the mouth, he then said something which was quite right: Look, he probably "lacks concision." We need the kind of people who can say something in a few brief sentences. Maybe the best expert on some topic is from Turkey and speaks only Turkish. That's no good for us. We've got to get somebody who can say something with concision, and this guy Chomsky just rants on and on. There's something to that.

Take a look at the February/March 1990 *Mother Jones*. There's an interesting article by Marc Cooper in which he does an analysis of the main people who appear as experts on shows. Of course, they're all skewed to the right, and the same people appear over and over. But the commentary is interesting. He talks to media people about this and they say, These are people who know how to make their thoughts concise and simple and straightforward and they can make those brief two-sentence statements between commercials. That's quite significant. Because if you're constrained to producing two sentences between commercials, or 700 words in an op-ed piece, you can do nothing but express conventional thoughts. If you express conventional thoughts, you don't need any basis for it or any background, or any arguments. If you try to express something that's somewhat unconventional, people will rightly ask why you're saying that. They're right. If I refer to the United States invasion of South Vietnam, people will ask, "What are you talking about? I never heard of that." And they're right. They've never heard about it. So I'd have to explain what I mean.

Or suppose I'm talking about international terrorism, and I say that we ought to stop it in Washington, which is a major center of it. People back off, "What do you mean, Washington's a major center of it?" Then you have to explain. You have to give some background. That's exactly what Jeff Greenfield is talking about. You don't want people who have to give background, because that would allow critical thought. What you want is completely conformist ideas. You want just repetition of the propaganda line, the party line. For that you need "concision." I could do it too. I could say what I think in three sentences, too. But it would just sound as if it was off the wall, because there's no basis laid for it. If you come from the

American Enterprise Institute and you say it in three sentences, yes, people hear it every day, so what's the big deal? Yeah, sure, Qaddafi's the biggest monster in the world, and the Russians are conquering the world, and this and that, Noriega's the worst gangster since so-and-so. For that kind of thing you don't need any background. You just rehash the thoughts that everybody's always expressed and that you hear from Dan Rather and everyone else. That's a structural technique that's very valuable. In fact, in my view, if people like Ted Koppel were smarter, they would allow more dissidents on, because they would just make fools of themselves. Either you would sell out and repeat what everybody else is saying because it's the only way to sound sane, or else you would say what you think, in which case you'd sound like a madman, even if what you think is absolutely true and easily supportable. The reason is that the whole system so completely excludes it. It'll sound crazy, rightly, from their point of view. And since you have to have "concision," as Jeff Greenfield says, you don't have time to explain it. That's a marvelous structural technique of propaganda. They do the same thing in Japan, I'm told. Most of the world still hasn't reached that level of sophistication. You can go on Belgian national radio or the BBC and actually say what you mean. That's very hard in the United States.

DB: *In your essay "Language and Freedom" you write, "Social action must be animated by a vision of a future society." I was wondering what vision of a future society animates you?*

I have my own ideas as to what a future society should look like. I've written about them. I think that at the most general level we should be seeking out forms of authority and domination and challenging their legitimacy. Sometimes they are legitimate. Let's say they're needed for survival. During the Second World War, we had a totalitarian society, basically, and I thought there

was some justification for that under the wartime conditions. Relations between parents and children, for example, involve forms of coercion. They're sometimes
justifiable. But any form of coercion and control requires
justification, and most of them are completely unjustifi-
able. At various stages of human civilization it's been
possible to challenge some of them but not others. Others
are too deep-seated or you don't see them or whatever. So
at any particular point you try to detect those forms of
authority and domination which are subject to change and
which do not have any legitimacy, in fact which often
strike at fundamental human rights and your understanding of fundamental human nature and rights. I
think if you look at the present scene, the future society
that I'd like to see is one where you continually do this,
and continually extend the range of freedom and justice
and lack of external control and greater public participation.

What are the major things today? There are some
that are being addressed. The feminist movement is addressing some. The civil rights movement is addressing
others. The one major one that's not being seriously addressed is the one that's really at the core of the system of
domination, private control over resources, production,
and distribution. The eighteenth-century revolutions
have not been consummated. Even the texts of classical
liberalism were talking about people being condemned to
work under command instead of working out of their own
inner need and not controlling the work process. That's at
the core of classical liberalism. That's all been completely
forgotten. But that ought to be revived. That's very real.
That means an attack on the fundamental structure of
state capitalism. I think that's in order. That's not something far off in the future. In fact, we don't even have to
have fancy ideas about it. A lot of the ideas were articulated in the eighteenth century, even in what are the
classical liberal texts and then later in at least the liber-

tarian parts of the socialist movement and the anarchist movement. I think that is a very live topic which ought to be faced. A vision of a future society from this point of view would be one in which production, decisions over investment, etc. are under democratic control. That means control through communities, through workplaces, through workers councils in factories or universities, whatever organization it happens to be, federal structures which integrate organized sectors over a broader range.

These are all entirely feasible developments, particularly for an advanced industrial society. The cultural background for them exists only in a very limited way but could be made to exist. That's a picture of part of a future society.

It's not the only one because there are a lot of other forms of hierarchy and authority which should be eliminated. The kinds of systems that have existed are state capitalist, of the kind we're familiar with, or state bureaucratic like the Soviet system with a managerial-bureaucratic-military elite that commands and controls the economy and the whole society from the top in totalitarian fashion. That's fortunately collapsing. Our system is not subject to any internal challenge, but it ought to be. The picture of a future society that evolves is one that you can then proceed to sketch out and has been sketched out in part.

DB: *You do hundreds of interviews and lectures and you're dealing with massacres in East Timor and invasions of Panama, death squads, pretty horrific stuff. What keeps you going? Don't you get burned out on this material?*

I could talk to you about my personal reactions, but again I don't see why they should interest anyone.

DB: *Is there an inner resource that you call upon when you're feeling despair?*

It's mainly a matter of whether you can look yourself in the mirror, I think. If you want to be encouraged, there are ways to be encouraged. Things are much better than they were 25 years ago, ten years ago. For example, 20 years ago I wouldn't have been able to go out to Manhattan, Kansas and find people who knew more about whatever-it-was than I did, who were active and involved. When I started giving talks back around 1964, it seemed totally hopeless. A talk would mean getting some neighbor to invite two people over and talk in the living room, or going to a church where there's one drunk guy who's coming in and some other guy who wants to kill you and the two organizers. When we organized public meetings back in those days at a university, I remember one at MIT when we announced a meeting on Vietnam, Venezuela, and Iran, in the hope that maybe you could draw in enough people to outnumber the organizers. Also, the hostility was extraordinary. The first public outdoor rally where I spoke was in October 1965 on the Boston Common, on an international day of protest against the Indochina War. It was organized by students, like most things, and was really the first major public event with a march and rally at the Common. There must have been 200-300 police, who we were very happy to see, I should say, because they kept us from getting murdered. The crowd was extremely hostile, mostly students who had marched over from the universities. They were ready to kill you. The demands were so tame, it was almost embarrassing to say them: Stop the bombing of North Vietnam. The bombing of South Vietnam, which was three times the scale, we didn't even talk about that. That went on up through the middle of 1966. You couldn't have an outdoor rally in Boston because it would be broken up by students and others. Then I felt totally helpless, I couldn't see any point to it at all.

DB: *So you are encouraged?*

Whether you are encouraged or not is a matter of personality, not of objective fact. In many ways things are a lot better. I think the cultural level of the country is much higher. Outside the educated classes, which are not changed, I think the moral and intellectual level of public discourse and public understanding has risen very considerably. I don't doubt that for a moment. And that's encouraging. If you want to be discouraged, you can think about the glacial pace of it, the distance that yet has to be traveled before you can make a serious impact on policy. These are questions of mood, not of objective reality. I don't see much point in paying attention to them.

Basically you take a kind of Pascal's wager. Take the environment. If you want to give an objective analysis, you can give an argument that in a couple of hundred years there's going to be nothing left but cockroaches. No matter what we do. That's possible. On the other hand you can try to do something about it, to change things. You've got two choices: Do nothing, in which case you can predict what's going to happen. Or do something, in which case maybe there's a chance.

DB: *You're committed to doing something.*

I try to be.

Prelude to the Gulf War

September 17, 1990

DB: *You take exception to, and I think you challenge the conventional mainstream media view that the Kuwait-Iraq crisis is the first major event of the so-called "post-Cold War era." Am I correct in that?*

That's right in a number of respects. First of all, I'm rather skeptical about the phrase "post-Cold War era," but even accepting that, the first major crisis involving military action in this era was the invasion of Panama. It was "post-Cold War" in the sense that—although the action itself was so normal as to be hardly more than a footnote to history—it's the first time in a long, long time, actually since 1917, that U.S. military actions, an aggression in this case, have not been justified on the pretext of defense against the Soviet threat. The pretext was never at all credible, but this time it was quite beyond anyone's imagination to construct. In that respect this was a "post-Cold War" invasion, use of military force. It had to be justified on different pretexts. In many respects it's rather similar to the Iraqi invasion of Kuwait.

DB: *Do you see any positive results evolving from the fairly united international effort to force Saddam Hussein to evacuate from Kuwait?*

I wish that I did see some, but I don't. I happen to agree with those international efforts, but the only reason they're taking place is because the United States is allowing them to take place. There's a lot of nonsense being produced now about how the U.N. is finally living up to its responsibilities in the post-Cold War era, with superpower conflict ending we don't have to worry any more

251

about Russian recalcitrance and we can put aside the psychic disorders of the Third World, and now the U.N. can finally do what it was designed to do. The fact of the matter is that for the past twenty years the major reason why the United Nations has not been able to do what it was designed to do is because the United States blocked it. The United States is *far* in the lead in vetoing Security Council resolutions and in voting often in isolation or virtual isolation on General Assembly resolutions on a wide range of issues, including the Middle East, aggression, observance of international law, disarmament, environmental issues, you name it. That's why the U.N. was unable to act.

But now the U.N. is more or less, actually less than we claim, acting in accordance with U.S. demands, so therefore it's able to act. It's as simple as that. The cynicism on this matter is mind-boggling. For example, on Sunday, September 16, the *New York Times Magazine* had a story about Daniel Moynihan praising him as the great exponent of observance of international law who has finally come into his own now that others have come around to understand the principles for which he has fought so hard all his life, etc. I've seen about a dozen articles like that about Moynihan, who just came out with a book on international law. It's perfectly true that in this book on international law Moynihan says it's a terrible thing we haven't observed international law, we should do it, etc. But there are a few slight omissions in this story. For example, the article in the *New York Times Magazine* praises Moynihan for his service at the United Nations, but they didn't say what he was doing there. What he was doing was ensuring that the U.N. couldn't function, and he describes that with great pride in his memoirs.

Referring to the Indonesian invasion of East Timor in 1975, he says that the United States wanted things to turn out as they did and that he had the assignment of making sure that the United Nations could not act in any constructive way to terminate or reverse the Indonesian aggression. He carried out that task with remarkable success. He then in the next sentence goes on to say that he's aware of the nature of that success. He says that two months later, reports surfaced that the Indonesian invasion had killed off about 10 percent of the population in East Timor over a period of two months. A proportion of the population which, he then goes on to say, is about the same as the proportion of people in Eastern Europe killed by Hitler. So he's taking pride in having stopped the United Nations from interfering with an aggression that he himself compares with Hitler's invasion of Eastern Europe, and then he drops it at that. This is the man who's telling us to observe international law and praising the United Nations for finally coming around to recognize its duty and to live up to its historic mission.

Putting aside his own stand, the stand of the interview with him and the praise for his book, front-cover story in the *Times Book Review* and other articles citing him as an exponent, an apostle of international law at the United Nations, that presses cynicism beyond its outer limits.

DB: *It would seem that the Gulf crisis would generate much interest in energy conservation—the institution of serious energy conservation measures in this country, developing alternative sources—but that doesn't seem to be happening.*

Not really, because it's not very relevant. The issue in the Gulf crisis is not a shortage of oil and it's not U.S. dependence on Middle East oil. It's pretty easy to see that. The U.S. position toward the Middle East has been, since the 1940s, that those energy reserves, by far the largest and the cheapest energy reserves in the world, would be dominated by the United States and its clients, and that no other force would be tolerated. Surely no armed force would be tolerated, had that been a realistic possibility.

And it wasn't tolerated after the British and French were pretty much expelled. There was a lot of talk about the Russians, but it was just talk. Crucially, no independent indigenous force would be tolerated. That was U.S. policy in the 1950s. It motivated the U.S. opposition to Nasser by the mid-1950s once it was recognized that he was an independent nationalist and wouldn't just play our game. It motivated the strategic alliance with Israel and with the Shah in opposition to what's called "radical national-ism," meaning independent nationalism, and on to the present. Why is that relevant? Until the early 1970s we barely imported any Middle East oil, but we had exactly the same position. In fact, if we didn't use one drop of Middle East oil today, we would have exactly the same position. The issue is who controls the world's major energy supplies, and it is understood that whoever con-trols the profits, whoever can administer production lev-els and prices, within narrow limits, because there isn't much of a range, has a very powerful lever over world affairs and over other countries, and we're going to make sure we have that. We could be completely self-sufficient and it wouldn't change this a bit.

DB: *I'm wondering if you could comment about media images. I'm thinking about the late 1970s with those horrific pictures of Ayatollah Khomeini gracing the covers of* Time *and* Newsweek, *and eleven years later the same issues of hostages, the Middle East and oil and the Butcher of Baghdad, Saddam Hussein, on the same covers, snarling and sneering at readers.*

In the 1960s it was Gamal Abdel Nasser who was the monster who had to be destroyed, part of the reason for the extreme enthusiasm about Israel's 1967 victory and U.S. participation in it. In fact, in the case of Saddam Hussein, we don't have to go back that far. On August 1, 1990 he was a favored U.S. client. The United States was offering him credit, lavishing support on him. The U.S.

was his major trading partner. We were the largest market for his oil. We were providing 40 percent of his food. The Iraqi-American business forum was praising his progress toward democracy. He was just a good guy. A day later he was the new incarnation of Genghis Khan and Hitler. No new crimes. True, the aggression in Kuwait was one new crime, but small in comparison with the record that he had already compiled.

What happened was he conflicted with U.S. interests. Period. That's what matters. He could invade Iran, murder thousands of Kurds with poison gas, set up one of the most brutal tyrannies in the world, if not the most— that was all just fine as long as he was seen as conforming to U.S. interests. When it became clear that he was another one of these radical nationalists who was going to go his own way, he picks up the mantle of Nasser, Qaddafi and Khomeini and anybody else who gets in our way.

DB: *How about Noriega?*

There it's kind of intriguing. For example, Bernard Trainor, a former Marine general and former *New York Times* military correspondent who's now head of some security studies program at Harvard, had an op-ed in the *Times* drawing the connection between Noriega and Hussein, saying Hussein, like Noriega, has to go. There is something in common between the two: they both got in the way of the United States. That's about the limits of what they have in common. Noriega was a crook, but a very minor gangster. Hussein, while we were supporting him, was one of the major monsters of the current period. But like Noriega, he opposed U.S. interests. Noriega was also a friend—still a gangster and a drug peddler and everything else—but a friend because he was seen as serving U.S. interests. When it became clear that he was following too independent a course, when he was starting to get in the way of the U.S. attack on Nicaragua instead of participating actively in it, when he was pursuing the Contadora process, he just had to go. So then his crimes, which are quite petty in comparison with the people we support, could be used against him. And now Saddam Hussein's crimes, which really are hideous, can be brought up against him. Two months ago, the same crimes had been committed, but they just didn't matter. He was progressing, and he was a perfectly acceptable, in fact favored, partner.

DB: *I'm interested in this issue of cognitive dissonance. But how can someone like Bush, for example, or his Secretary of State Baker or the earlier cited Daniel Moynihan, how can they be talking about international law and violating the rights of sovereignty of nations as a grave crime, etc.? How do they reconcile that stand with U.S. actions in Panama, for example, or Grenada?*

The World Court proceedings condemned the United States for the unlawful use of force, and a whole record all the way back. Just take Panama. On Sunday, September 16, 1990, the press announced with great pleasure that the Security Council had voted a severe condemnation of Iraq for its break-in at the foreign embassies. That's quite right. When they broke in, the press was just outraged. This was an attack on diplomacy itself, the *New York Times* said, and for the first time demanded that he be tried as a war criminal. The U.N. resolution was published in full and with great prominence.

I haven't seen anyone point out the obvious. That's the second time that's happened this year. In mid-January the United Nations Security Council voted a resolution condemning a country for violating diplomatic immunity in a case very similar to this one. Mainly, U.S. troops broke into the Nicaraguan compound in Panama and messed it up. The Security Council had a resolution which was vetoed by the United States. That's it. There was also a Security Council resolution condemning the invasion vetoed by the United States. There was a General Assembly resolution condemning the invasion. In fact, just more recently, the Catholic Church in Panama has described the U.S. invasion as the worst tragedy in the history of the country, and a government commission has also condemned the invasion. Going back in the United Nations, as I mentioned before, the United States is very far in the lead in preventing it from acting on issues of observance of international law, aggression, etc.

To get back to your question: how can they do these things? It depends on the individual, but there are several possible answers. Some may simply be total cynics. Most likely they are people who have acquired or had naturally a certain technique which is almost a filter that you have to pass through in order to get to a leadership position. That is that you be capable of erasing totally from your mind anything that conflicts with your need to serve powerful interests. You've got to be able to erase it, and then you don't have cognitive dissonance.

DB: *But the level of conformity is startling, even by U.S. standards, on this issue. I kept waiting at the daily press conference that Bush held in Maine and now in Washington for one single reporter to get up, even if he didn't believe in what he was saying, to just challenge the administration line on this issue about international law and the sanctity of borders, etc., bringing up the issue of Panama. Not one of them, not one, came forward.*

No, and what's more I have yet to see an op-ed or an editorial running through the record on this and pointing out the utter hypocrisy of it. Incidentally, I know that such op-eds have been submitted to major newspapers, but they have been turned down.

DB: *Some years ago you said that anti-Arab sentiment is the last vestige of respectable racism in the United States today. Do you see any elements of that racism in this current crisis?*

I think it is just flagrant. The reaction is utterly racist. Of course you find this in outright racist journals like the *New Republic,* which is reeking with anti-Arab racism, but that's always the case. Even in parts of the media that try to retain a level of minimal respectability on this, the anti-Arab racism just screams at you. This has been true for a long time, but it's quite apparent now.

DB: *I happened to be listening to a Christian religious broadcast, and there were comments about "Islam breeds violence" and "The Koran sanctifies terrorism and holy wars." It was rather astounding to hear all this stuff.*

That's typical of a racist culture. Christianity doesn't breed violence? Is the history of Europe very pretty?

DB: *Where is Israel, the strategic asset, in this crisis? Why is it seemingly on the sidelines?*

"Seemingly" is the right word. It remains a base for U.S. power. If the United States decides to go to war, as it very well may, plunging the area into total chaos and possibly catastrophe, Israel will be a major strategic reserve. But right now, the United States would much prefer for Israel to keep a low profile and they've surely been ordered to do that. The reason is that the very fragile pretense of an Arab force is crucial for propaganda purposes, and that would collapse instantaneously if Israel were to take an active part. In fact, probably the whole Arab world would be inflamed. The United States would probably find itself involved in counterinsurgency.

DB: *I'm interested that you use the term "Arab world," because it's mystified me. You don't hear about the "Slavic world" or the "Hindu world" or the "Buddhist world."*

Or the "Christian world."

DB: *Is this part of that racist framework? And we use it.*

Sure, we use it. I use it. The so called "Arab world" is as complex and diverse as the European world.

DB: *What about the internal feuds within the region? Some people are rather surprised to find, for example, someone like Hafez al Assad winding up against Saddam Hussein.*

Assad has been a sworn enemy of Hussein for a long time. They represent two wings of essentially the same secular nationalist, actually internationalist Arab movement, the Ba'ath party, but different wings, and they've been at each other's throat for years. Syria was the only major Arab state to support Iran during the Iraq-Iran war. So it's just a continuation of it. It's interesting that all of a sudden Assad has become a good guy in America. This morning there's an article in the *New York Times* saying that of course, he's not very nice, but much better than Saddam Hussein. Two months ago, Saddam Hussein was much better than he was. In fact, they're pretty much on a par, but he's on our side, so therefore he's got real promise.

DB: *Hasn't Bush and his administration really painted itself into a corner in comments like "Iraq's occupation of Kuwait will not stand, it will not be tolerated"? Is he giving Saddam Hussein any avenue to compromise?*

I think in my view that's a rather odd way to put it, because there have been several offers from Iraq on a negotiating track that could be followed to end the conflict with Iraqi withdrawal, and they've been turned down by the United States. So it's not a matter of the United States offering a possible compromise. As it is right now, it's a matter of the United States refusing to permit a diplomatic track to be pursued. There was a rather remarkable front-page article in the *New York Times* by their chief diplomatic correspondent, Thomas Friedman, a couple of weeks ago, August 22, saying that there's a great concern in Washington, which he supported, that others might find the diplomatic track too tempting. On this issue, I think you can see a real difference between the United States and most of the rest of the world—not all, Kuwaiti nationals and Israel agree with the United States, and some others do—but most of the world is tending in a different direction. That's over what is the crucial issue right now. There is a general hope that economic measures of some kind, some form of embargo, will succeed in compelling Iraq to withdraw and reverse the aggression, but suppose they don't? Then what? There are then two ways to achieve that end. One way is war and the other is diplomacy. The way I read the international situation, most of the world prefers diplomacy, and the United States is gearing up for war. There apparently are diplomatic options and a diplomatic track. We can't be sure of that, since every such opportunity has instantaneously been shut off and in fact barely reported, but there certainly have been proposals floated that look like possible diplomatic options.

DB: *Wasn't there an Iraqi offer to talk about withdrawal from all occupied Arab lands?*

That was on August 12. That was the first of them. Exactly how serious it was we don't know, because it was instantly rejected. There were several others, too. There was an Iraqi proposal on August 19 to treat the Kuwait affair as a problem of the Arab world and the Arab League and have it settled in the same manner as Syrian forces in Lebanon and Moroccan forces in the Western Sahara. That was rejected out of hand as well.

There was an argument for rejecting it, namely that in that arena Saddam Hussein could expect to be highly influential, in fact perhaps to prevail. That has some logic to it, except for one small point. He was simply stealing a leaf from the U.S. book. Every time the United States intervenes in the Western Hemisphere, it immediately stands up and denounces the rest of the world for trying to get involved. So it will veto Security Council resolutions calling for an end to hostilities on the grounds that this is a Western Hemisphere affair and we can do it ourselves. You guys keep away. Why? Because we can hope to prevail as long as it's just Western Hemisphere. We've done the same in the Middle East, for example, trying to bar U.N. intervention in Cyprus when Turkey invaded Cyprus, in fact earlier, back in the early 1960s, keeping it a NATO issue.

A third, however, and more important proposal from Iraq was on August 23, and again, we do not know much about it or how serious it was because it was pretty much suppressed. But on August 23 a proposal was brought to Washington by a former high U.S. official with Iraqi connections calling for—and this had terms that were quite forthcoming—an Iraqi withdrawal from Kuwait, an end to sanctions, freeing of anyone who was detained, the hostages, no precondition that the U.S. troops withdraw or any other precondition. The only terms that Iraq insisted on in this proposal were one, some form of guaranteed access to the Gulf, and two, control of the Rumailah oil fields, which are about 95 percent inside Iraq and 5 percent inside Kuwait on what has always been a contested border. That proposal was described by a White House spokesman, who was quoted in the press, as "serious and negotiable." It certainly sounds that. How serious and how negotiable it is we don't know because it was instantaneously rejected by the United States and largely suppressed by the press. The offer had apparently been leaked to the *New York Times,* which didn't publish it. It was then very prominently published a week later by *Newsday,* a Long Island newspaper, and at that point the *Times* had to refer to it, but it buried the thing and dismissed it as baloney in a paragraph and that was the end of it. It hasn't been referred to since. There are other proposals. There are several proposals attributed to the PLO in Jordan calling for Iraqi withdrawal and a plebiscite and other possibilities. How realistic they are, again, we do not know because as long as the United States rejects them, and as long as the media won't report them, we do not know. But the logic of the situation is pretty clear. If the embargo does not succeed in a limited time, then the options will be war or diplomacy. If diplomacy is cut off, it will be war.

DB: *If sanctions don't work, if, say, six months from now...*

I don't think the United States will wait six months. Just imagine the situation, say, two months from now. Let's imagine what it's going to look like. We can't be certain, but here's a possibility, not implausible. Two months from now we may find a huge American army, 200,000 men, suffering in the desert, not much fun, isolated, dying of the heat, the tanks not functioning. The U.S. economy heading into a tailspin. Germany and Japan, our major rivals, doing business as usual. They really don't want to have any part of this and regard it as a bilateral arrangement between the United States and Saudi Arabia. The embargo is starting to leak. Turmoil increasing in the Arab world, which is likely. Conflicts developing between the U.S. military forces and the local population, which is also likely, even if they're superbly well behaved there are too many opportunities for conflict. Just imagine that situation. What does George Bush do at that time? Either you withdraw the army, which is unimaginable, or you use it.

DB: *Do you favor the military option in getting Iraq out of Kuwait?*

The military option? It would be crazy. First of all,

unless it were authorized by the U.N. Security Council, which is highly unlikely, it is illegal. But aside from law, which has never bothered us, it would be wrong and crazy. For one thing, it isn't clear that the United States *has* a military option. Western military analysts are by no means certain of that. Western military attachés in Baghdad, for example, have been arguing that it would be extremely costly for the United States to attempt a forceful removal of the Iraqi army. Quite apart from the uncountable number, we have no idea how many people would be killed in the operation itself, the longer term, the broader effects are quite incalculable. It could have catastrophic effects throughout the entire region, up to in fact destroying large parts of the world's energy reserves. It's an extremely grave and ominous possibility. Quite apart from the fact that nothing remotely similar has ever been done in comparable cases of aggression in that region or elsewhere.

DB: *I didn't follow something you said. You said that even if the U.N. Security Council voted in favor of military action it would be illegal?*

Unless the U.N. Security Council voted in favor of action, authorized and directed the action, it would be illegal.

DB: *How does this crisis affect the Palestinians and the intifada?*

I think it's a catastrophe for the Palestinians. If there is a war, Israel might use the opportunity, and I suppose be authorized by the United States, to invade Jordan, which they've been itching to do for a long time. Both major parties in Israel and the U.S. government regard Jordan as a Palestinian state, and their long term goal would then be to invade Jordan, then remove much of the population of the occupied territories to the Palestinian state and bring in Russian immigrants while expanding their natural borders, etc. It's not unlikely in the context of a war. Even if there's no war, I think the situation will end up with an even tighter alliance between the United States and militarily strong forces in the region committed to opposition, of any form of Palestinian or other indigenous nationalism.

DB: *Do you think that Saddam Hussein's invasion of Kuwait vindicates the right, the Likud line in Israel, that "you can't trust the Arabs, they're terrorists, they're barbaric aggressors," etc.?*

Within Israel itself?

DB: *Yes.*

I think it strengthened that position. There's been a shameful response on the part of the so-called peace movement. The most prominent example is Yossi Sarid, whose column in Israel about how that's the last time I talk to the Palestinians, they can forget about me, was reprinted in the *Wall Street Journal*. Segments of the Israeli peace movement have followed him on that.

Not all, I should say; he was pretty harshly criticized, too. Shulamith Aloni, for example, who is a leading civil libertarian for many years in Israel and from Yossi Sarid's party, had a couple of interviews in which she pointed out quite honestly that she doesn't care at all about the Palestinians, doesn't care really what happens to them, and never has. All she cares about is the Jews and Israel, and she will continue to talk to the Palestinians because she cares about the Jews and Israel. She furthermore went on to say, without mentioning Sarid's name, that, speaking of the Israeli peace movement, we like to pretend that we've done things for the Palestinians and they're being ungrateful, when in fact we've done nothing for them. We've done things only for ourselves. We did nothing to help relieve their suffering until it started to harm us. We never cared about it, and they have nothing to be grateful to us for. Let's not make pretenses about that.

She also said something which is immediately intelligible to an Israeli audience, although I don't know if people would understand it here. She said, people are comparing Saddam to Hitler. This is not the first time that nationalists in the Middle East have expressed their support for Hitler. She was referring, of course, to the Prime Minister of Israel, Yitzhak Shamir, who was the head of a group, LEHI, the so-called Stern Gang, which made overtures to the Nazis in 1941 not out of expediency but out of agreement, offering to become the outpost for the Third Reich in the Middle East. This is very well known in Israel but maybe not known here. Others have also been extremely critical. The Israeli satirist B. Michael, a very prominent satirist, had a column in which he ran through the list of monsters who Israel has cheerfully supported, essentially asking, what's the difference between supporting them and supporting Saddam Hussein? Do we talk to ourselves? There have been others as well. But the peace movement, such as it is, has been much weakened and deeply split over this issue.

DB: *Coming back home, is there anything that people can do here in the United States?*

There's a lot. I think we should face the likelihood that we are moving towards a situation in which the choices are going to be pretty stark: diplomacy or war. If we don't want war, with all of its catastrophic consequences, we have to be preparing the grounds for diplomacy. There are possibilities right now and there will be increasing possibilities over the next couple of months. If they continue to be turned down by Washington, they will be suppressed by the press. After all, that's their job: to serve power, not to tell the truth. That means it's going to be a little hard to find out about them and hard to gain publicity for them or develop support for pursuing them, but that has to be done, or the alternative will be a war with possibly quite catastrophic consequences.

World Orders: Old and New

November 18, 1990

DB: *What are the common threads that you see running between the old world order and the new world order?*

Virtually everything is common. There have been a few changes. They're not sudden. There's one change that's been developing over a thirty year period, and that's the relative decline of the United States in economic power relative to its major industrial rivals: German-based Europe and Japan and its network of dependencies. It's been obvious for about 20 years that the world has been drifting towards what's now called tripolarity, three major economic powers. That was all accelerated by the Vietnam War and further by the Reagan administration. The United States no longer has the position of overwhelming dominance that it had 30 or 40 years ago. That's been a slow, continuous process. By the 1970s it was pretty well in place and has become even more so through the 1980s. So that's one change, but there's nothing sudden about that.

A second change in the mid- and late 1980s is the collapse of the Soviet Union, which means that the Soviet satellites are freed up. The Soviet tyranny collapsed internally. The Soviet military system has declined and is no longer really effective in world affairs. That changes the world order in several respects. For one thing it means that there is a sense in which it's true that the West has won the Cold War. One major element in the Cold War was the fact that the Soviet Union had blocked off a certain region of the world from investment, exploitation of resources, etc. This region that they had blocked was traditionally heterogeneous, but most of it was a kind of colonial backwater, a quasi-colonial dependency of Europe to a large extent. That's not entirely the case. It's not true of Czechoslovakia, but most of it was. A large part of the Cold War was the unwillingness of the West to accept the extrication of this section of the world system from exploitation by the Western industrial powers, and now that's over. It'll probably move right in the direction of the Third World, a region for providing cheap resources and cheap labor and a brain drain, because they have a good educational system. Their future will probably look something like Brazil or Mexico, as things are now going. So that's a change in the world order. It means that there's another region open, the Third World has expanded enormously.

That has its effects with regard to the tripolar economic system because the United States is not now in a position to be the leader in gaining from this new area of exploitation. Germany and Japan are well ahead. They have excess capital, which the United States doesn't have. They're close by. That's going to lead to major changes over the coming era. Germany may become a much more powerful country if it has a colonial hinterland nearby to exploit. Japan will sooner or later be exploiting the resources of Siberia, which are close at hand and valuable. Japan has the capital and the technology, and Siberia is relatively underdeveloped, so it's sort of in the cards that sooner or later they'll be moving there. That will give them for the first time independent sources of energy and minerals which will make them a much more significant world power.

The United States will be doing what it can to get into these regions, but it's not in a very favorable position to lead the way, to put it pretty mildly. So that's going to be a change in the world order, and it will affect the development of the tripolar structure over time.

The other effect of the Soviet disappearance from the world scene is that the United States is left as the only military superpower. Up until now the Soviet Union provided a deterrent to U.S. military force in two respects. For one thing, the United States always had to be somewhat cautious in the use of military force because it would always appear that you might get involved with the Russians. That would be dangerous, because the Russians could strike back, and you don't want to do anything that's harmful to yourself. You can kill other people, but you don't want to suffer. So there was a limit. That limit's gone. Now there are no limits.

The second aspect of this deterrent was that the Soviet Union to some extent offered support for targets of U.S. attack, and that helped them sustain themselves. That's what's usually called "Russian aggression." They helped the Sandinistas or Cuba sustain a U.S. attack. That's gone, or at least it's limited and will probably soon be gone. That frees up the U.S. again to use military force more effectively. That's been quite evident in both of the two major post-Cold War interventions. The first was in Panama. It was post-Cold War in the sense that it was impossible even to conjure up a pretense that it was to defend yourself against the Russians, the usual pretense. That was so far beyond anybody's imagination that they didn't even try. They had to make up new pretexts. In that sense it was post-Cold War. The use of force in Central America is usually pretty free because the Russians are nowhere nearby, but this time even more so. Elliott Abrams, for example, pointed out publicly that this was the first time the U.S. had been able to use military force without any concern at all about the Russian reaction. That does free us up more to use military force. I have been writing about this for a couple of years, quoting strategic analysts and people who had seen that this was going to come. The decline of the Soviet Union frees us to use military force, and it's a good thing, they add. No more deterrents, no more containment of the U.S.

The same is true in the Gulf. We would have been

much more hesitant to introduce massive conventional forces if there were a concern that the conflict might lead to interaction with the Russians. Now we can be quite free. We can put in massive ground forces, conventional forces, right on the borders of the Soviet Union without any concern at all that there will be a Soviet reaction. So both of these illustrate the same point: that targets of U.S. attack are now much more vulnerable than they were in the past, because the military power of the United States is now, dominant as always, but now it's absolutely unchallenged.

So we have a new world order, if you like, with one military superpower, three major economic powers and a new region of exploitation opening up. The military superpower does not have the economic base any longer to carry out its military actions alone. It therefore has to somehow coerce its allies into paying the costs. We also see that in the Gulf, the efforts made to try to compel Germany and Japan to pay part of the costs of the operation. The issue is not so severe in the Gulf because the enormous rise in oil prices means that U.S. clients like Saudi Arabia have plenty of cash on hand. But in other cases it will be, and that's been noted. Lawrence Eagleburger, Deputy Secretary of State, testifying before Congress on the new world order a couple of weeks ago made that very explicit. He said the new world order is based on a new kind of invention in diplomacy, namely, we carry out the military action, they pay for it. So I think that's roughly the contours of the new world order.

DB: *There have been many examples of aggression and occupation in recent decades. We can enumerate them ad nauseam. Why is the U.S. behaving differently with the Iraqi aggression, occupation and annexation of Kuwait?*

The United States behaves quite consistently with regard to aggression. It's fine if it's in perceived U.S.

interest. It's bad if it's opposed to perceived U.S. interests. It's very simple. No inconsistency at all. People who sense an inconsistency, I think, are quite wrong. Consistency is close to perfection. In this case, Iraq transgressed, violated a fundamental principle of world affairs, which is that the energy reserves of the Middle East have to be firmly in the hands of the United States energy corporations and trusted U.S. clients like the Saudi Arabian elites. The imperial settlement of the Middle East left the oil resources in the hands of small families that would closely link to the Western imperial powers. That meant that the mass of the population does not really benefit from its own resources. Rather, the West benefits from them because the Saudi elite and the emirates and Qatar are basically sectors of London and New York. That arrangement is allowed to continue. We don't care if the Saudi elite administers the oil prices because that's just like having it done from New York.

We do care very much if an independent nationalist moves in to exert some influence over the resources of the region and threatens to use them for domestic purposes. We oppose that anywhere in the world. We always oppose independent nationalism in the Third World because it interferes with the fundamental role of the Third World, which is to be exploited for the benefit of the West. But in the Middle East it's particularly important, because these resources are really crucial. Latin American resources we could live without, but the value of Middle East resources has been understood since the 1940s. It's enough just to quote State Department estimates. They describe Saudi Arabian oil as "a stupendous source of strategic power" and "one of the greatest material prizes in world history," and there's a whole string of rhetoric in that style. It's quite correct. That is for several generations into the future the world's major cheap and readily available energy. No nationalist is permitted to move in. It doesn't matter what their politics are.

In Iran in 1953 we overthrew a conservative nationalist parliamentary regime. After August 2 of this year we are opposed to a guy who happens to be a murderous tyrant, but he was just as much a murderous tyrant the day before and we supported him. We thought he was wonderful because he wasn't interfering with American interests. It's very simple and straightforward. It's been a consistent policy for years.

DB: *So the critical policy issue is not one of aggression or defending borders, but one of controlling oil, control of the spigot.*

It's obvious the United States has no opposition to aggression. There's case after case of annexation or aggression where we've either carried it out ourselves or some client state has carried it out and we've been perfectly happy with it. Just a few months ago the United States invaded Panama. That's aggression. We imposed a puppet regime of our choice. It's still under U.S. military control, in fact it describes itself as a country under military occupation. That's probably what Saddam Hussein would have done with Kuwait if there hadn't been U.N. sanctions. He probably would have done exactly the same thing: moved in and established a puppet regime, kept enough force in the background so they would do what he wants and then pull out. That's the easy way to administer a country. We obviously didn't object to the invasion of Panama. The world did. We had to veto two U.N. Security Council resolutions condemning it.

But the world is irrelevant. Turkey invaded northern Cyprus, virtually annexed it. The United States supported that. We've been interfering with U.N. efforts to settle the Cyprus problem since the early 1960s. Turkey invaded a sovereign republic, broke it up and took what it wanted, which was fine. Very similar to Kuwait. They killed a couple of thousand people. They looted the place. They looted antiquities. They tried to destroy any relic of

Greek civilization. They drove out a couple of hundred thousand people. Rather similar to Iraq in Kuwait. But nobody even talks about it. When the president of Turkey came here a couple of weeks ago George Bush hailed him as a peacemaker, even though his actions were just what Saddam Hussein had done.

In the case of Israel: Israel attacked Lebanon, killed many more people than Saddam Hussein did, killed about twenty thousand people in that attack. It viciously bombarded a capital right in front of TV cameras. It still occupies southern Lebanon. The United States vetoed a whole series of U.N. Security Council resolutions to try to terminate that aggression and to try to settle it, because we were in favor of it. Israel holds on to the occupied territories. It has annexed some of them. The United States supports it. Morocco invaded the Western Sahara, essentially annexed it. The United States thinks that's fine because Morocco is an ally. Indonesia, the worst case in the modern period, invaded East Timor. That was near genocidal. They annexed it. A couple of hundred thousand people killed, about the worst slaughter since the Holocaust relative to the population. Carter gave them aid. Everybody applauded. Wonderful.

The United States cannot conceivably claim that it's opposed to aggression. In the West it can claim it, because we have a very disciplined intellectual class. In the Third World it is regarded with ridicule. Of course everybody with their eyes open can see that the United States is one of the major violators of the principle that aggression is wrong, so that's not an issue. As to borders, same thing. If somebody changes the borders in what we see to be our interests, fine, no problem with that. If they change the borders in ways that are contrary to what are seen as U.S. interests, that's a horrible crime and you have to have Nuremberg trials. It's almost unfair to call this hypocrisy because it's so transparent.

DB: *What has the role of the corporate media been in the Gulf crisis?*

That's been interesting. There's a substantial sector of corporate America that doesn't like what's happening and sees that we're getting in over our heads and the American economy could suffer badly and their interests could suffer. The media have to reflect that. It's kind of striking that for about two or three months it was just like goose-stepping on command, virtually no criticism, just little murmurs here and there. By now, there's an undercurrent of criticism in the media reflecting these concerns. It's not going to be good for us. We'd better pay attention. We're isolated. We're paying the cost.

However, the crucial questions will never be asked in the media. What's driving us into the war right now? Washington is on a high moral horse, standing for all sorts of magnificent principles. A new world order is at stake. The future of peace and justice, aggressors can't be rewarded, all this kind of business. If that were true, if any of that stuff had even a shred of validity to it, you could make a case that we should go to war. You do not compromise on serious principles. If a new era of peace and justice is really threatened by this, maybe we ought to pay the cost. That's an argument.

On the other hand, if the whole thing is a total fraud, then that class of arguments collapses and there's no barrier to moving towards a negotiated settlement, a diplomatic settlement. Here the media play a crucial role. I don't mean just the media, I mean the whole intellectual class. As long as they don't challenge that moral posturing about principles, then we're probably going to go to war. The choice is going to be very soon. We can't keep that big army there for long. You certainly aren't going to withdraw it if great principles are at stake. That can never be questioned. You look everywhere you like and nobody will question that. Even people who are saying, let's get out.

For example, the December 6, 1990 issue of the *New York Review of Books* has an article called "How to Get Out of the Gulf" by George Ball, who's been a critical, intelligent, knowledgeable voice on many of these topics with government and corporate experience. If you cut away the first paragraph, the article makes a good deal of sense on a method for getting out of the Gulf. You can question the motives on which he bases it, but it's doubtless a serious proposal about how to get out.

What about the first paragraph? The first paragraph starts off by saying, for the first time in the Cold War period it is possible to put to the test the Wilsonian principles of collective security which until now have been barred by an automatic Soviet veto at the United Nations. But now the Russians are out of it. They're not going to veto everything at the United Nations, so we can pursue our goal of collective security. That's part of the posturing of moral superiority. That's a question of fact. You can look back at the U.N. and find out whether an automatic Soviet veto has barred its peacekeeping function. If you look back, what you find is that an automatic U.S. veto has barred its peacekeeping function, and the point isn't even ambiguous. In the early days of the U.N., when the United States basically ran the world, it was true that the Soviet Union vetoed things, because we had an automatic majority and we were using the U.N. as a weapon against them. But in the last 25 years or so the United States was quite alone and way ahead of the pack in vetoing Security Council resolutions and voting against General Assembly resolutions and trying to undermine U.N. peacekeeping functions. There's nobody even close. The only country that has done anything at all significant in this respect is Britain in its effort to support the racist governments of Southern Africa. The Russians have for the most part voted with the overwhelming majority and supported the peacekeeping functions of the U.N.

But you can't say that. Because if you say that you'll

lift the veil and begin to see what role the United States plays in the world. That degree of enlightenment is unacceptable. The failure to provide that enlightenment may very well drive us to war, because if in fact we're standing for collective security and we can do it for the first time because the Russians aren't stopping it, then a lot is at stake. We can't abandon the search for collective security. So I think Ball essentially gives away his argument in the first paragraph. Any intelligent administration propagandist can come back and say, I don't care about the article after the first paragraph, but look at your first paragraph. Look how much is at stake. Finally we can lead the world to collective security, and you're saying we should abandon it because of narrow self-interest. Unacceptable.

I must have read dozens of articles on the amazing sea change in the United Nations, all making these same claims. The Russians aren't impeding it, the Third World is irrelevant. We can now do what we've always wanted to do. I've not seen one, not one anywhere, which pointed out the simple, unambiguous, indubitable fact that it's the United States that's been blocking it for the last 25 years. In fact, the cynicism on this issue has reached such a point that it's mind-boggling even for a skeptic like me. The guy who is brought out constantly as the great exponent of world order is Daniel Moynihan, who we've talked about before. He's the very man who says in his memoirs [A Dangerous Place], with great pride, that he succeeded in frustrating the United Nations and in rendering all its peacekeeping actions null and void. In the case of the Indonesian invasion of Timor, he says, that was my job and I did it. That's the man who's now hailed as the advocate of international law. Just showing that there's *no* level to which the intellectual community won't sink in its commitment to serve state power.

DB: *Why do you think the United States is so opposed to the so-called "linkage issue"?*

Linkage refers in this case to a connection between withdrawal from the Gulf and the settlement of other regional problems, crucially the Arab-Israeli problem. The United States has no opposition to linkage as such. We're always talking about the importance of linkage. But in this case we're against linkage, and the reason is we're against a diplomatic settlement in the two cases that are to be linked. Linkage has to do with the diplomatic settlement of the Gulf crisis and the Arab-Israeli crisis. The United States is opposed to a diplomatic settlement of each of them, and therefore it's certainly opposed to a joint diplomatic settlement of them. That's what lies behind the opposition to linkage.

In the case of the Arab-Israeli conflict, the United States is virtually alone in the world, and has been for a long time, about 20 years, in barring any meaningful peace process, any negotiated political settlement. The extent of U.S. political isolation would appall people if they were aware of it, so therefore they're not aware of it. It was made clear once again, as it has been for a long time, at the last session of the United Nations, December, 1989, where there was a General Assembly resolution voted on a political settlement of the Arab-Israeli settlement. The vote was 151 to 3, opposed by the United States, Israel, and Dominica. That's the way it's been for a long time, the United States and Israel against virtually the whole world on a political settlement. The United States just doesn't want it. What we want is for Israel to maintain effective control over the territories and to ensure that there's no Palestinian self-determination. That's U.S. policy. Official U.S. policy is that there already is a Palestinian state, Jordan, and that there can't be a second Palestinian state. Therefore, we don't want that issue brought up, because if it's brought up there will be pressure for a diplomatic settlement and we don't want a diplomatic settlement.

In the case of the Gulf, the United States is also

pretty isolated, apart maybe from England, in opposing a diplomatic settlement. There the reason has to do with the so-called new world order. A diplomatic settlement is of no particular benefit to the United States. The U.S. strong card is not diplomacy. That's why the United States is usually against diplomacy and negotiations. Force is our strong card. If there's a victory by force, that is a victory achieved by the United States and places the U.S. in a strong position for world control. If you can establish that force is the way to rule the world, we win, because we're way ahead of everybody else in force. It's a version of what Nixon once called the "madman theory." It was revived in the Reagan administration. If you get the world scared of you, you can do a lot of things. There's plenty of reason to be scared of us. We have plenty of violence at our command. We also have the biggest economy, but in the area of force we're unchallenged.

DB: *There's another element that has changed since the Nixon years, and I think that's quite evident in this crisis. Because of the economic weakness of the United States now, we're essentially shaking down states in a kind of international extortion, with Egypt, for example, waiving that $7 billion debt. That seems to be a major difference.*

There's a major difference. Already in the days of Nixon it was eroding, but we still had enough of an economic base to carry out the military adventures. Now we can't, and we've got to get others to pay for it. Germany and Japan, mainly. Actually, it's even a little more complex than that. Back in the 1950s we could do anything we felt like. We didn't ask anybody when we invaded South Vietnam in the early 1960s.

By the time of Nixon, it was already problematic, because the United States at that time had already become one of three. Still the biggest of three, but one of three. The Nixon reaction to this had several facets. One was to break down the old economic order, to break down the convertibility of the dollar and institute import protection, to break down the Bretton Woods system. The other reaction was military. It had to do with delegating repressive authority to carry out repressive actions to surrogate states. That was the Nixon doctrine. Other powers are "cops on the beat." They do the local job and we run the show. That was a reflection of U.S. weakness. It was recognized that we can't carry out the intervention ourselves, so we'll have surrogate states. In the Middle East that meant Israel and Iran under the Shah. They were the gendarmes, to make sure nobody gets out of control. But we'll keep control of the whole business.

DB: *Within Kissinger's overall framework of world order.*

Within the overall framework of world order that we run and others pursue their regional interests, like Europe and Japan. Now it's changed. Now we're not delegating the intervention authority any longer. We're doing it ourselves again. But now we're doing it as mercenaries. The changes in the economic order have been such that the United States can function primarily as a mercenary state. As Hessians, as the editor of the *Chicago Tribune* described it with pride. He said we can be the world's Hessians. Somebody has to run the Third World and make sure that nobody raises their head and that there's no independence. We can do that because we have a monopoly of force. We will simply coerce our allies into paying for it. They're going to rely on us for the force to control the world. We can turn that to our advantage, as the Hessians, by forcing them to give us economic concessions, like purchase of Treasury bonds and shoring up our economy and also to pay for our military operations. That's the new world order. That fits very well with things that are happening in the world.

Another aspect of the new world order is that everybody knows that there's a serious internal infrastructure decline. The cities are falling apart, the educational system's collapsing. One consequence of that, well understood by business, is that there's going to be a shortage of skilled labor. Skilled labor means everything from typists to managers and researchers and product designers. People who are coming out of the ghettos are not equipped to do those jobs, by and large. They're semi-literate. They're living in criminal societies. That means that the United States is not going to be able to sustain those functions. To some extent you can overcome this by brain drain. Now the immigration laws are being changed so that we can try to attract people who get their educations elsewhere. The idea is other countries, primarily Third World countries, pay the costs of the education and we take the benefits of it. So you go out to your favorite computer store now and the chances are that the technicians who are fixing it are from Turkey or India. Those countries pay through funding their education, we benefit. It can work up to a point. But you have to be able to resupply the work force internally to some extent. There's one kind of work force that we can resupply, with the ghettoes the way they are: mercenaries. It could go that way.

DB: *Do you think it's noteworthy, somehow a departure from the norm that the ruling circles have had difficulty defining the U.S. role, the raison d'être for the Gulf intervention? The rationale keeps shifting from not rewarding aggression to oil to hostages to jobs, etc. etc.*

That reflects one of the few things that changed with the end of the Cold War. The end of the Cold War didn't change very much, because it was always a subsidiary feature in world affairs. One thing that changed was ideological. Since 1945, in fact since 1917, every U.S. intervention and every buildup of the military system has always been reflexively justified in terms of defense against the Bolshevik threat. That began with our support for Mussolini in 1922 and it's been the case virtually without exception since. It's like a reflex. You want to invade some country, you're defending yourself against the Russians. Pour more money into the computer industry through the Pentagon because you need it to defend yourself against the Russians.

And it worked fine, until the late 1980s. By the late 1980s it became harder and harder to use this justification. They could use it when they invaded Grenada. When they invaded Nicaragua they still got away with it. But by 1988 or 1989 it was ridiculous. They didn't even try when they invaded Panama. So now it was narcoterrorism. That's the problem that you're pointing to. They're building up for an attack in the Gulf, and you cannot make any pretense that it's defense against the Russians. They're just flailing around for other excuses. Nobody ever gave the real reasons for the war against Nicaragua. The Russians were there as a pretext. Now you don't have an easy pretext. They're searching around for one, and it's not easy to find. They can't come out and say, look we have to have our hand on the spigot, because that's the way you control the world, and we need a victory by force because that's our strong card. You can't say that.

DB: *You've long maintained that U.S. policies are contributing to Israel's destruction. Do you still believe that?*

Yes. I think that the Israeli victory in 1967 was the worst thing that ever happened to them. Israel's willingness to join, by about 1970, the new system had been pretty well settled with Kissinger's takeover of foreign policy directions. Israel went along with that. The idea was that Israel should be a strategic asset, essentially a mercenary state available to serve U.S. interests. In return we would give it military and economic power to carry it off. Notice that that's kind of a microcosm of U.S.

relations with the rest of the world now. That's our mercenary state and we sustain it. We want to be the world's mercenary state and they're going to sustain us. Of course, the difference is that we're going to be strong enough to threaten them. Israel was never a military threat to us, but we're going to be a military threat to the rest of the world. That is a parallel. Israel agreed to that. What they got in return was control over the territories and sustaining their economy, which is rather artificial. That was a devil's bargain. I think that's driving them to destruction. It's going to make the country unlivable and may sooner or later lead to its actual destruction, if not in this crisis then in some future one.

DB: *And this situation that Israel finds itself in, does that cause you any personal sorrow or discomfort or pain?*

Plenty. Since childhood this has been more or less the core of my own existence and involvement. Up until I was a teenager I was much more involved in the affairs of what was then the Jewish community in Palestine than any other issue. I lived there for a while and could very well have ended up there. Quite apart from caring what happens to anybody, I have personal reasons in this case. I think that since about 1968 or so I've had a very ominous feeling about it. That's when I started writing about it. First of all, I thought it was wrong, but also I thought it was disastrous. If you look back at what I wrote at that time, I wouldn't change a word of it. In 1968-69 I was writing about a perfectly predictable cycle of repression, resistance, harsher repression, more resistance, punctuated by regional wars, leading finally to destruction. I don't think anything much has changed.

DB: *You've also said that popular antagonism in recent years has been rising toward Israel. You've noted that it's tinged with some anti-Semitism and you've contended that the so-called*

Israeli lobby is reviving anti-Semitism.

I think the Israel lobby is reviving anti-Semitism and there's a certain sense in which they're doing it consciously and willfully. You get a picture of the reasoning if you read publications of the Anti-Defamation League. Forty years ago the Anti-Defamation League was a bona fide civil rights group primarily concerned with problems of Jews. That's fair enough. Every group has its own concerns. But it was a bona fide civil rights group. Now, as described casually in Israel, it's part of the Israeli lobby. The way they've redefined anti-Semitism is very revealing and helps answer your question. There's a book worth reading, *The Real Anti-Semitism in America,* published early in the 1980s by the Anti-Defamation League, written by the person who was then its research director, Nathan Perlmutter and his wife. They describe what the real anti-Semitism is. They point out that by conventional measures anti-Semitism has been declining very significantly in the United States. That's true. Anti-Semitism has reached a historic low.

They concluded that that's misleading because there's another kind of anti-Semitism which is increasing, and that's the *real* anti-Semitism. This is exhibited, for example, by the National Council of Churches when they criticize U.S. defense budgets and by peace groups that condemn U.S. intervention in Central America. The real anti-Semites in his own words are the people who "give war a bad name and peace too favorable a press." That's the real anti-Semitism. The logic is impeccable, by their standards. The interests of Jews are the interests of Israel. The interests of Israel are the interests of a powerful, militaristic Israel. Those interests are served by a powerful, militaristic United States. Therefore, anyone who criticizes the militaristic posture of the United States is really an anti-Semite. That's a syllogism. With that conception of anti-Semitism, the extent to which the population of the United States becomes opposed to aggression, violence, terror, militarism, war machines, etc., and is concerned with issues of peace and justice, is the extent to which they are anti-Semitic by the League's terms. That's going to build up a special kind of anti-Semitism.

We saw this in the last campaign, in 1988, very dramatically. About two months before the election, in August 1988, it was discovered that the Republican campaign committee had a bunch of Nazis running the group called the ethnic outreach group, which tries to get support among ethnic populations. It was being run by Ukrainian and Romanian ex-Nazis, Holocaust deniers, the usual array. That caused a minor flurry. It was striking that the Democrats never made an issue of it. Some of them were fired and returned in other positions. The Democrats never used it because probably they were told, essentially, by the Jewish organizations, to lay off.

The meaning of this was expressed very aptly in a *New Republic* editorial. The *New Republic* is another agency of the Israeli lobby. Its editorial said that it was true that these things were found, but this was what they called "antique and anemic" anti-Semitism. So Nazis and Holocaust deniers and people who want to put the Jews in gas chambers, that's "antique and anemic" anti-Semitism, not really very important. What we should be concerned with is the anti-Semitism exhibited in the Democratic Party, because at the convention they had allowed debate of a resolution calling for Palestinian self-determination. That's the serious anti-Semitism. These Nazis, they don't matter very much any more. Nazism, who cares about that? But you call for a Palestinian state, that's real bad stuff. We should worry about the anti-Semitism in the Democratic Party, not the fact that the Republicans used these Nazis.

This framework for understanding anti-Semitism is common. For example, for several years right here in the Boston suburb of Brookline there's a program, the National Institute of Education, the Department of Education runs in which they support innovative educational programs in high schools. There was some kind of competition. There was a proposal put in year after year by some Brookline group on the Holocaust, an educational series with video and classes and lectures on the Holocaust. It always got the highest ratings, and it was always turned down. I mention this because it was all revealed right before the election and had the same fate: nobody cared. It was turned down because right-wing Republicans like Phyllis Schafly and others who were advisors and commentators were writing in that the program was unfair to the Nazis, didn't adequately present the Nazi point of view, was unfair to the Klan, was arousing anti-Western sentiments, was raising the wrong kind of questions. You just can't treat the Holocaust honestly, is what they were saying. Finally the only way in which William Bennett could turn it down was to cancel the whole program. Since it had won all the support it could get from reviewers, the only way to keep from funding it was to cancel the program, the entire competition, which they did. All of this came out right before the election. Not a peep out of the Democrats. In other words, since these people are all adequately pro-Israel, it doesn't matter if they are Nazis or anti-Semites.

Again, this is defining anti-Semitism in a particular way. If support for the rights of Palestinians is anti-Semitism then there are many anti-Semites in the United States. The general population has been about 2 to 1 in favor of a Palestinian state, as is most of the rest of the world. So that makes them all anti-Semites, by this definition. And I think it's having its effects. I can tell both from personal experience and even from polls. In my experience, the dislike of Israel in much of the country is palpable, to the extent that I don't even talk about it in most places any more. In fact, I often find myself defending Israel in public against unfair attacks which have an anti-Semitic tinge to them. And I think that that's going to increase. If people are told that if they object to the fact that Israeli soldiers break bones of children, they're by definition anti-Semitic, they can say, well, OK, then I'm an anti-Semite. That's going to be the reaction. It's even shown up in the polls. Some have been published in which the positive attitudes towards Israel have declined very sharply and radically, and I think that's going to continue. If Israel wants to be, prefers to be, a militaristic, mercenary state maintaining its rule over a subject population by violence and totalitarian measures and to do the dirty work for the United States throughout the world, they're not going to be popular.

DB: *I'm sure you've seen these ads in the* New York Times *and elsewhere, for example, one is from the American Jewish Committee, published on November 12, 1990. It says that Israel is "judged by a double standard," that there's a tremendous amount of "moral hypocrisy" and that "Israel is held to a standard that is not applied to other countries."*

I agree with that. Israel is given the kind of leeway that no other country in the world has. For example, if Russia had treated Jews the way Israel treats Palestinians, we would probably have nuked them. Israel is permitted to get away with treatment of Palestinians that would never be tolerated anywhere.

DB: *That's not the thrust of this ad.*

I realize that that's not the thrust of it, but in fact, it's correct. Israel is described in the press as the "symbol of human decency," *(New York Times),* "a country of unique moral values." True, they make a mistake sometimes, but look how noble they are, etc. No other country that carries out atrocities is considered that way. Their argument is an interesting one. It's also presented by people like Thomas Friedman and others. Their claim is that Israel is put under a spotlight, that every little thing they do is judged, and other countries nobody pays any attention to, like who cares about Syria? And there's a certain truth to that.

But that's a curious argument. By that argument you could prove that the press in Boston are anti-Boston racists. If there's a corrupt judge in Boston who is exposed, there will be an article about it. If there's a corrupt judge in Seattle there won't be an article about it. If a policeman kills a civilian in Boston, a big article about it. If it happens in Karachi, they will never report it. Does that prove that the press is anti-Boston? No. It proves that the press focuses on Boston because it's important to the people of Boston. The press focuses on Israel because Israel wants it that way. They have tried to get the press to focus there. The want the correspondents in the Middle East to be in Tel Aviv and Jerusalem, because that way they can control the news and they can run what they call their *hasbara* system, their propaganda system. They know how to handle journalists, treat them nice, get them to see things your way, you want them to focus on Israel constantly so that Israel is in the limelight. The reason is you want the Americans to keep paying and the United States to treat Israel like—you can't say "treat them like another state," because they get much more than any American state does—they want the American people to keep subsidizing Israel to the tune of $1000 per person annually or something roughly like that, if you count everything. But to do that, you've got to keep it in the spotlight. So they want it there. And they get a tremendous amount of favorable publicity that way. Every issue in the region is seen from their point of view, not from anybody else's point of view. I remember a couple of years ago, maybe still today, ABC News had three bureaus in Asia. One was in Japan, one in Tel Aviv and one in Jerusalem. That's Asia. That's the way Israel wants it.

Of course, if you do it that way, you're going to suffer from just what Boston suffers from: when you have a corrupt judge or a policeman who kills somebody, people are going to read about it but not an equivalent crime in some corner of the world that's not covered. You can't have it both ways. It's true that atrocities in Syria aren't covered much in the American press, just as atrocities in Karachi are covered less than in Boston, because Israel is treated like Boston. Israeli elections get more coverage in the U.S. press than Canadian elections. That's because they want it that way. On the other hand, notice that although atrocities in Syria aren't covered as much as they are in Israel, you'd have to look very hard to find one kind word about Syria in the American press. Horrible as Syria may be, it's not total hell. There are a lot of favorable things that you could say about the worst country you could imagine. Those are never said. Nothing good is ever said about Syria or, for that matter, virtually any Third World country.

On the other hand, the overwhelming mass of the coverage about Israel is very favorable and very much in their interests. To the extent that they get negative coverage, it's for the same reason that Boston gets negative coverage in the Boston press. They can of course exploit that. They like that. Because then the tremendous focus on Israel means they control the news, they control the agenda, and if they do something wrong and it's criticized, they can say the world's anti-Semitic. So they have it both ways. It's a nice trick, actually.

DB: *Do you still believe that the leaders of Jewish organizations in the United States are opportunistic? I recall you saying you would be one of the few remaining to defend Israel when the chips are down.*

This is a guess, and people differ, so it's not 100 percent. I think sooner or later the United States is going to turn against Israel because the U.S. relation to Israel is opportunistic, it's not based on any moral principle. States aren't moral agents. It's based on the assessment that Israel is beneficial to U.S. interests. That assessment can and may change, and if it does they'll just dump Israel. My prediction is that in that case most of the most hysterical advocates of Israel will go along with the U.S. government. I wouldn't be surprised if I end up being one of the last people defending them because my attitude toward them is based on something different. It's not based on U.S. interests or an interest in associating with U.S. power.

I can see this happening. In 1982, during the war in Lebanon, although the United States supported the war strongly, by the end of August it was becoming harmful to the United States, and Reagan essentially forced them to call it off. When the Sabra Shatila massacre occurred it was very bad for the United States in the Arab world in general, and therefore support for Israel declined. They carried out worse massacres in Beirut. You don't carry out big massacres like that in front of television cameras, that's really stupid, like killing the Jesuits in El Salvador. You had to turn against it. It was interesting to note that the most passionate supporters of Israel started criticizing it, people like Irving Howe, who a couple of months earlier had been described in the Israeli press as such an extreme lover of Israel that when everyone turns against it he'll still be waving the blue and white flag. In fact he had been an outrageous apologist for Israeli atrocities. After Sabra Shatila I recall, in two days, he had three different statements and letters and articles in the *New York Times* disassociating himself from it. There are a whole string of opportunists who chose that moment to pull away and say, this isn't us, we supported something different. I think to the extent that Israeli fortunes decline in the United States, you'll find a fall-off in support, including in the Jewish community.

DB: *In a conversation I had with you a couple of years ago at UCLA you said something that I've always wanted to ask you* *about. We were talking about the Armenian genocide and you made the observation that Israel "didn't want anyone elbowing in on the Holocaust business."*

Israel has been very strongly opposed to efforts to bring the Armenian genocide into consideration. The extent of this is really astonishing. I keep learning new things about it all the time. For example, in 1982 there was a conference on genocide in Israel. It was organized by a childhood friend of mine. He is a psychologist there. The conference was dealing with all kinds of genocide. The Israeli government put pressure upon it to drop the Armenian genocide. They allowed the others, but not the Armenian one. The honorary chairman was to have been Elie Wiesel, and he was pressured by the government to withdraw, and being a loyal commissar as he is, he withdrew from the conference because the Israeli government had said they didn't want Armenian genocide brought up.

Just recently, a well-known Holocaust historian in Israel, Yehuda Bauer, told the Israeli press that Wiesel had called him from New York at that time pleading with him to drop out of the conference because the Israeli government didn't want it because it was dealing with the Armenians, and he agreed to that and felt very bad about it in retrospect. That gives an indication of the extent to which people like Elie Wiesel were carrying out their usual function of serving Israeli state interests, even to the extent of denying a holocaust, which he does regularly.

Why are they so fixated on denying the Armenian holocaust? That's very simple. Part of it is that they want to monopolize the image for their own purposes, but the other part of it is that this is the Armenians. They were massacred by the Turks. The Turks are allies, and you don't want to alienate allies, because that's much too important. So if they happened to carry out a genocide, that's not our business. They're our allies. Therefore you don't talk about the Armenian holocaust.

Take people like Bernard Lewis, a major Middle East historian and historian of Turkey, very pro-Israel. Just out of curiosity I looked up his historical account. He has a standard history of Turkey. He has one sentence, I think, on the Armenian genocide, some kind of evasive sentence. Well, maybe he honestly believes it didn't happen. That could be. Maybe he has facts. But the treatment of it is rather intriguing and I suspect it can be traced to the same kind of pressures, just judging by other things.

DB: *Did you know that Robert Dole in the Senate introduced a mild resolution commemorating 1990 as the 75th anniversary of the Armenian genocide? The Israeli government worked with the Turkish government to lobby against it. [The resolution was defeated in the Senate.]*

I knew about that. The Israeli government has always lobbied for its friends, and in this case the Turkish government is a friend and ally, with anti-Arab concerns. Yes, the Israeli government and its local Jewish affiliates lobbied to prevent that from being recognized. If you get to the more fanatic sectors of the Jewish community, they do the same with any other genocide.

Take the gypsies. Nobody supports the gypsies. You don't have to worry about alienating anyone. There isn't much study of the gypsies because nobody cares about them, and you know how everybody hates them anyhow, so they don't study it. But there is a Romani intelligentsia that's done research on the treatment of the Romani people by the Nazis and it looks pretty parallel to the way the Jews were treated. There are people who just flat out deny that in the most vulgar fashion. I noticed an article in the *American Jewish Congress Weekly,* a pretty liberal part of the Jewish community, a couple of months ago by some guy named Edward Alexander, from Americans for a Safe Israel, quasi-Kahane, right-wing nuts. He simply had a phrase: The Nazi genocide of the gypsies is an "exploded fiction." These gypsy stories are just fairy tales. That's exactly like the people who say the Nazis never did anything to the Jews. It's just fairy tales. If people say that about the Jews, we react with contempt, but if you say it about the gypsies, it's just fine, because who cares about them anyhow? I don't know much about him, but I suspect the motive there is to monopolize the Nazi genocide because you can use it as a weapon for Israel. People like Elie Wiesel go along with this all the time. That shows us how much they actually care about the Holocaust.

DB: *I sense in your work and observing you when you give lectures and talks that you see yourself as a presenter of information and analysis, but you're very hesitant to tell people what to do. What's the source of that reluctance?*

I don't think I'm in any position to tell people what to do. I felt the same way back in the 1960s when I was talking to young people whose lives were on the line. What do you tell them to do? That's for them to decide. It's easy for me to tell somebody to go be a resister and spend a couple of years in jail or go into exile and destroy your life, but what right do I have to tell people to do that? If you tell people to get seriously involved in dissidence, they're going to change their lives. This is not the kind of thing you can dip your toe into and then walk away from. If you're serious about it, it's going to affect you. It's going to change your life in ways which are serious. By certain measures, you'll suffer harm. You can face repression, economic reprisal, vilification, marginalization—there are a lot of unpleasant things that can happen.

From another point of view there are compensations, but they're mainly moral compensations. You'll be able to look yourself in the mirror and say, I've done something decent with my life. I don't feel in any position to tell people how to make those choices. I wouldn't tell my own children how to make them.

The Global Protection Racket: Reflections on the Gulf War

May 21, 1991

DB: *On Sunday, May 19, 1991, there was a welcome home parade in Hollywood for returning Gulf War troops. More than a million people attended. Jimmy Stewart was the co-chair of the parade, an actor who has starred in some war movies. He said that it's been a wonderful year for the U.S. and we should all be proud. Another attendee, who is also an actor, but in real wars, was General William Westmoreland. He said, "I don't think we've ever seen a time in history when the country is so elated and happy about the great success of a war." I'd like you to contrast those two rather euphoric assessments with your own observations from traveling around the country and giving lectures to people. You've said that you've found support for the war rather thin and problematic.*

I might also contrast it with another view that's rarely heard, that of the Iraqi Democratic Opposition, who were pretty well blanked out of discussion in the U.S. One of them finally was granted an op-ed in the *Wall Street Journal* in early April, Ahmed Chalabi, a banker now based in London, speaking for the conservative elements of the Iraqi Democratic Opposition, who have always been rebuffed by Washington and banned from the press.

He opened his *Wall Street Journal* piece by saying that for the Iraqi people the war has brought us the worst of all possible worlds, with the country devastated, Saddam Hussein more firmly in power than ever, butchering rebels with tacit U.S. support. So that's another view, that of Iraqis who are interested in and have been fighting for democracy in their country, with no help from the U.S., needless to say.

293

Around the U.S., I have been traveling a lot and going to many places which are regarded as very conservative or patriotic or whatever term you want to use for it. I have found that there's a good deal of surface support for the war, but my impression is that it covers a good deal of uneasiness. The commitment to the government policy is very thin. There is euphoria about one thing, that's for sure, namely that the U.S. emerged without a very heavy toll of casualties. One has to remember that the population was sold a bill of goods in which Iraq was presented as a major military power poised to virtually take over the world on the way to becoming impregnable, as Paul Starr describes it in the latest issue of *The American Prospect,* a sort of left-liberal quarterly. The population believed that there was this huge military power there, heard Schwarzkopf give interviews in which he described how we were outmanned and outgunned and were going to fight anyway.

Then this miracle took place, due to the incredible courage and brilliance of our leader and his generals, and we managed to overcome this immense colossus without the vast casualties and destruction on our side that were predicted and anticipated as part of this disinformation campaign. Under those conditions, part of the euphoria is quite genuine.

DB: *I've heard you speak on a number of occasions and read your articles in Z. Throughout this entire period, you've had many references to fascism and fascist-like policies and the Nazis. You've talked about the deep Nazi-like character of the intellectual class in this country. I can hear detractors saying, Well, there goes Chomsky off the deep end again.*

Actually, I don't think I've made any references to the Nazis. But I have talked about the open advocacy of fascist values, and I think that I'm correct. I've also mentioned that the media and the intellectuals behaved very much in the manner that one would expect of a totalitarian state. This is not to say it *is* a totalitarian state. In fact, quite the contrary, it's a very free society, which makes this behavior even more interesting. But these are questions of fact. So is it expression of fascist values or not to have articles in the national press, say the *Washington Post*, saying that one of the great achievements of the war is that now people properly appreciate the martial virtues and that the power of the president has reached unchallengeable heights, stating that this is good, and that we have overcome what Norman Podhoretz [of *Commentary*] once called the "sickly inhibitions against the use of military force"? Are those fascist values or aren't they? I think those are fascist values exactly. Those are exactly the values we hear in fascist societies. Did the media and the intellectuals behave in the manner that one would expect in a totalitarian society? Well, yes, I think so. I've reviewed a lot of evidence which leads one very strongly to that conclusion.

DB: *In the month following the Iraqi invasion of Kuwait we did an interview, and I was rather startled by the depth of your conviction at that time that the U.S. was absolutely going to war. What informed your views?*

In part it's just a general reading of U.S. policy. George Bush had nothing against Saddam Hussein. The policies were designed pretty much to keep him in power. And if not him, then some clone, some equivalent. That's pretty well understood. So it's not Saddam Hussein that was a problem. The problem was that he had demonstrated independence, and anyone who demonstrated independence, who doesn't follow orders, becomes an enemy who has to be destroyed. You can't just settle it. You have to teach the right lessons when you settle it. The lessons that have to be taught are several. There are lessons for the Third World. First, Don't raise your head or you're not going to be just returned to your box. You're going to be smashed and destroyed. So just keep to your place. Keep to your function of supplying cheap labor and resources. Teaching that requires force, not diplomacy.

As I've mentioned in other interviews, the U.S. is characteristically opposed to diplomacy. If you look at U.S. policy on other issues you find also that it has typically, not universally, tried to avoid and undercut diplomatic solutions and to rely on a settlement through the demonstration of the effectiveness of force. There are good reasons for that. This was true throughout the whole Vietnam War, for example. The U.S. continually undercut diplomatic negotiating possibilities, possibilities for peaceful settlement, meaningful elections, anything of that kind. It was dramatically true during the Central America years. I don't think anyone even debates that, or if they do they're not serious. The U.S. undercut the Contadora agreements, it was opposed to the so-called Arias plan, the Central American peace agreement of August 1987. When that plan was nevertheless ratified by the Central American presidents, much to the consternation of Washington, the U.S. at once moved to undermine and destroy it and succeeded. It continued right up until it got its way through force in the elections to violate the regular agreements of the Central American presidents, the World Court, etc. The same has been true in the Middle East. For years the U.S. has been virtually alone in blocking the kind of political settlement of the Israeli conflict that essentially the entire world has been calling for.

Use of force over diplomacy is characteristic, and not because of any weird cultural features, but simply because the U.S. plays with its strong card when it is in conflict, which is violence, not diplomacy. To achieve your ends through diplomacy you must be putting forth policy that has popular appeal. Diplomacy, negotiations and other peaceful means depend on the appeal of what you are proposing, ultimately. That's not all, but to the extent that you rely on peaceful means, it's because you think you can persuade, and the U.S. knows it can't persuade.

There's no way to persuade Third World people that they ought to suffer and be subordinated and fulfill a kind of service role. On the other hand, in the area of force, the U.S. reigns totally supreme. In fact, in *any* confrontation, but surely in a confrontation with a Third World country. So it's entirely natural that the U.S. should try to shift confrontations to the arena in which it will be very successful: military force. It wants to teach that lesson.

Where it's not military force it's economic warfare. In the case of Panama, Cuba and Nicaragua the U.S. has resorted to illegal economic warfare because that's also a domain in which the U.S. if it does not totally dominate, is at least very powerful in. Along with that goes the need to teach another lesson, namely, that's the way that conflicts ought to be resolved. Not just this one, but all of them, because that's where we're strong.

Those are general reasons for assuming right off that there was going to be a resolution through force. But particular reasons also emerged very quickly. Within days, even before anybody had any background information about what was going on, it was clear that the U.S. was gearing up a military force that went way beyond any tripwire function needed to enforce sanctions. Sending a major military force to the desert is a way of saying, We don't want sanctions to work. Sanctions take a little time. In a case like this, probably not much time. In fact, they probably had already worked by the end of August. But anyway, they take some time. Sending a major military force is a way of saying, We're not going to wait, because that force can't be maintained there. By the end of August it was not even a question. It was publicly stated through the State Department spokesman in the *New York Times,* the chief diplomatic correspondent Thomas Friedman, who is basically the voice of the State Department, that the U.S. must block the diplomatic track because that might defuse the crisis, with a few token gains for Iraq. He enumerated the gains, which everyone knows about: border settlements of conflicted issues, etc. That's just a way of saying, Look, we don't want any settlement. The Bush administration said flat out, There will be no negotiations, no diplomacy, which means no sanctions, because sanctions are the pressure behind pushing a diplomatic settlement. So it was already evident by certainly the end of August, if not before, that the U.S. would not tolerate—maybe it would have no choice, but it would try not to tolerate—a peaceful settlement of this. The ends of U.S. goals in the region would not be achieved that way.

As you say, I was writing about it at the time. It didn't seem to me very questionable. Now that more information has come out we see that that's exactly what was happening. It became more and more obvious through the months: no possibility was going to be given; if the U.S. could control what was going to happen, it would block any peaceful resolution. That went right to the end, February 23.

DB: *What would have been a response that you would have been comfortable with to the Iraqi attack on Kuwait?*

We now know the following: that within a few days after the Iraqi attack there were meetings of the Arab states. We don't have definite knowledge of what happened there, only information that's leaked, but it looks as though there were interactions with Iraq, trying to get it to withdraw from Kuwait. Apparently under U.S. pressure, Egypt and Saudi Arabia blocked those negotiations. One thing that I think should have been done is certainly not to block, in fact, to facilitate those efforts to arrange for Iraqi withdrawal within the regional context through the Arab states. By August 9, a week after the invasion, a back channel offer had come from Iraq to withdraw in connection with the settlement of the two disputed border issues, the access to the Gulf and the control of the Rumailah oil field, which remember is virtually all in Iraq. The only dispute over the Rumailah field was about a two mile penetration into Kuwaiti territory over a never settled border. So these are negotiable issues, plainly.

The access to the Gulf issue I think everyone would agree is readily negotiable. There are easy ways to think how that one could have been worked out. No linkage, nothing about other issues. According to Robert Parry, an investigative journalist, there was a National Security Council meeting on August 10 which rejected that offer. It was then pursued further by both Iraq's Ambassador and Foreign Minister and Americans like Richard Helms, the former head of the CIA. He and others on the American side said that it was clear that the State Department wasn't interested.

Another response that I would have preferred was to an Iraqi offer to withdraw entirely from Kuwait. Maybe you don't have to accept the offer as it was stated, but a counteroffer would have been, say, Withdraw and we'll discuss these issues. In fact, a reasonable offer would have been to live up to the actual wording of the major U.N. Security Council resolution, 660, the first resolution. Remember, it didn't just call for Iraq to withdraw from Kuwait. It had two things in it, only one of which anybody talks about. Iraq should withdraw from Kuwait and there should be immediate negotiations between Iraq and Kuwait to solve the disputes between them. That's the right position, I think. I was in favor of that resolution. Unfortunately, the U.S. undercut it. But the way to favor that resolution in the first week, within a few days after it was passed, would have been to encourage regional powers to pursue their own efforts to bring that resolution to realization, to respond to the Iraqi offer of August 9 by reiterating U.N. 660 and saying, Good, you withdraw and you and Kuwait move immediately to settle these two issues that you've brought up. That would have been a very constructive response, and it's very likely that it would have worked. You can't be certain, because you don't know until you try.

In the process of such negotiations doubtless other issues would have arisen, which is entirely legitimate. They should arise. There are all kinds of regional issues, in particular the arms level issues are definitely regional issues. All such issues are regional and must be dealt with on a regional, if not a global scale, as everyone agrees. So those are, within the first week, quite reasonable options which could have been pursued.

There is a general question of principle: Do we want to direct the conflict towards the arena of force or towards the arena of peaceful settlement through negotiations? That decision was apparently made, if not instantaneously, at least within the first few days. I think that decision should have been made the opposite way. But of course I think the same on the other issues, too, in which the U.S. has insisted on the use of force, and for good reasons. If you recognize that your power is violence, not diplomacy, not negotiations, not options that the general population is going to find appealing, then you want to block diplomacy and move to violence.

DB: *Did the war sustain your thesis about the tripolar post-Cold War world?*

It's first of all not my thesis. It's a description, not even arguable. In my view this was obvious twenty years ago and more or less expressed in the trilateralism of the 1970s. I don't really think that's a contentious thesis. The main features of the world system that has been developing through the 1970s and up until today is that there are three major economic blocs and one military force. There is also a fourth important element, namely the Gulf oil producing region, which is a tremendous source of capital.

Those are among the major elements in the current world system. They interacted throughout this crisis in about the manner one would expect. The state that has the monopoly of military force insisted on using it. It has a lieutenant, namely the British, also a declining economy but a respectable military force, one with what the British like to call a "manly tradition" of smashing the natives in the face for hundreds of years. They have virtually put it in those terms. So they have a sturdy national character. They know how to kick the little brown guys in the face. They've been doing it for a long time. They're our lieutenant. They're really not part of Europe.

So the major military power, the one with the virtual monopoly on force, and its lieutenant moved at once to make force the arena in which the conflict would be settled. They pressed very hard on the other two major economic blocs to pay up to support this operation, which was going to be costly. That reflects their conception of their role as basically mercenaries for the world's rich and privileged. That matter was described with surprising frankness in the international business press, sometimes delicately, sometimes rather crassly. I thought the more crass expressions of it were the more honest.

My favorites, I guess, were a series of columns by the financial editor of the *Chicago Tribune* who ended up finally saying, Look, the U.S. should sell protection. We should run a protection racket. This is Chicago. Everybody knows what that means. We run an international protection racket. The other two major powers, the other two rich guys in the world, basically want the same thing we do: for the Third World to keep its head down and do the work we want, and sometimes those guys get rambunctious and get in our way. So we call the Mafia and they kick them in the teeth or break their bones. That's us. We kick them in the teeth. They pay us a war premium, like an insurance policy. He suggested the Federal Deposit Insurance Commission as a model. Continental Europe and Japan will pay us a premium, and if somebody's getting in their way, they will call us and we'll smash them up. We're doing it now. Some Third World upstart is trying to get his hands into influencing oil production and price, so we'll smash him up properly. Then you guys have to pay for it. That's the way protection rackets work. It's quite natural that to the U.S. and Britain the idea of a mercenary role should be appealing. Look at the current states of the economies and their strengths and weaknesses and it falls pretty naturally. So that reflected itself as expected.

As to this other major source of capital, the oil producers, they don't have much in the way of choices, but they're coming along as expected. The way the U.S. and Britain have controlled the world energy system, or a large part of it, is by setting up what the British back in the 1920s called an "Arab façade" behind which they could essentially control Middle East oil production. The method is use of family dictatorships too weak to strike out on their own, dependent on external power for maintaining them. In return, we run a protection racket there, too. We protect them in several ways. Ultimately it is just by our own force. Of course, they pay for it. And they pay constantly. Their task is to ensure that the production and pricing levels stay basically within the range that the U.S. wants. Sometimes we push it up, sometimes we push it down, but basically within that range.

Also, crucially, we demand that they direct a very substantial part of the profits that come from oil to the British and the American economies. Right in the middle of the Gulf crisis one Saudi prince bought out about ten percent of the stock of one of the major collapsing financial institutions here, Citicorp. We don't know how much is going into treasury securities, etc. But we do know that corporations like Bechtel are going to make a real killing on this. Bush's proposal at least was to sell eighteen billion dollars worth of armaments. There's going to be a bonanza of construction and rebuilding what we destroyed. Meanwhile they'll just pay out plenty of cash. If they don't pay out directly it will go into treasury securities and shares in U.S. and British businesses. Saudi Arabia, which actually went into debt on this one, had to arrange a loan. The loan was arranged through the Morgan banks. Loans to Saudi Arabia are not like loans to you and me. They are a big contribution to their welfare. In general, the U.S. and British did about as well as you would expect. The U.S. and its lieutenant increased their leverage in world affairs and also got at least a temporary shot in the arm for their economies. All of these are factors in the world system.

I guess the last part of the new world system that should be mentioned, which I've discussed with you before is that the Russians aren't part of the game any more, no longer deterring our use of force. That's another aspect of the new world order.

DB: *It's clear why the U.S. and Britain were so enthusiastic for the Gulf War. But what explains the French enthusiasm for this war?*

I don't think enthusiasm is quite the right word. The French are mainly enthusiastic about making money and increasing their power. They try to pursue a partially independent policy, partly because of memories about the glory of France and partly for simple reasons of self-interest. The tactic that Mitterand followed, a reasonable one from the point of view of a cynic like him, or any statesman, is to keep making gestures to the Arab world, saying, Remember, we're on your side. So when it comes to business opportunities later, don't forget us, because we're on your side.

Up until the war France was standing apart. They weren't part of the unified command. The command in the desert was the British and the U.S. That's it. Two powers.

The French were in the background, with planes, this and that, but basically they weren't part of it. They kept making gestures which they knew perfectly well wouldn't get anywhere. But these were gestures intended in part for the domestic population, which was not enthusiastic about the war, to put it mildly, but in part to the Arab world. That went right up to the evening before the war, when France made a proposal at the U.N. which it knew that the U.S. and Britain would veto, and it was a meaningless proposal. But it was cheap, a cheap gesture, and I would interpret it as meaning, Look, you fellows over there in North Africa and the Middle East, don't forget us. We're really your friends, even if we're going to go join the war.

The minute the war started, of course, France joined it to try to get what it could out of that. I think the reasons are pretty much what the business magazines said. They knew there was going to be contracts and business deals coming from the Gulf states, and they wanted a share of it. First gestures to the rest of the Arab world, such as North Africa, that they were passionately against the war, saying, We're really on your side. At the last minute we send the Foreign Legion and get our licks in so we're not cut out of the contracts in rebuilding Kuwait either. On the side, try to show that France is a force in world affairs, which helps you to think you're glorious.

DB: *Do you give any credence to the speculation that the U.S. set up Saddam to invade Kuwait?*

Personally, I don't. I think there is evidence that could be read that way, but I don't find it convincing. The weight of the evidence, to me, shows something different. It seems to me to show that George Bush and James Baker, the main policymakers, were stridently in support of Saddam Hussein right through July. The evidence keeps coming out about that. A couple of weeks ago the

London Financial Times had a long story, a big front page story, that they had unearthed jointly with ABC News, in which they described how in November 1989 Bush and Baker had intervened strenuously to ensure that a billion dollars in credits were given to Saddam Hussein. That intervention was internal and bureaucratic. The Commerce Department, the Treasury Department and the Export Import Bank, which guarantees credits, were all opposed. They weren't opposed because Saddam Hussein gasses Kurds. Nobody cares about that. They were opposed because they recognized that he was not going to be able to pay it back, that he just wasn't creditworthy. It's clear that lots of that money was going into purchase of weapons. Bush and Baker intervened to overrule them and to ensure that he did get that billion dollar shot in the arm. That continued right through 1990.

In February 1990 the Iraqi Democratic Opposition tried to get some sort of support, at least verbal, from both Washington and London for a call for parliamentary democracy in Iraq. They were rebuffed in both places. Through 1990, the same continued. Congress a couple of times and elements of the Labor Party in Parliament tried to bring up Saddam Hussein's atrocities, atrocious human rights records, etc. They were rebuffed every time by the governments. They didn't want anything like that. No condemnations, no sanctions, nothing. The aid to Iraq continued right until the end. Up to August 1, the White House was still authorizing high technology shipments to Iraqi installations, including installations that were later bombed on the grounds that they were producing nuclear and chemical weapons. That went right through the last weeks of July and into August 1. All of that is consistent with the assumption that Bush and Baker were continuing the policies of the administration through the 1980s.

The policy was described by Middle East specialists of the Reagan and Bush Administration clearly, after the war, of course. Geoffrey Kemp, for example, said,   We knew he was an S.O.B., but he was *our* S.O.B. In this *Financial Times* story that I mentioned they quoted Peter Rodman, the National Security Council official advisor involved in the Middle East, saying, We knew that Saddam Hussein was a "murderous thug," but it looked like he was on our side. I think that all of this evidence is quite consistent. It goes right through the Glaspie-Kelly testimonies, whatever little details you could argue about. The part of it that was agreed upon is that April Glaspie, following State Department orders, essentially told Saddam Hussein that the U.S. had no particular objection to his rectifying border issues like the two outstanding ones, the issues over the Rumaila field and over the access to the Gulf, by intimidation, even by force if necessary.

The U.S. had no particular objection to his raising the price of oil. There's only one way to do that, given market pressures, and that's intimidation. She gave a figure of $25 a barrel or more. I think that's consistent with U.S. policy. Raising the price of oil has very complicated effects. In some ways it's harmful to the industrial countries, in other ways it's helpful to the U.S. and England. One way in which it benefits the U.S. and England is that they are both high cost oil producers, and as the price of oil goes up their own oil production becomes much more valuable. Take Alaska or the North Sea. That's high cost oil. You can make a profit on that when the price goes up. Another thing is that the profits to the Gulf states tend to flow back to the U.S. and England through the purchase of armaments, treasury securities, investments, etc. So it's a mixed bag when oil goes up. It's a delicate calculation, but it's much more beneficial to the U.S. and Britain than it is to their major rivals, Germany and Japan.

I don't see any big problems understanding U.S. policy. I think this is almost predictable behavior. On the other hand, I don't see any evidence that the U.S. expected Saddam Hussein to invade Kuwait and take it over. I think Saddam Hussein may have interpreted it that way, but if so that's again an understandable error on the part of a tyrant who's closed off from any advice and acts on his own intuitions. It was perhaps like Hitler calling for a two front war. Probably his generals told him it was crazy, but he saw himself as smarter than they were. Once Saddam Hussein had done that, the gears quickly went into motion in the usual fashion when a Third World murderous thug oversteps the bounds and is no longer our S.O.B. but his own S.O.B. In that case he has to go.

Whether a Third World leader is a thug or an angel is irrelevant. If he's his own angel, then he has to go, too. That's the way I would read the evidence. I would agree that there are some things that are not explained in these terms. This is a very conservative interpretation, just as I assume the facts are as they appear to be on the surface. As they appear to be on the surface they kind of hang together.

There are a few things that don't entirely fit this version of events. One is based on leaks from people like Pierre Salinger and others. I don't know whether to believe them or not, this kind of new journalism style with unattributed quotes. You can do what you like with it, and a lot of it is probably disinformation from intelligence services fed through willing journalists, but whatever one makes of that stuff, and I don't think it has high credibility, there does seem to be indication that Kuwait responded with surprising arrogance and inflexibility to Iraqi moves in late July. Other responses would easily have been imaginable that might have eased or deterred the crisis.

That's not explainable on the terms that I just outlined. It would be explainable if there were some kind of Kuwaiti plot to lure Saddam Hussein into Kuwait. I agree that the evidence could be read that way. It seems to be a very dubious interpretation, built on reeds, and it's extremely unlikely. I don't think states operate that way, to tell you the truth. I don't think that's the way any state operates, except on very rare occasions. Also, if they did it, it would have been extremely risky. There was no way to know how it was going to come out. There was no way to be certain that the Arab friendly tyrannies would be able to control their own populations. Once you set off a military conflict, it becomes extremely unpredictable. The level of weaponry is too high, the level of catastrophic power is enormous, the uncertainties in the political system are vast. It would have been an enormous risk for not very much gain.

In fact, let me just repeat that I don't think they had any reason to be upset about Saddam Hussein. He was acting the way they wanted him to. He was a good trading partner, purchasing Western goods, playing the game the U.S. wanted him to.

DB: *The U.S. has had a relationship with the Kurds that's been rather mixed, to say the least. Beginning in the early 1970s, through Massoud Barzani and the Kurdish movement inside Iraq at that time. Can you talk about that?*

The relationship with the Kurds goes back a little ways beyond that. In the 1920s that was British turf, not U.S. turf, and we might remember that it was the British that used poison gas largely against the Kurds. Against others too, but largely the Kurds, as part of their terror campaign when they tried to establish the state of Iraq under British control, as they cut it out of the Ottoman Empire. That was Winston Churchill's contribution to peace and joy among nations. He was the official who authorized the use of poison gas and bitterly denounced the "squeamishness" of people who were opposed to using the modern means of warfare.

There's an older history, too. But starting around the early 1970s there was a Kurdish revolt supported by Iran. The Shah at that time was the main U.S. ally. He wanted to cause some trouble for Iraq. One of the ways of causing trouble was to sponsor a Kurdish revolt in the north. The U.S. then under Kissinger went along with that, helped out. Later revelations by the Pike Committee were leaked and published in the *Village Voice,* though as far as I know I don't think they were published in book form in the U.S. They were published in a book in England, by a small publisher. Nobody wanted to see this stuff, but it was a very important report. The Pike Committee report, which had a lot of documentation, included cables and other statements, with the names blanked out, but it's obvious who it is, between Kissinger and Iran, making it very clear that neither the U.S. nor Iran wanted the Kurds to win. In fact, they didn't want the Kurds to win, they wanted them to fight and bloody Iraq, but not to win. That was crucial. They were frank about that. This was intended as pressure on Iraq to settle some border issue about access to the Gulf.

When Iraq backed off and accepted the Iranian demands, Iran, the U.S. ally, canceled its support for the Kurds. The U.S. also canceled its support. They were left then to be slaughtered. Iraq knew that this was going to happen and was prepared for it, so it began the slaughter right off. Very similar to what we've just seen. The Kurdish leader, Barzani, didn't understand this at all. He was so pro-U.S. he once said that this new Kurdistan should become the 51st state. He was shocked, as the Kurds were generally, to see how crudely they were sold out by the U.S. once they were no longer needed. The U.S. refused to provide even humanitarian aid, not even that, to the Kurds as they were getting slaughtered by Saddam Hussein. The Iranians forced back Kurdish refugees. It was a pretty bloody and ugly scene. That's when a U.S. high official, later allegedly identified as Kissinger, made the famous statement, apparently in secret Congressional testimony, that we shouldn't confuse foreign policy with missionary work. Our foreign policy was to inspire a Kurdish rebellion but make sure that it didn't succeed, and then when it was no longer needed pull the rug out from under them and get them slaughtered by Saddam Hussein. That's foreign policy. You didn't want to raise questions about missionary work or talk to the Maryknoll fathers. You're in serious company now.

Actually, I admire Kissinger for saying that. I don't think one should denounce him. He's just honest. And in fact, he's right. Foreign policy is not missionary work.

Later, in the early 1980s, the record is murky. We don't have much evidence. There have been no leaked congressional reports about it. There may have been some kind of tentative arrangements made between the Kurds and Saddam Hussein, in the context of the Iran-Iraq war. At that time again Iraq was weak and needed quiet in the north. It didn't want a revolt up there. So they had an autonomy arrangement with the Kurds. That one fell through by about 1984, which was just about the time that the U.S. was making its dramatic shift towards support for Saddam Hussein. The reasons why that fell through, why Iraq backed off from that agreement, have never been well documented, but general belief reported recently by the *London Economist* is that this was under Turkish pressure. The Turks have never wanted independence for the Kurds. About a quarter of the population of Turkey is Kurdish, although they don't concede it, and their own repression of Kurds is vicious, stepped up again during the Gulf War. But it appears they were worried about these moves towards independence and what effect they'd have within Turkey. Apparently they have a threat that they hold over Iraq, namely, they control the pipeline and, during the war, that was the way in which Iraq couldn't send oil through the Gulf, but it could send it through the Turkish pipeline.

Apparently Turkey threatened to close the pipeline if Iraq proceeded with these arrangements, and at that point Saddam Hussein backed off and that one fell through. All of this must have been with U.S. support.

Turkey is a close U.S. ally. At that time Saddam Hussein was becoming a U.S. ally. On this we only have indirect evidence, but that's the way it looks. I mentioned a *London Economist* report which gave it this way as fact, without giving their own sources. That was the second one. The third one is what we have seen in the last couple of months.

DB: *Why do you think it took the Bush administration so long to respond to the Kurdish situation in northern Iraq?*

I don't think that they would have responded at all if they hadn't been getting embarrassed. The U.S. war policy was designed primarily to target the Iraqi troops that were in the southern part of Kuwait. They were mainly peasant conscripts with no interest in the war, third line troops, mostly Kurds and Shiites. They were in holes in the sand trying to survive this incredible bombardment. When the U.S. stopped the bombardment they tried to flee and of course got wiped out in the horrifying flight through the desert. That was attacking mainly Iraqi peasants, Kurds and Shiites. In fact, it's quite possible that the U.S. killed more Kurds then than Saddam Hussein did in the north. We don't know the numbers, but it's not impossible.

The major Iraqi forces, the elite forces, were essentially not untouched, but left intact. As soon as the cease fire was announced, there was a revolt in the south and in the north. They first turned to the southern revolt, the Shiite revolt, and crushed that one, very brutally, probably more brutally than the attack on the Kurds. That was almost within eyesight of the American military forces and the correspondents. The people fleeing had plenty of horrifying stories. But nothing was done about them. In fact, to this day nothing has been done about them, because there was no pressure to do anything. Therefore the Bush administration could follow its instincts and do nothing for them.

After having crushed the southern rebellion—not totally, it's still going on—Saddam Hussein moved his elite troops to the north. The U.S continued to watch quietly, doing nothing about it, not even enforcing its own alleged agreement that he was not supposed to use helicopters. He turned to attacking the Kurds, who had by then taken over large parts of northern Iraq. Hundreds of thousands of Kurds fled. They ended up in the mountains and the press started providing these horrifying reports on the scene of what was happening.

Meanwhile Bush was fishing, as you remember, and didn't have any particular interest in it. He was showing what a vigorous outdoor sportsman he is. After a couple of days of this it started getting embarrassing, and I'm sure his PR agents told him, Look, it doesn't look nice while during the TV reports of the dying Kurdish children you're out casting for trout. They just had to put on some show of interest. Then they began to move towards humanitarian gestures. There's no reason to believe that there's any actual concern for the victims. You can tell this in part from the reaction to the Shiite massacre. Since the press didn't make a fuss about that one, the Bush administration has done nothing about it, although you can practically see it.

Another clear indication that it wasn't the issue of the massacre of the Kurds that was a problem, that Bush continues, like other statesman, to accept Kissinger's dictum that foreign policy is not to be confused with missionary work, is what happened in Turkey over the last couple of months. George Bush, you'll recall, has been praising Turgut Ozal of Turkey as a great peacemaker and a great statesman and humanitarian, etc. He's now getting honorary degrees in the U.S. Naturally, and predictably, knowing anything about Turkey and the Kurds, you would have predicted back in August that Turkey is going to step up its repression of the Kurds. It's going to use this new found glory, and the fact that attention has shifted elsewhere, to step up its repression of its own Kurdish population to an extreme. Apparently it did so.

Since the press isn't interested, we don't know much about it, but we know enough to have some picture of what's happening, from relief workers, European medical assistance groups in Turkey, human rights activists, lawyers, and others. The picture looks like this: in August 1990, right after the invasion, Turkey rescinded the laws which granted at least technical civil rights to the Kurdish population that had been instituted under European pressure. There's almost total censorship and always has been. In Turkey that's not a joke. You get arrested and you're tortured and never seen again.

The next thing that happened is Ozal started stepping up the bombing of Kurdish areas. Maybe hundreds of villages were bombed, cities were bombed, napalmed. According to the reports from mainly European human rights workers and medical and relief workers there, probably hundreds of thousands of Kurds were fleeing up to the mountains in Turkey over the winter, trying to survive the winter somehow. They couldn't return to their bombed out homes and villages, with the fields destroyed. They're starving up in the mountains. This was December and January. Maybe hundreds of thousands of them. Meanwhile, according to the U.N., by the end of January, about two hundred thousand Iraqis, that would mean mostly Kurds, were already up in the mountains fleeing from the U.S. bombardment. That means there could very well have been on the order of half a million Kurds up in the mountains in the peak of winter trying to survive at the end of January.

There was some humanitarian aid from Japan, a little from Germany, virtually nothing from the U.S., no attention to it. It's true that that was not as barbaric as Saddam Hussein's later assault against the Kurds, but it was bad enough. Nobody lifted a finger on that one, for the very simple reason that there was no pressure to do it. If there's no pressure, you don't do it.

DB: *What's your assessment of the peace movement's response to the Gulf crisis and war? I know you've described it as "reactive" and "sporadic," but could it really be anything else?*

I think it would have been very hard to do anything else, given the resources and capacities that were available, the means of intercommunication, the information, the almost total closing of the media and the journals, etc. You can always second guess this or that, but I don't think it could have been very different. There's room for debate as to what position the peace movement should have taken. I think it should have been very forthright in condemning the invasion. In my view, and while my friends differ, the peace movement should have supported sanctions. I think it was even legitimate to support an initial early dispatch of tripwire forces to Saudi Arabia. It's not clear whether Saddam Hussein would have gone on. He didn't know, I don't think. It doesn't make sense to try to predict that. It would have depended on what happened the first few days. A clear indication: Look, you can't go on. You've got to get out of Kuwait. I agree with that.

In my view, those moves, in the first few hours, could be justified, and the pursuit of sanctions. What kind of sanctions? That's a question too. Not the peace movement, but the National Council of Churches and the World Council of Churches came out quickly and forthrightly against the sanctions, and rightly, in my view. Not against the idea of sanctions, but against sanctions on food and medicine, which they called unconscionable, and I agree. That's never been used, even in much more severe cases of aggression and human rights violations than this one. But some kind of sanctions, some kind of pressure, and certainly an end to any arms shipments or any other kind of shipments other than food and medicine, an embargo on oil, that's legitimate. I think any lingering conception that there's anything positive or progressive to say about Saddam Hussein should have had no place in the peace movement response. He was, in fact, a murderous thug, and it was right to oppose him all along on those grounds.

Then, after that, I think more attention should have and could have been given towards making clear the apparent possibility of the diplomatic track and negotiations possibilities and bringing out what the government was up to. It's easier to say it in retrospect than at the time, but frankly I don't think it would have made much difference. I think given the circumstances, even if the peace movement had followed whatever the optimal tactics might be, I've got my ideas about that, others have other ideas, I suspect the outcome couldn't have been very different. The propaganda portraying Saddam Hussein as a major threat to our existence, even survival, was so overwhelming that no response to that could have had much effect. The suppression in the media of the negotiation possibilities, and the flat refusal to discuss them, that couldn't have been overcome by any peace movement activity, no matter how it was carried out. I don't think that there would have been much of a way to counter the sense on the part of the population that there was a threat to their lives, their homes, their future, their children, the world, unless we go to war to stop this new Hitler before he conquers the world. That probably would have been very hard to change without a very different political culture and climate.

DB: *The historical engineers have been busy at work over the last few months, as you well know. One of the things that has been rewritten and massaged is that the United States somehow fought the Vietnam War with one hand tied behind its back. This has gotten into the popular culture.*

You're right about the historical engineering. That slogan is an interesting one: We fought the war with one hand tied behind our back. Actually that's true. I agree with that. There was a deterrent to the use of U.S. force in Vietnam. It's very interesting to see how the U.S. fought the war in Vietnam. The major war in Vietnam, which has not yet penetrated U.S. political culture, we're much too brainwashed to face the truth on this one, was the U.S. war against South Vietnam. That was the core of the U.S. war, the attack against South Vietnam which went on for years and years and has never been recognized. There is no such event in American historiography, even on the left. That war was fought with no hands tied anywhere. There was no fear of any retaliation, no concern that we might get involved with the Russians. In fact, there was no political cost, no deterrent, and therefore the war was fought freely. The U.S. did what it wanted. If you want to bomb dikes, bomb dikes. If you wanted to carry out saturation bombing in heavily populated areas you did so.

It's kind of interesting to look at the *Pentagon Papers,* which show that in all this elaborate discussion of just how to carry out the bombing of North Vietnam and how to fine tune it, etc., there's virtually nothing about the bombing of South Vietnam, which was *much* heavier. In 1965 three times the scale of the bombing of the North, and it continued to be much heavier, much more vicious. No discussion. Reason? No cost. So there are no hands tied anywhere. The same with the "pacification programs," the terror programs that the U.S. carried out in South Vietnam. No cost, therefore no constraints.

In the southern part of North Vietnam, below the twentieth parallel, the same was true. There the place could be turned into a moonscape. No problem. And that's pretty much what happened. When you move farther north in North Vietnam, then the political costs and the deterrent effect began to mount. For one thing, there was a political cost to the bombing of the North Vietnamese capital. After all, it's a country recognized by other countries who weren't too happy about their embassies being bombed, etc. So you could get gestures of opposition by European allies. For another, as you got closer to the Chinese border, it was never very clear how the Chinese were going to react. Forgotten here, but China knew it, was that for years we were bombing an internal Chinese railway, the major Chinese rail link between southwestern and southeastern China, passed right through North Vietnam. That's the way the French built the railroads in the colonial period. That's as if some foreign power were bombing a major railroad between Chicago and New York that happened to pass through Canada, bombing the Canadian part of it. We wouldn't be too happy about that. There was also a question how the Russians would react when we were bombing Russian ships in Haiphong Harbor. There was in fact a deterrent from the Russians and Chinese, who could have poured in masses of troops. Remember, the U.S. is a global power. We intervene in areas where we don't have overwhelming conventional force advantage. So it's dangerous. The Russians could have done something somewhere else in the world, too. There's the political cost in Europe.

The popular focus, including the peace movement, was on bombing North Vietnam, not on South Vietnam. That's part of the weakness and primitive character of the peace movement at the time is that they fell for all this propaganda. You see it in the tactics. So there's something to the idea that they fought with one hand behind their back, but in North Vietnam, not in the south.

But what's particularly interesting in the slogan is that you should raise it. You could say the same thing about the Russians in Afghanistan. They definitely fought with one hand behind their backs. If they had used nuclear weapons, there would have been a strong U.S. reaction, so they were constrained in the use of force. But if we heard Russian generals pointing that out: We fought with one hand behind our back in Afghanistan because there was always the danger that the Americans would have done something somewhere, we would be angry, and rightly. What's interesting about the U.S. is this scandalous idea that we were constrained in the use of violence in one sector, the northern part of North Vietnam, because of the deterrence of the Russians and the political cost, that there's something *wrong* with that. Everyone who participates in this debate on either side is accepting that premise. It's the basic premise that's being accepted: Look, the U.S. has the right to use as much violence as it wants anywhere. Some people like George Bush, are saying, we couldn't do it, so that's bad. People on the other side, the liberals, are saying, what do you mean? We did, we used as much violence as we could, so there's no problem. That's the debate. And that debate is all on the assumption that we're a violent terrorist state, an aggressor, lawless, and we do what we feel like, and if anything constrains us that's a problem. That's a shocking debate.

DB: *A couple of other myths have been put into circulation. The media lost the Vietnam War. I know you've studied that one very carefully. Also that the peace movement in this country somehow mistreated returning Vietnam vets, humiliated them, spat on them, etc.*

Those are interesting stories. As far as the media are concerned, there have been extensive studies of the media in the war. I've done it, other people have done it. I think the results are pretty conclusive. The media were very servile. I was very surprised to see an editorial in *The Nation* the other day comparing the coverage of this war with the Vietnam War and implying that during the Vietnam War there was somehow courageous, honorable, revealing coverage. There were journalists on the scene who were honest. You could find a scattering of journalists on the scene who did something. But by and large the media were extremely subservient. That's one of the reasons why no such concept as the U.S. attack against South Vietnam exists in the U.S., because the media never reported the events in such a way that you could understand even that elementary fact.

If nobody in Russia knew that the Soviet Union had attacked Afghanistan, if everyone assumed it was a Russian defense of Afghanistan where they couldn't win because one hand was tied behind their back, we wouldn't bother doing any investigation of the Russian media and the Afghan war. The same is true here. If you do a closer analysis you find the same: the media, including television, contributed to hawkishness. They made the population more hawkish. It goes right through the Tet offensive.

It wasn't until major sectors of U.S. power, corporate sectors, turned against the war that the media began very timid criticism. What's called exposé, the kind of thing that David Halberstam, Neil Sheehan did in the early 1960s. That's just saying, It's not working. It ought to work better. Here's a way to do it better. That's not criticism. There were some exceptions, like Richard Dudman of the *St. Louis Post-Dispatch,* Ray Coffey of the *Chicago Daily News,* and a couple of others, but they were scattered. By and large the media were extremely supportive. Walter Cronkite, the whole bunch of them, right through to the end. In fact, it continues in subsequent years.

Of course, from the government point of view, or from the point of view of advocates of the war, the media were never subservient enough. But remember, that's also true of totalitarian states. Take Russia and Afghanistan. In a book that Ed Herman and I did on this we quoted some of the commentary of Russian generals and high communist party officials on the way the Russian media covered the Afghan war. They were bitterly critical of the Russian media for having stories about the suffering of the Russian helicopter pilots and soldiers and the atrocities. It read very much like the condemnation of the U.S. press. Let me just say that the criticism of the U.S. press for having lost the war has a very totalitarian, quasi fascist flavor to it. If people don't like the term, I'm sorry, but that's the right term. That's how we described the Russian case, and to be honest that's how we need to describe it in our case.

As for the reaction to the soldiers during the Vietnam War, that's also interesting. The peace movement wasn't a membership organization. I can't say, "members of the peace movement" did this or that. Maybe somewhere somebody spat on a soldier. But it is so uncharacteristic that it's way out on the margins. I kind of expect it would have been a government provocateur. The peace movement was very supportive of the soldiers. It was the peace movement which set up G.I. coffee houses and support groups. And don't forget that the soldiers were not passive instruments. The army had its own internal opposition to the war, and a very powerful one. The Vietnam Veterans Against the War, the War Crimes trials, those didn't come out of the peace movement. They came from the G.I.'s on the scene.

The U.S. made a tactical error in the Vietnam War. It sent a conscript army. Every imperial power knows that you do not send conscript armies to fight colonial wars. Colonial wars are vicious, murderous wars in which you're killing civilians and murdering babies. There's no other way to do it. For that you need professional killers. Either professional killers or people who are so far away from the action that they don't see what's happening, like B-52 pilots. That's OK. They don't have to see what's going on. But if you want to fight a colonial war on the ground, you need professional killers like the French Foreign Legion and the Gurkhas, etc. But not conscripts. The conscripts are too much part of the civilian culture, and in particular part of the youth culture. They came out of the same background as domestic protesters. A peace movement developed inside the army.

In fact, by the late 1960s the military officers were calling for withdrawing the army from Vietnam because they were afraid their whole military was going to collapse. The G.I. coffee houses and so on were just supportive of G.I.'s. Many of them were setting up places where soldiers could break out of the ugly controls of the military, to which they themselves were opposed. That continued. The War Crimes trials were carried out by soldiers. The peace movement people participated. I joined in.

Attacks on soldiers took place, but on the part of the right wing and the mainstream. The right wing denounced the soldiers or disregarded them because they didn't win. They didn't win the kind of war they wanted. They were supposed to come back conquering heroes, and they didn't come back conquering heroes, so they were basically either ignored or denounced from the right. As far as the mainstream is concerned, they treated them very shabbily. The press, the Congress, etc., treated them rotten, but not the peace movement. That was the mainstream and the media.

Take reporting of atrocities. What's the atrocity that comes to everybody's mind? My Lai. My Lai was a mainstream liberal event. It was splashed over the front cover of *Life* magazine. On the other hand, it was not a peace movement issue. The American Friends Service Committee, the Quakers, had a clinic right near the My Lai massacre. They said, We knew about it right away. Remember, it didn't come out for about nineteen months, until Sy Hersh broke the story, finally. The AFSC said, We knew about and we never were particularly interested in it because that kind of stuff was going on all over the place. Furthermore, that wasn't the main thing. The main thing was the air attacks.

That was the general peace movement attitude. The criminals were not a bunch of crazed G.I.'s out in the field, with people shooting at them from every direction and not knowing if they were going to live the next minute. What they did was horrible, but they're not the real criminals. As I've stated in other interviews, the real criminals are the guys sitting in air conditioned offices plotting B-52 raids on villages, or sitting back in Washington laying out the grand strategy of slaughtering people in South Vietnam. But the media and the whole liberal establishment took a different line. They went after the G.I. on the ground, after the weak, defenseless ones. You can't pardon what they did, it was horrifying. But you can understand it. What you can't understand is the generals, the commanders and the civilian officials above them, that's the part that's completely unpardonable.

Of course, it was only in the peace movement that this point was made, because the planners were the people who have to be protected. They're the people with power. The half educated G.I. on the ground you can go after. That was pretty standard. So the whole babykiller line, that's right-wing and liberal media, mainstream criticism. Insofar as there was a peace movement as an organized force, it wasn't pushing that distortion. It was saying, Let's go back to where the decisions and choices are being made. My Lai was part of a major operation, Operation Wheeler Wallawa, which killed nobody knows how many thousands or tens of thousands of people in real massacres. Operation Speedy Express, to take another example, the media bypassed, although it was a peace movement issue. That made My Lai look like a tea party.

DB: *Let's talk about something else. You were four years old and out walking with your parents in Philadelphia one day and you came upon a textile workers' strike that made quite an impression on you.*

We drove past in a trolley car, as I remember. Whether I was four or six I wouldn't say. It was one of the strikes in the mid-1930s, which were often pretty violent.

This one I particularly remember, I didn't understand what was happening and asked my mother what was going on. It was mostly women, and they were getting pretty brutally beaten up by the cops. I could see that much. Some of them were tearing off their clothes. I didn't understand that. The idea was to try to cut back the violence. It made quite an impression. I can't claim that I understood what was happening, but I sort of got the general idea. What I didn't understand was explained to me. Also, the interpretation was not that far out of the general understanding. My family had plenty of unemployed workers and union activists and political activists and so on. So you knew what a picket line was and what it meant for the forces of the employers to come in there swinging clubs and breaking it up.

DB: *You've remarked that during the Depression crossing a picket line was as outlandish as stealing food from a beggar. Things have changed in the culture since then.*

Not just during the Depression, but for many years after. People were brought up to understand that. It has changed.

DB: *Why did it change?*

There was a good example yesterday. We went down to this working class high school [Tiverton, Rhode Island]. I talked to the students and some of the teachers. The teachers came from the same working class background that the students did, but a generation older. One of the teachers I was talking to was describing the difference between her understanding of the world and that of her students. Although they come from the same working class background, a depressed New England mill town falling apart, she grew up a generation back still in a culture where you had an understanding, an instinctive appreciation of working class solidarity and the needs of poor people and the need to work together and build unions. That's just in your bones. Whereas the same working class kids today don't understand it at all. That's the experience I've had. I'm a generation earlier than the teacher, but in my childhood and adolescence that was just taken for granted. Poor people and suffering people can only defend themselves against power and get a share of what they deserve by working together, and working together means things like picket lines, unions, and so on. That's the way you do it.

Today it's very different. I remember a couple of years ago here, during the Eastern strike, when Frank Lorenzo was trying to break the union, he at one point lowered air fares to New York. The fares were ridiculously low. People were just flocking to Eastern, including radical kids. I remember talking to student activist groups about this and saying I didn't understand it. Granted, the pilots and stewardesses aren't Mexican farm workers, but still, it's working class people and the machinists' union is behind it. How can you guys cross the machinists' union's picket lines? The reaction I kept getting was, we're on the side of the working man and working woman, and we don't see any reason why they should be pushed around by these union bosses. If they want to go to work that's fine, the unions shouldn't be able to stop them from going to work.

At this point you hardly know what to answer. You've got to begin from kindergarten and explain what it means to have a class struggle and to fight against oppression and to work together with others. That's been lost. And not by accident. A lot of thought and effort went into it. It began right in the 1930s, with major public relations efforts on the part of the propaganda wing of the business community, the public relations industry, etc. to try to break down that kind of consciousness and solidarity. It began right off in the 1930s, probably at the very same time I was watching that strike, right after the

Wagner Act in 1935. The Wagner Act was labor's first and also its last real legislative victory. It gave labor the right to organize and various protections. It frightened the business community for two reasons. For one thing, it was an exercise in democracy, which is always frightening to elites. They don't want democracy. Secondly, it allowed for CIO to carry out serious union organizing, and that was frightening.

The reaction was instantaneous. Within a year management had developed what were called scientific methods of strikebreaking. The basic idea was to try to mobilize popular opposition to the strikers around vacuous slogans, patriotic slogans like harmony, Americanism, togetherness, that kind of thing. This was tried out first, I think, in the Johnstown steel strike, the Bethlehem steel strike in Pennsylvania, which the CIO lost. I think it was 1936. The idea was to flood the community with propaganda. The basic tone of the propaganda is that it's us against them. We are the corporate executive, the sober working man who wants to just do his job, the housewife in the kitchen, the clergyman, the grocer, that's us. It's true, one of them plays on the golf course and the other drinks beer in the bar, but basically we're all together. Those are just cultural differences. So there's us on one side, and on the other side are these disruptive elements that are trying to break up the harmony, Americanism, the friendliness, our nice lives, and we've got to mobilize to defend ourselves against these disruptive elements. That flooded the press, the radio, the churches. It worked. It was later called the Mohawk Valley formula. Later there were other ingredients added, like human relations. You bring the workers to appreciate the fact that they're really on the same side as management, we're all in this together, we're all friends. Things like the attack on un-Americanism, which actually had earlier roots, were then revitalized in a very dramatic way.

I don't think there's any other country in the world

that has a concept analogous to un-American. People being un-French, un-Spanish, they would probably laugh if they even understood what we meant in those countries. Actually it doesn't mean anything here either. Un-American doesn't mean anything, but that's precisely the point. Just like harmony doesn't mean anything.

DB: *Like "Support our troops."*

Like "Support our troops." It doesn't mean anything. They're just empty slogans. In fact, support our troops is just the contemporary reflex reaction, exactly the same as We're all in this together. Don't ask the question: Do you support the program, the policy? That's what you want to deter people from thinking about. So have them scream Support our troops, and then the peace movement will debate, do we support our troops or don't we support our troops? Does it mean anything?

The public relations industry puts a lot of effort and money into this. And it's not just the business community. It's also the academic community, the intellectual community, etc. There are substantial commitments to try to undermine independent thought, to break down any conception of solidarity, of the interests that unite people in achieving their goals. You want to break all of that down and end up with an atomized society in which nobody thinks of anything except their own individual gain, maybe a little bit of charity on the side, a thousand points of light, but certainly nothing like fighting for a common goal. That stuff has been very effective.

Sometimes you see it come out in pretty striking ways in polls. There was one rather interesting poll about a month ago which asked people, What's the most important thing in your life? It came out roughly like this: the top choice, over 40 percent of the population, was My relation to God. The second choice, around twenty five percent, was personal health. The third choice was a happy marriage. Satisfying work was I think about five percent. Respect in the community was about two percent. That's roughly what the numbers were like. I think that would be very hard to duplicate in any modern industrial society, anything remotely like that. When you think what it means, I think it's not obscure. The idea of meaningful work is not an option. The idea of respect of the community doesn't mean anything because there aren't any communities. You are alone. You are alone, you are gaining commodities, you're a passive worker, you follow orders, there's no community, there's no such thing as satisfying work, certainly there's no such thing as any control over your work, they don't even know what that would mean. You follow orders, you're a passive worker. Your life, insofar as it exists, is maybe individual acquisition of commodities. That's a pretty sick commentary on a society, especially a rich, wealthy, privileged society like this one.

DB: *You've told me that toward the end of the academic year you get deflated, dispirited and somewhat dejected. What do you do for yourself to rejuvenate and to recuperate from the stress of the year and all the talks and teaching that you do?*

I'm pretty sure every activist goes through this. The year has a rhythm. That's the way life works. It's basically September through June, that's where the big time activity is, peaking in the fall and the spring. When it winds down, and also for me, being in academic life the school year winds down, you have a little time to try to look at the debris that's been piling up and try to catch up a little bit and also to think about what you've been doing for the last year, which I don't have time to think about in the moment because it's just going on from minute to minute. When you ask yourself, when you think, the last ten months I've been really killing myself, racing every minute, not a second off, tense, ugly, there are a lot of rewards, but also a lot of unpleasant things, certainly a lot of

tension. If you ask yourself what it's all about, what have
you achieved, the answer can always seem to be, not very
much. Maybe some small gains here and there, maybe
some other losses somewhere else, often huge losses, and
it's hard not to ask yourself what it's all about. It's pretty
easy to become depressed when you ask yourself what it's
all about. I'm sure that I'm not alone in going through that.

How do you deal with it? People have their own ways.
Sometimes I do things the wrong way. That's why I ended
up in the hospital a couple of years ago. But one has to
understand that as things are there are going to be at best
small victories, fending off some atrocities, improving
things a little bit here and there, making things less bad
than they might have been or a little better than they
might have been, maybe gaining some clarification and
understanding yourself, maybe helping other people gain
some. That's about it.

Bigger goals are beyond reach for now. But the
achievements can be pretty substantial. Take the Marin
County Task Force where we both were a couple of months
ago. It's a small group of very dedicated people who have
been defending Salvadoran human rights activists and
others who have been defending Salvadoran refugees.
Maybe when they think about it, it doesn't feel monumen-
tal, like they haven't changed the world. But they have
certainly saved plenty of lives and helped create a space
in which other people can survive and work. That's not a
small achievement. There are places where huge atrocities have gone on. Timor is one of the worst. But they could
have been a lot worse. The reason they're not is because
there are a few people, mostly a handful of young people,
who did and continue to devote themselves to it. Occasionally that will compel a newspaper to cover it. Occasionally
it will cause some protest in Congress and give the kind
of deterrent effect that allows people some space to live.
The development of these communities of engaged people
in the U.S. is important.

Pascal's Wager

October 15, 1991

DB: *You've often commented that it was the impact and work of solidarity organizations, church groups, etc. that inhibited the Reagan administration actions in Central America. Why weren't they a factor in the Gulf War?*

For one thing because there was no time. In fact, the Bush administration was kind enough to tell us exactly what was going on. Right at the moment when the ground campaign started, there was a very interesting leak, obviously from the administration; I don't know why they leaked it. But they leaked a section of their first international strategy report that was done for the Bush administration. When a new president comes in there's always an assessment of the world by the CIA and the Defense Intelligence Agency, etc. This was one that was done in the first weeks or months of the Bush administration. One section of it was leaked and buried in the *New York Times*. It had to do with conflicts with Third World countries, very much like the Iraq war. What it said is, in the case of much weaker enemies, and of course they're the only kind that you fight, we must not only defeat them but defeat them decisively and rapidly, because anything else would undercut political support and would be embarrassing. So that's a recognition of their understanding that there is no political support for intervention, and if you let anything drag on long enough for people to open their eyes, you're going to be in trouble.

I think that's pretty much what happened in the Gulf War. Up until a few days before the war, polls were still indicating about two to one opposition to war, if you interpret them correctly. That is, if people were asked up to a few days before the war, would you favor a negotiated withdrawal of Iraqi forces in the context of consideration of regional issues, Israel, Palestine, etc., the population was in favor about two to one. That figure was very misleading because those poll questions started by saying, George Bush is opposed to a negotiated settlement. If you want to load a poll question, just say the President thinks X, what do you think? You automatically get a big X factor. So we have to discount for that.

The other piece, and this is much more important, is that the people who were answering that question, must have assumed, I'm the only one who favors a negotiated settlement, because virtually no one had articulated that view. In fact, rejection of a negotiated settlement was virtually universal in the media and in Congress. Nevertheless, by about two to one people favored it. Furthermore, it's very unlikely that anyone who said yes to that question knew that just a week before Iraq had once again offered a withdrawal proposal which had been rejected by high U.S. officials. There's no reason to question it. It was a withdrawal proposal essentially without conditions except for an international conference. Just imagine that the media hadn't been doing their job. Suppose that they'd been telling people what's going on in the world and allowing opportunities for discussion of the real issues. You wouldn't have had two to one; you would have had ten to one support for a settlement that was on the table, that the U.S. had rejected, especially if it had been discussed. So that's right up to the war.

Then comes January 15. You start kicking ass. Everybody's excited. We're killing lots of people. Meanwhile there was still this big buildup, remember, about Iraq. The most powerful country in the world, they're going to murder us all, etc. People were really terrified. I could see that traveling around the country. You go to the most reactionary place in the country and people are cowering in terror behind their fatigues and yellow rib-

bons that Saddam's going to come and get them. That was
a real fear. People were frightened. Schwarzkopf was
giving interviews about how we're outmanned but we're
going to fight anyway and how the Iraqis had this fantastic weaponry that no one's ever dreamt of before and this
kind of business. The thing was precisely organized so
that there was no combat. That was very critical. There
was never any war at all. That was a complete misnomer.
By the time that the ground campaign began, there was
basically nothing there except wreckage, so they could
walk through. American combat casualties were on the
order of those incurred in Grenada, hardly more. Under
those circumstances you could get support.

Of course, in that period, a couple of weeks of bombardment of an enemy who was about to destroy us
allowed no time or opportunity for building up any consciousness or anything else. I think the administration
understands that. If you want to fight a war these days,
first you have to build up the enemy to be larger than life
and you have to terrify everyone. And you have to do it
very quickly. Then you have to arrange a conflict with no
combat and get it over very fast. That's a very narrow kind
of war, and I don't think they have any other options.

Going back to your question, under such
circumstances, with monolithic propaganda systems,
there's simply no possibility of developing any serious
opposition quickly. The solidarity movements developed
over years of activism and distribution of information and
setting up separate contacts and people going down to
Central America to see for themselves. You can't do that
overnight.

DB: *But there's something else at work here in terms of
comparing Central America and the Middle East. There's an
enormous amount of ambivalence and conflict when it comes to the
Middle East. I've talked to activists who say they feel more kinship
with Central America. There's language affinity and religion and*

those kinds of issues, and they don't feel that about the Middle East.

There's something to that. And there is a background of endemic anti-Arab racism which is extreme. But notice that the administration was able to do the same thing with Panama, again in the same way. Just a few months earlier, after all, Noriega was again set up to be a figure larger than life. Look back at the commentary by Ted Koppel and others, saying Noriega was one of the worst slimes in history, greatest danger we faced, etc. This was in the context of this phony drug war, which really had terrorized the country. You could see that by polls and lots of other evidence. Here's this Hispanic narco-trafficker who's going to come and destroy our lives. That worked the same way, a very rapid, very destructive attack with no combat. Then you forget about it.

Although what you're saying is quite right, anti-Arab and anti-Muslim racism is much more extreme than anti-Hispanic, you could use that racism too. Noriega was turned into a demon with plenty of racist caricature. You recall all the business about the pineapple face on National Public Radio, the mixed breed, etc. The media just accepted that completely. Some of it was horrifying. For example, CNN at the time of this juvenile attack on the Vatican embassy, which was much praised here, the television stations all had gotten in high rise hotels nearby, they had set up their studios so they could see all the fun stuff. I think it was CNN that had hanging out their window a banner with a pineapple on it. Another pure racist caricature of the official enemy, the kind of thing you might expect in Nazi Germany. But that was just taken for granted. And it was also described as good clean fun. If we want to blare rock music at the Vatican embassy, that's good clean fun.

DB: *You and Ed Herman in* Manufacturing Consent, Necessary Illusions, *and elsewhere described a propaganda model. In* *terms of what you've just been discussing, was there any break from that form?*

It was startling, a textbook example. Prior to August the media had been very soft on Saddam Hussein. During the period when the U.S. government was strongly supportive of Saddam Hussein, and the Bush administration was barring any Congressional critique of his human rights record and they were sending him high tech aid, much of it for military purposes, the media had very little coverage. Almost all of the exposure of this stuff is after August. They never even reported it. There was one television correspondent, Charles Glass, who had been trying for years to get ABC to publicize material that he was collecting and getting in indirect ways on Iraqi biological warfare facilities and U.S. aid to Iraq, etc. Occasionally he would get a little spot in there, but it was almost always followed by a Pentagon denial and few others were interested. That was typical for a long time. So that's the first phase. When the U.S. government supported Saddam Hussein the media were pretty quiet.

Then comes the second phase, August to January. You've got to build up war fever. At that point, the task was to suppress the fact that there's no reason for going to war. You want to go to war, you have to give a reason. It's a serious matter. The question is, do you pursue peaceful means? That's always the question. Do you try to reverse aggression or other crimes by peaceful means or do you go to war? The only argument given by the administration on this issue was, we believe in principle, and principle cannot be compromised and you can't negotiate with an aggressor.

Principle has nothing to do with it. George Bush has a whole history of either carrying out or supporting aggression. Any ten year old would have ridiculed his stand. But the media never ridiculed it. Every time Bush made that kind of statement—there will be no negotiations so we can't compromise—there was huge applause across the spectrum for the tremendous, amazing American stand on principle. He would say there will be no negotiations, and you would have a hundred editorials saying, he's going the last mile for peace and pursuing diplomatic means to the limits, etc. There was almost complete suppression of the fact that no reason was ever given for going to war, no reason that wouldn't be ridiculed by a literate teenager.

Secondly, the options for a peaceful settlement were suppressed as we discussed in other interviews. They were barely mentioned outside of this Long Island *Newsday* article. It's doubtful that one percent of the population ever heard of them. More information came out later, which makes it even worse. So the task of the media at that time was to prevent the possibility of recognizing that there are alternatives to war.

There was one issue that was discussed, because it was discussed in Congress: Shall we let sanctions go on for a longer period? That was discussed, but that's a technical question: Will sanctions ultimately work? The fact of the matter is that sanctions had worked, as far as we knew, probably by mid-August, when the Iraqi offers for withdrawal started. But those offers couldn't be discussed. The media created the context in which the war could take place. I mentioned those poll results. If the media had not done their job so successfully, there would have been overwhelming support for pursuing the apparent possibility of a diplomatic peaceful settlement. People supported it even without the media letting anyone know about it.

Comes January through the end of February, the six weeks of what they call the war, actually the slaughter. During that period, of course, the media were just cheering for the home team. You didn't expect anything at that time, and you didn't get anything.

Now comes the even more interesting period, the

period after the ceasefire. The U.S. war tactics were to attack the civilian infrastructure. That gives the U.S. a hold over the population in the post-war period. We can keep the screws on them because we've carried out what amounts to biological warfare. They will starve and die of disease unless they do what we want. So that's the purpose of that tactic. The second part of the war strategy was to attack the conscript army in the south, mostly unwilling Shiite and Kurdish peasants, as far as we know, and they were just slaughtered. Meanwhile, the elite units remained intact. After the war, the next task was to watch while the elite units, which had been more or less freed, were set to work to do their jobs, namely to suppress the popular rebellions. That started in the south. There was a big Shiite rebellion in the south, right under the nose of Stormin' Norman watching them. The U.S. didn't lift a finger. The Republican Guards and helicopter gunships massacred people in southern Iraq right next to the U.S. forces. Nothing happened. After they had succeeded in that, they moved to the north and the same units attacked the Kurdish rebels in the north. Everybody watched. Nothing happened.

But to get away with massacring Kurds is a little more difficult than to get away with massacring Shiites. Shiites, after all, are just Arabs, so basically nobody cares. Kurds have Aryan looking features. Television correspondents talked about the blue eyed children, etc. So there was a lot of public pressure built up about the Kurds. Finally, the Bush administration had to back off from its open support of the massacre and move to tacit support, namely they pretended to move in to stop it. But meanwhile, the whole time that the helicopter gunships and the Republican Guard tank units were slaughtering Kurds, Stormin' Norman was giving interviews over television about how we wiped out the elite units and grounded the helicopters. George Bush was out fishing.

As I stated in a previous interview, in outlining that

humanitarian considerations weren't even a remote factor in the administration response, the media had a problem with this one. The Shiite rebellion in the south was no big problem, because nobody cares about that massacre. The suppression of the Kurds was tricky, and it's interesting to see how they handled that one. Here we have a situation where George Bush is supporting Saddam Hussein, tacitly, while he is massacring the Kurds and others who were involved in a popular uprising aimed at bringing about democratic change in Iraq. Here's George Bush supporting his old buddy, Saddam Hussein, while once again he smashes up and destroys by enormous violence the possibilities of any democratic outcome in Iraq. How the media were going to handle that one is intriguing.

What they came up with was the line that yes, we're the most dedicated humanitarians in the history of the human race, obviously, and of course we give everything for democracy, but we also have to recognize the need for pragmatism and stability. Pragmatism is a nice word which means, do anything you feel like. Stability is a nice word which means, impose the kind of order we want. So we need pragmatism and stability.

I did an analysis of especially the *New York Times* on this, and it was kind of interesting to see how they handled it. Their Middle East correspondent, for example, Alan Cowell, I think it was April 10, had a long article trying to deal with the fact that after having allegedly opposed Saddam Hussein, the butcher of Baghdad, we're now standing by while he wipes out the Kurdish opposition. What he said is, there's a remarkable degree of unanimity among the Arab coalition partners and the U.S. on the need to follow the pragmatic policy of maintaining stability and order in Iraq, which means ensuring the rule of Saddam Hussein and not these disruptive elements.

Apart from the cynicism of Cowell's conclusion, an obvious question comes to mind: What about this unanimity? Everybody was giving the same line: it's a realistic, pragmatic position supported by the Arab coalition partners. Of the eight Arab coalition partners, six are family dictatorships. That doesn't make them countries. They're just family dictatorships set up by Anglo-American imperial settlement to manage the oil resources for us. So that's six of them. The seventh one is Hafez al-Assad, a clone of Saddam Hussein, a murderous minority tyrant, so he's not going to object on principled or humanitarian grounds, so that accounts for his view.

The only one of the eight coalition partners that can even be called a country is Egypt, which is a tyranny, but by the standards of the region a relatively benign tyranny which has a semi-open press. Out of curiosity I checked the press in Egypt the day before this column about the amazing unanimity. The major journal in Egypt, *Al Ahram,* which is sort of like the *New York Times,* basically a government journal, had an article on the U.S. support for Saddam Hussein and bitterly denounced it. It said the U.S. support for the Butcher of Baghdad, what they called the "savage beast," simply shows what Egypt has been alleging all the time, namely that the U.S. and Britain were in this war for totally cynical purposes having nothing to do with democracy or freedom or anything else. Further, the purpose was to reestablish hegemony over the region, and that they'll work together with the savage beast himself if necessary to suppress any democratic tendency.

That's April 9. April 10 we learn that all the Arab coalition partners are in agreement with us on supporting Saddam Hussein to restore stability. Then you get the smart guys, like Thomas Friedman, the diplomatic correspondent of the *Times,* giving the analysis. To his credit, he was pretty straight about it. What he said is that for the State Department, for which he speaks, the "best of all worlds" would be for military elements in Iraq to take over and restore the "iron fist" that Saddam Hussein had used before, much to the satisfaction of Turkey and Saudi Arabia, and of course the United States. So what he's saying is the best of all worlds is what we had until August 1990, when Saddam Hussein with his iron fist was maintaining stability. True, he was gassing Kurds, and so on, but that didn't stop it from being the best of all worlds. What we want is to return to that. Of course, we'd prefer not to have Saddam Hussein do it, because that would be a little embarrassing. It would be nice if we could find somebody equivalent to impose the iron fist and we'd still have the best of all worlds, crushing any opposition, ensuring stability, integrating it into the U.S. program for the region. A pretty straight account if you pick through what he's saying.

So the media handled this one, too. I was curious to see if they'd be able to rise to the situation, after having built up this huge hysteria about the beast of Baghdad, and suddenly we have to support him while he's wiping out the popular opposition. It was carried off, justified on grounds of our higher morality, our recognition of the need for stability and pragmatism. This whole story, from beginning to end, is an amazing achievement.

In fact, just to add another little fillip, throughout this whole period the Iraqi democratic opposition have been in exile. You can't survive under a regime of the best of all worlds. But they're there, and they're perfectly respectable, bankers in London, architects, quite articulate. They have always been excluded from the media. You can understand why. They have always been opposed to U.S. policy. In fact, their positions have always been pretty much those of the peace movement. Prior to August 1990 they were opposed to George Bush's support for Saddam Hussein. They were rebuffed by Washington, they refused to talk to them when they came here to request support for calls for parliamentary democracy in Iraq. They got cut out of the media. From August through February, they were opposed to the buildup for war. They didn't want to see their country destroyed. They were calling for a political settlement, and even calling for a withdrawal of troops from the region. You could read their reports in the German press, the British press, or in Z magazine. But they were totally blanked out of the American press. I don't know if there was a word about them, in fact. If there was, I couldn't find it.

From January through February, nobody's talking. Afterwards, of course, the Iraqi democratic opposition was in favor of the popular uprisings, openly in favor of them. The media closure, rejecting any voice from that opposition, wasn't one hundred percent, because the *Wall Street Journal* allowed a couple of openings. There were other people who are called Iraqi dissidents who as far as I know are not associated with them. However, the major Iraqi democratic opposition, which is organized and is in London and Germany, was essentially shut out, aside from these few post-war openings in the *Wall Street Journal*. That again is interesting. Here is a significant democratic force, courageous people, human rights activists being rebuffed. What's going on?

More examples of the U.S. rebuffing struggles for democracy can be seen in Kuwait. Right now, Kuwait has been carrying out a pretty brutal repression of all sorts of people. Any non-national Kuwaitis, the so-called *bedun,* who had lived there for generations but have never been given Kuwaiti nationality, the Palestinians, plenty of others. A lot of torture, repression, etc. There's some coverage of it in the press, but of course the most interesting part is what's brought out in an occasional letter to the editor by someone from Human Rights Watch. Namely, that George Bush is openly supporting the repression. Aryeh Neier, the head of the Human Rights Watch, had an article in *The Nation* where he pointed out that Bush's statements condoning the terror are appearing in the front pages of the Kuwaiti national newspapers, saying, even George Bush says it's OK, so let's continue.

DB: *Bush says the war wasn't about democracy, it was about aggression.*

Right. He's more or less saying it's understandable, what the Kuwaitis are doing. When he was asked why he didn't say something about democracy, the White House response was, that would be interference in the internal affairs of another country. They even said that in private letters to the Sheikh he has not mentioned the word democracy because of his concern for non-interference at such a level of delicacy. You can't even suggest the word "democracy" in a private communication.

That's not the way he's dealt with Cuba, Nicaragua, Iraq, Panama, this great believer in non-intervention. Again, the fact that the press can mouth these words without ridicule boggles the mind. Just the other day, in the aftermath of the overthrow of democratically elected government in Haiti, Bush was asked about sanctions. He said you can't impose sanctions because it will hurt the people of Haiti. That was in the last paragraph of the *New York Times* article with no comment. This man is saying you can't impose sanctions because it would hurt the people of Haiti? After his record with regard to sanctions? Cuba's under blockade and embargo. Nicaragua was strangled to death. In Iraq people are dying of hunger and disease. We could go on and on. And this man comes out and says you can't impose sanctions because it would harm the people in the case of a military takeover. And nobody makes a comment. You've got to admire the discipline.

DB: *If the media are indeed so servile and quiescent as you suggest, why then did the Bush administration, during the war period, go to such lengths to control them, to concentrate them in pools, to send monitors with them in the field, to control their movements and to actually censor their reports?*

No system of power is ever satisfied. During the Afghan war in the pre-Gorbachev period, the old Stalinist period, the Soviet high command and the Communist Party were bitterly condemning the media for being unpatriotic, not waving the flag enough, undermining the war effort and feelings at home. There is no degree of servility that will ever suffice for any system of power. I haven't checked, but I'll bet you that if you went back to Goebbels' Ministry of the Interior under the Nazis you'll probably find that they were criticizing the German press for not being patriotic enough. In fact, the press is regarded as adversarial. From the point of view of people in power, that's true. If it doesn't simply sing their praises every minute of the day, that's intolerable.

DB: *Polls show that people strongly supported these controls on the media. It doesn't take a genius to know that there's a palpable public hostility toward the media. How do you account for that?*

The kind of hostility that you have in this country is interesting. There's hostility toward the media, toward Congress, toward just about every institution except one, namely the corporate system. No hostility toward that. That tells you exactly who runs the country. It's perfectly OK to criticize the media, Congressmen, the courts, and the cops. You can say the President's a clown. You can do anything except criticize the actual center of power. You're not even allowed to know that it exists. It's invisible.

It was very striking in the Orwellian terminology that was designed in the 1980s how special interests are talked about, which we've discussed in a previous interview. Just to recap, the Democrats are always being accused of being a party of special interests, meaning labor, women, youth, the elderly, everybody. But if you check back you find one striking omission from special interests: never anything about corporate power, business power. That's not a special interest. That doesn't exist.

The omission seems true of scholarship, too. Some years ago, in the 1970s, there was a very rare academic study of corporations and foreign policy. The person wrote an article, a standard mainstream political scientist, in one of those journals. He started by reviewing standard works looking at this question. He took the two hundred leading works in international affairs and foreign policy to see what they had to say about corporations and foreign policy. He discovered, to his amazement because he was pretty naive, that they avoided the topic. He said 95 percent of the studies never mentioned corporations and foreign policy. Five percent gave it passing mention. There was plenty of talk about women, clergy and foreign policy, but somehow nobody ever talked about corporations and foreign policy. He went on to speculate as to this strange oversight. He concludes that if scholars start looking at corporations and foreign policy they'll probably find that there's some influence there.

That shows the discipline of the scholarly profession. You want to make sure that you never study what's important. It would be much too dangerous. The field of diplomatic history, which is an interesting field, spends an awful lot of time on personalities. I've been in debates about this with radical historians who strongly disagree with what I'm saying here. But in my view the concern about the personal decisions and the personalities of the leadership is about as interesting as discussion of the personalities of the Chairman of the Board of General Motors. Undoubtedly it has some hundredth order effect on the decision being made, but the overwhelming effects are institutional, having to do with the institutional structure in which he's working. Whether George Bush believes what he's saying, or did Ronald Reagan remember this, who was the particular advisor who said this, what did he have for breakfast that morning—yes, these are all hundredth order questions, about as interesting as the personalities of these people, which are not very gripping. But they tell you very little about policy. However, that's the way the academic professions have to work, all the way over to the radical critics for the most part, not entirely, but very far over.

You get it in the general public. If Massachusetts has a serious economic crisis, who do people hate? Take a look at this morning's *Boston Globe*. It talks about the popularity of the governor after his cutback of services. Why? Because he's attacking the people who everyone hates most, namely state employees and the poor. That's who everybody hates. Are they the cause of economic problems? Or is there some other factor involved in what happens in the New England economy besides the poor and state employees? Of course, people hate the media, too. You're allowed to hate them. In fact, you're allowed to hate everyone except the people who don't exist, namely the ones who in fact run the show, the ones who have concentrated decision making power, who make investment decisions, who set the framework within which the government operates, who own the media, control them and set the conditions under which they work. Those institutions you're not allowed to hate, or even know of their existence.

In fact, part of the propaganda system promotes the idea corporations are comprised of people just like us. There's "us" on the one hand, going from the corporate executive to the honest sober worker to the housewife and so on. That's all us. And then there's "them," the state employees, the poor, the Congress and all these bad guys who are trying to make life tough for us. That's the picture. It is not painted that way by accident. There has been an enormous effort made, probably a billion dollars a year spent on advertising, public relations in the broadest sense, to try to create these images on movies, sitcoms, outright propaganda, scholarship, all framed in these terms, and pretty consciously. People in the public relations industry know what they're doing, and they wouldn't be doing their job if they didn't carry this out.

DB: *Obviously you have a strong background in science. You collect data and information, you analyze it and draw certain conclusions. I think it's the latter where people may disagree with you. But I was interested to see a review of your latest book* Deterring Democracy *in the October, 1991* Progressive *by its publisher, Matthew Rothschild. Ostensibly someone who's favorably inclined toward your views, he was critical. Joshua Cohen and Joel Rogers in a* New Left Review *(May/June 1991) article about you also found your theories rather weak when it comes to the specific area of the media. Rothschild goes to the extent of suggesting that you have a conspiracy theory about the media.*

In the book you mention, there is very little talk about the way the media work. There's just discussion of examples. Elsewhere I have talked about why they work the way they do, but not in this book. But it's interesting that he would call it a conspiracy theory. Because in fact what I've argued, together with Edward Herman very explicitly, is that there are institutional factors that operate to constrain the way the media function. The criticism by Cohen and Rogers that you mentioned, actually it's the opposite of how you put it. They say I don't go far enough in talking about the institutional factors.

But Rothschild's review is concerned because I *do* discuss the institutional factors and I don't spend enough time on the particular decisions that are made by a particular editor, reporter, government official, etc. In the book in question I just took for granted the institutional factors, which are barely mentioned and which have been discussed elsewhere, although there is one long chapter of the book which is devoted to the ideology behind this, from the seventeenth century right up until today, which is concerned with the reasons why you have to institute propaganda and thought control, in order to marginalize the population. Maybe he would call that a conspiracy theory, but I don't.

But the fact the people move at once to the words "conspiracy theory" is revealing. A conspiracy theory must be something bad. Therefore if somebody's moving to a conspiracy theory it means that something's wrong. On the other hand, if you look at the institutional factors that constrain decisions and at the actual record of thinking about the topic, that tells you too much. So you have to not see that. And in fact Rothschild doesn't see it.

You can imagine what would happen if people reacted to economic analysis this way. Let's go back to the General Motors case. Some economist is talking about General Motors's decisions. He talks about the general concern for increasing market share and profits, what happens if you build this kind of car and not that kind of car, concern over costs, etc. Suppose somebody came back and said, that's a conspiracy theory, because you didn't interview the executive to find out what happened in the director's meeting on such and such a day, who said this, etc. That would be a joke.

There are major factors having to do with the way the systems function which overwhelmingly determine the way the media are going to work. I've discussed them elsewhere. Cohen and Rogers, in their critique, say I don't go far enough in that direction, which could be right.

DB: *How do you filter poll data? I know in your public talks when you cite polls you always add a word of caution. What advice would you have for someone using poll data?*

Contrary to a lot of critics, I don't think poll data is faked. I think it's quite accurate, within the limits of possibilities. You have to look carefully at what question was asked. You can get quite different results by just slightly changing the nature of the question. That's why you have to look with caution. In the polls around mid-

January which asked people about a negotiated settlement of the Iraq withdrawal, it was important to notice that the poll question started: the President is opposed to this. What do you think? Once a question is asked that way, you know that there's already a large bias introduced, because there's going to be a strong tendency to support the President in times of crisis. So you have to factor that out. Poll results are interesting, but you want to check them carefully and look at how they're asked, what the backgrounds are, what the framework is within which they're asked, etc.

Let me give you another example. A lot of people on the left cited polls during the 1980s saying that the population was very strongly opposed to support for the *contras*. It wasn't false, but it was misleading, because much of the population didn't even know which side we were on. What the population was largely opposed to was support for anybody. Why should we support groups? That's not relevant to this issue, and that factor has to be separated out before you use material like that.

DB: *Over the years you've been subjected to a number of personal attacks. I don't want you to go into a detailed response because you have done that elsewhere. But I'm curious about your perception and understanding of the nature and character of these attacks. What motivates them? Why do they persist? I'll just give you two examples. On March 16, 1991 you spoke for KPFA and the Middle East Children's Alliance in Berkeley. This prompted a letter from seventeen UC Berkeley academics who condemned you and called you "a defender of the PLO, even when it was carrying out murder missions against Jewish children." You also have the current case of a national bestseller, Alan Dershowitz's* Chutzpah. *In various passages, he calls you an "anti-Zionist zealot, anti-Israel, anti-American, and anti-Western." Did he leave anything out?*

I didn't read it so I can't tell.

DB: *But what about these attacks? How do you respond? How can you respond?*

You really can't. There's no way to respond. Slinging mud always works. Again, it's partly institutional, but in this case partly personal, too. In the case of the Berkeley professors, the letter came out about six weeks after I was there, and it was a letter, remember, to bookstores, saying that they should not allow this stuff to be heard. I've also been told, although I'm not certain, that there was an attempt to get them to withdraw my books from the stores. I think that's very understandable and I appreciate it. These are people who know perfectly well that they don't like what I say. They know that they don't have either the competence or the knowledge to respond, so the only thing to do is to somehow shut it up, prevent it from being heard because you can't respond to it. Therefore you say I supported the PLO, etc. Most of them probably don't know what I said about anything. But the author of the letter, Robert Alter, knows perfectly well that I condemned the PLO for those atrocities, probably more harshly, certainly more knowledgeably then he did. But that doesn't matter. Facts are irrelevant.

Turning to Dershowitz, there's partly the same story. Again, he knows that he can't respond to what I say. He doesn't have the knowledge or the competence to deal with the issues. Therefore, the idea is to try to shut it up by throwing as much slime as you can. There's a famous story attributed to Sam Ervin, a conservative Senator, who once said that as a young lawyer he had learned that if the law is against you, concentrate on the facts. If the facts are against you, concentrate on the law. And if both the facts and the law are against you, denounce your opposing counsel. Dershowitz is not very bright, but he understands that much. If you can't answer on the facts and if you can't answer on the principles, you better throw dirt. In his case there happens to also be a personal reason.

He's been on a personal *jihad* for the last twenty years, ever since I exposed him for lying outright in a vicious personal attack on a leading Israeli civil libertarian. Despite pretenses, he's strongly opposed to civil liberties. Using his position as a Harvard law professor, he referred to what the Israeli courts had determined. But he was just lying flat outright. This was in the *Boston Globe* [April 29, 1973]. I wrote a short letter refuting it [May 17]. He then came back [on May 25,] accusing everybody of lying and challenging me to quote from the court records. He never believed I had them, but of course I did. I quoted the court records in response [June 5]. He then tried to brazen it out again. It finally ended up with my sending the transcript of the court records to the *Globe* ombudsman, who didn't know what to do any more with people just taking opposite positions. I translated them for him, and suggested that he pick his own expert to check the translations. The ombudsman finally told Dershowitz they wouldn't publish any more letters of his because he had been caught flat out lying about it.

Ever since then he's been trying to get even, so there's just one hysterical outburst after another. That's not surprising, either. He's basically a clown. In that case there's a personal issue overlaying the political issue, which is much more interesting. This personal stuff is not interesting. But if you look at the Anti-Defamation League or the Berkeley professors, and there are plenty of others, it's the Sam Ervin story. You know you can't deal with the material. Either you ignore it, or if you can't ignore it, then defame the speaker. That's the only way you can deal with it if you don't have the brains or the knowledge or you just know your position can't be defended. I think that's understandable, and in a sense you can appreciate it. That's just the hallmark of the commissar.

DB: *The three themes that characterize these attacks on you*

are your support for the PLO and its terror and your apologia for
Nazi and Khmer Rouge genocide.

They're all fabricated. In the case of the support for
the PLO, I've been a bitter critic of the PLO. There's no
doubt about this. In the case of the Khmer Rouge, I've
rarely said anything alone, but Ed Herman and I, who
wrote about this several times, not only condemned their
atrocities but said that they were comparable, made a big
point of comparing them to the Indonesian slaughter in
Timor, which is the worst massacre relative to the population since the Holocaust. What people are upset about
is that we said: let's tell the truth about both of these.

The reactions have been interesting. On the Timor
side of the analogy, total silence, because that was U.S.
supported. On the Khmer Rouge side, there's a claim that
we supported the atrocities when we said we should tell
the truth about them instead of lying about them in the
service of the state.

The Faurisson case is also interesting [over which it
has been alleged that I supported the position that Nazi
gas chambers did not exist]. My position on this has been
articulated way back before this incident with him ever
happened. In fact the introduction to my first book, *Amer-*
ican Power and the New Mandarins, talks about this years
before any of this ever came out. It discusses Nazi apolo-
gists and people who deny the Nazi crimes and points out
that even to enter into discussion with such people, even
to enter into the arena of debate, is to lose your humanity,
although sometimes you have to do it. This issue of Faurisson is a case in which a fascist law was applied, namely,
a person was punished for falsification of history. That's
standard Stalinist, fascist doctrine, and I happen to oppose Stalinism and fascism, on this issue as on many
others. So just as I support the right of American war
criminals to teach in American universities, even at the
time when their research is being used for war crimes, I

support the right of people to say whatever horrendous thing they like, even if one doesn't like it.

So for example, if the Journal of the American Jewish Congress publishes, as it recently did, an article claiming that the Nazi genocide of the gypsies is an exploded fiction, I don't say that the American Jewish Congress's editors should be brought to court for Nazi apologetics and for denying an act of genocide which was in fact quite comparable to the Holocaust. If they want to publish their disgraceful lies, they should have the right to do so. If they were brought to court, I would defend their right to say what they want. People who are opposed to freedom of speech, or who have their own motives for trying to silence critics, will naturally turn this into whatever they want to.

DB: *Ed Herman has suggested that these attacks on you and the persistence of the criticism is in fact a tribute to your effectiveness, and that's why it's going on.*

I think that's reasonable. Incidentally, it went on long before this. From the first time I opened my mouth the attacks started.

DB: *On Indochina?*

Yes. It starts right in 1969. Let me give you an example. In the first book that I wrote, *American Power and the New Mandarins,* in the first edition there's a slight error, namely I attributed a quote to Truman which was in fact a very close paraphrase, almost verbatim paraphrase of what he said in a secondary source. I got a note mixed up and instead of citing the secondary source I cited Truman. It was corrected within about two months, in the second printing. There isn't a scholarly monograph that doesn't have a similar error somewhere. There have been at least a dozen articles, if not more, using this to denounce me, to prove that you can't believe anything that's said by anybody on the left, etc. These are very desperate people. A commissar culture is a very desperate culture. They know they cannot withstand criticism, and therefore you've got to silence it.

It doesn't just have to do with me. Let's take this current attack on so-called political correctness. The real story is what I mentioned before, about the academic studies of corporations and foreign policy. There is almost total control, iron, rigid control, over curriculum and thought to a remarkable degree on the part of the commissar culture. But since the 1960s, there have been a couple of breaks. A few things have opened up. For example, you can no longer be openly racist and sexist, no longer talk about the discovery of America as the most magnificent thing that ever happened to the human race, etc. There are various constraints on that. The commissars are very upset about it. The idea that there might be independent thought somewhere, that's very dangerous. Therefore a huge attack has been launched on the left fascists who are taking over the university and the culture. There's a hundred articles talking about how we used to have this free country and free universities, but now it's being run by left-fascist monsters. When you read hundreds of attacks of them and virtually no defenses, you have to wonder: Since the left fascists now run the place, how come they're being denounced a hundred to one?

Another interesting thing about that attack is that they're always called "left fascists." Suppose we accept the whole story. When George Bush gave a speech at the University of Michigan denouncing the people who were silencing everyone with intimidation because of alleged racist and sexist remarks, he called them "the left." Everybody calls them "the left." Why? The assumption is that if anybody's anti-racist and anti-sexist and in favor of respect for other cultures, they must be on the left and therefore we must be against them. That itself is an interesting assumption. But it all fits together.

The point is that the people who have authority and privilege are naturally terrified of any break in it. In the 1960s, when students started asking questions instead of just taking notes, the faculty acted as if the universities were being burned. Libraries were being burned all over the country because a student asked a question. It's a natural reaction on the part of people who are used to 100 percent obedience. It's like, to go back to something we talked about before, the Soviet high command and the Russian Communist Party denouncing the Soviet media for their lack of patriotism. From the point of view of power, no degree of subordination ever suffices. If anything can't be totally disregarded, you are going to launch a big campaign to destroy it because it just might be heard.

Again, very interesting differences between democratic and totalitarian societies in this respect. They behave quite differently. For example, in the Soviet Union, pre-Gorbachev, the *samizdat,* the underground journals, had extremely wide circulation. There are some estimates that they may have reached almost half of the more educated population. In a democratic society, you'd never permit that. You can read *Z* magazine or listen to your program, but if you reach .01 percent of the population, that's considered dangerous. In a totalitarian state you can reach 50 percent and they don't care very much. It wouldn't have been that much trouble to shut down the *samizdat.* It just wasn't worth it. As long as you have people controlled by force, the assumption is that you don't care much what they think.

DB: *You told Bill Moyers in an interview that given a chance you would do some things differently. I was wondering if you were thinking about the Faurisson affair?*

No, what I was thinking about there was in fact what I told him. In the case of the Indochina war, which is the main one, I started much too late. I didn't get involved in that in a serious way until 1964. I'd say the same about many other things. Take the Timor atrocities. I didn't write about them until late 1978. They had been going on for three years already. There are plenty of things like that. And yes, there are a lot of things like that that I would have done differently if I had thought about it. I'm sure that there are others right now that I'll think about later.

DB: *You wouldn't include that letter you wrote to Serge Thion, defending free speech even in the most loathsome circumstances? That is, what he later used, without your knowledge and permission, as an avis to Faurisson's pretrial Mémoire en défense, when he was tried for "falsification of history," after publishing arguments that the gas chambers did not exist.*

If you ask me, should I have done it, I'll answer, yes. In retrospect, would it have been better not to do it, maybe. Only in the sense that it would have given less opportunity for people of the Dershowitz variety, who are very much committed to preventing free speech on the Arab-Israel issues, and free interchange of ideas. I don't know. You could say on tactical grounds maybe yes, but that's not the way to proceed, in my view. You should do what you think is right and not what's going to be tactically useful.

DB: *You have said often that every American President since the end of World War II could be considered a war criminal under the Nuremberg principles.*

Every one of them, without exception, has been involved either directly or indirectly in atrocities and war crimes. Take Carter, who was the least violent of them. Nevertheless, it was the Carter administration which gave the crucial, decisive military and diplomatic support for the Indonesian slaughter in East Timor, still going on, incidentally, which may have wiped out something like a quarter of the population. That's not the only case. The

Carter administration supported Somoza, contrary to a lot of claims, right up to the end, until they realized that they couldn't hang on to him any longer. At the very end, after Somoza's National Guard had slaughtered about 40,000 people, the Carter administration was trying to figure out how to save the National Guard, even if they couldn't save Somoza. When they couldn't save the National Guard, they spirited them out of the country in planes with Red Cross markings, which is a war crime in itself, in order to set them up elsewhere. This is the best of administrations. About Reagan and Bush we don't even have to talk. But all the way back, this is the way it's been.

DB: *What about Bakunin's "instinct for freedom"? You've written that you'd "like to believe that people have this instinct for freedom, that they want to control their own affairs, they don't want to be pushed around, ordered, oppressed, etc. They want a chance to do things that make sense, like constructive work, in a way they can control and control with others." Then you write, "I don't know any way to prove this. It's really a hope about what human beings are like, a hope that if social structures change sufficiently, those aspects of human nature will be realized."*

There is no way to prove it or disprove it. We don't know anything about human nature. If we're rational we know that it exists and undoubtedly there are very powerful biological constraints on the way we think, what we do, what we conceptualize, what we imagine and our fears and hopes, etc. But about what they are, you can learn more from a novel than you can from the sciences. You operate on the basis of your hopes. I think no one has ever said it better than Gramsci in his famous comment that "you should have pessimism of the intellect and optimism of the will." That's the only reasonable strategy.

DB: *You sometimes close your lectures with reference to what you call Pascal's wager.*

Pascal raised the question: How do you know whether God exists? He said, if I assume that he exists and he does, I'll make out OK. If he doesn't, I won't lose anything. If he does exist and I assume he doesn't, I may be in trouble. That's basically the logic. On this issue of human freedom, if you assume that there's no hope, you guarantee that there will be no hope. If you assume that there is an instinct for freedom, there are opportunities to change things, etc., there's a chance you may contribute to making a better world. That's your choice.

Pearl Harbor

November 16, 1991

DB: *Alexander Cockburn likes to tell the joke that the two greatest disasters that befell U.S. power in the twentieth century were the Japanese attack on Pearl Harbor and your birthday, both on December 7. About the Pearl Harbor attack: you have a kind of non-traditional view of the events leading up to that.*

I wrote about it a long time ago, in the 1960s. What I think is not very far from what is actually in the scholarly literature. First of all, let's be clear about what happened. It's not quite the official picture. About an hour before Pearl Harbor Japan attacked Malaya. That was a real invasion. The attack on Pearl Harbor was the colony, the military base on a colony of the United States. An act of aggression, but on the scale of atrocities, attacking the military base on the colony is not the highest rank. The big Japanese atrocities in fact had already taken place. There were plenty more to come, but the major ones, the invasion of China, the rape of Nanking, the atrocities in Manchuria, and so on, had passed. Throughout that whole period the U.S. wasn't supportive, but it didn't oppose them very much.

The big issue for the United States was will they let us in on the exploitation of China or will they do it by themselves? Will they close it off? Will they create a closed co-prosperity sphere or an open region in which we will have free access? If the latter, the United States was not going to oppose the Japanese conquest.

There were other things going on in the background. By the 1920s, which was of course the period when Britain was still the dominant world power, Britain had found that they were unable to compete with Japanese manu-

facturers. Japanese textiles were outproducing Lanca-
shire mills. As soon as that became evident, Britain
dropped its fancy rhetoric about the magnificence of free
trade. Nobody supports free trade unless they think
they're going to win the competition. Britain hadn't supported it before it had won the industrial game, and it was
now going to withdraw its support. In 1932 there was an
important conference in Ottawa, still the British Empire
then, remember. There was an empire conference and
they basically decided in effect to close off the empire to
Japanese exports. They raised the tariff 25 percent, or
something absurd. This in effect closed off India, Australia
and Burma and other parts of the British Empire.

Meanwhile the Dutch had done the same thing. This
is the 1930s. The Dutch had done the same with Indonesia, the Dutch East Indies. The United States, which was
a smaller imperial power at that time, had also done the
same with the Philippines and Cuba. The Japanese
imperialists' story was they were being subjected to what
they called A, B, C, D encirclement: America, Britain,
China, which was not being penetrated properly, and the
Dutch.

There was some truth to that. The Japanese idea
was: they're just denying us our place in the sun. They've
already conquered what they wanted, and now when we're
trying to get into the act as latecomers, they're closing off
their imperial systems so we can't compete with them
freely. That being the case, we'll go to war.

It didn't happen like that mechanically. The invasion
of Manchuria preceded the Ottawa conference, but these
things were going on. There was an interaction of that sort
which continued up until 1941. The Japanese were being
constrained by the imperial powers. They were carrying
out more aggression to create for themselves a domain
that they would control. That aggression led to more
retaliation from the imperial powers. Things got pretty
tight.

At the end there were negotiations between the United States and Japan with Cordell Hull, Secretary of State, and Admiral Nomura. They went on until very shortly before Pearl Harbor, and the issue was always basically the same: will Japan open up its imperial system to U.S. penetration? At the very end they actually made some kind of an offer to do that, but they insisted on a quid pro quo, namely, that the United States reciprocate. That led to a very sharp response from the Americans. They're not going to be told anything by these little yellow bastards, is what it came to. Shortly after came Pearl Harbor.

There is a complicated interaction throughout the Pacific War. Had the Japanese not been so murderous and near genocidal in their conquest of Asia, they might have had more Asian support. They did gain a lot of support in the countries that they invaded, like Indonesia. A lot of the Asian nationalists supported them. It was only when they showed themselves to be so utterly brutal that they lost most but not all of that support. They were regarded in essence as liberators, getting rid of the white man who'd been on our neck forever. So it's a complicated story.

In fact, it's even more complicated. I remember that in the late 1960s the Rand Corporation had just published translations of Japanese counterinsurgency manuals that they had used in trying to suppress Manchuria. I compared them with the counterinsurgency manuals that the United States was then putting out, and the practices as well, in South Vietnam. They were remarkably similar. There are things that don't change much.

At the time I was kind of skeptical about World War II. I used to go down to the Philadelphia Public Library which had a big collection of all sorts of weird radical journals and read stuff which had all sorts of interpretations of what was going on, from it being a phony war run by—I don't want to make any insults, but you'll guess who I'm talking about. In those days they were around, too.

There was a conspiracy between the Bolshevik ruling class and the Western ruling class to destroy the European proletariat and that was what the war was really all about, and other theories. Some of the theories were kind of nutty, but not totally nutty. They had aspects like comparable stuff today that were not without some insight.

As the liberation of Europe began you could see what was happening. So in 1943 the Americans restored fascist sympathizers in Italy. In 1944, in particular, when the British came into Greece, there was no mistaking what was going on. By December 1944 even somebody who was just reading the newspapers could see that they were destroying the resistance. The people who fought the Nazis the British are now destroying, so they were replacing the Nazis. So we go.

That attitude of mine at that time was colored by the Zionism. Here's the British imperialists, the British lion, perfidious albion, look what they're doing to the Jews in Palestine, to the Greeks. It was hard not to have that association when you're a fifteen-year-old Zionist activist. I wouldn't claim I understood anything that was happening, but you could see things. In 1945-46 Dwight MacDonald's *Politics* came out, which was a real eye opener. That's classic stuff.

DB: *Were you reading it then?*

I read it maybe a year or so later, probably 1946-47, when I was a college student. That had a tremendous impact. I don't know what I'd think about it if I read it now, but at the time it had an enormous impact. He was a marvelous writer, very evocative, and he exposed lots of hypocrisy. Some of the stuff I read I'll never forget. For example, I remember one very pompous liberal writer named Max Lerner. MacDonald, who was very anti-fascist—nobody exceeded him in anti-fascism—described something that happened, whether he was there or heard about it I don't know. It was in Germany. Apparently Max Lerner was going along with the American forces. They came across a group of refugees, starving women with knapsacks on their back, German refugees trudging along the road, looking for some place to survive. MacDonald describes how Lerner got down from his jeep and started to interrogate these women about their war guilt. It was very incisive, it captured very dramatically a lot of the hypocrisy and self righteousness of the conqueror-liberators. It raised lots of questions. That was true of all of his writings. One of the things there was the responsibility of intellectuals thing which I later picked up.

DB: *You are invariably asked in lectures and interviews to draw connections between your work in linguistics and your politics. I'm not going to ask you that question.*

Thanks [chuckles].

DB: *But what's really interesting is why the question is asked.*

That is an interesting question. The question is continually asked. What's more, there are also answers given to it by everybody except me. There are also some sensible answers. But it's not because of the sensible answers that the question is being asked. I think there are two reasons. One reason is that there's an assumption that you can't just be a human being. You can't be interested in genocide because you don't like genocide. It must be coming out of something else.

There's also an assumption that unless you're a professional expert on something, you can't be talking about it. So there are any number of reviews, including favorable reviews, I should say, reviews from activists on the left will review a book of mine and say, oh, my god, this propaganda analysis is fantastic, because he can use

linguistics to deconstruct ideology or something like that.
I don't even know what the word "deconstruct" means, let
alone how to use it.

You sat in on my class two days ago. You can see the
connection between that and writing about ideology. I
might as well be doing algebraic topology for all that has
to do with ideology. But people have to see some connection. It must be that I can do this because I'm a professional linguist. And the implication is, you can't do it if
you're not a linguist. That's the bottom line. It's telling
people tacitly, you can't do it. You can't think about the
world. You can't understand the world. You can maybe
have feelings, but leave it to the experts. Here's this guy
who's a professional linguist, he can talk about ideology.
If you go to the political science department, they'll explain to you about politics, but you, the ordinary people,
you're totally incapable. I'm not suggesting that the people
who write the favorable reviews would accept this position. In fact they reject it strongly, I'm sure. But I think
hidden underneath there, it's there. Otherwise why
should anybody look at anything I write and say I'm
deconstructing ideology, whatever that is supposed to
mean, because of my professional expertise as a linguist?

DB: *The Commander in Chief in New York on November
12, 1991 said the Congress is "pushing the same old tired liberal
agenda to a country that is hungry to build on what we've done
abroad and bring that success at home." There indeed seems to be
an increasing hunger in the U.S., but it's not of the variety that
Bush is suggesting. A record number of Americans, almost one in
ten, now rely on food stamps to put food on the table. You've
written about the great success in Iraq. Of course that's an ongoing
triumph. Perhaps you could review some other areas, such as
Grenada, Panama, Nicaragua and East Timor?*

Iraq was a disaster from the point of view of any
values that were professed. Of course, it was a disaster

from the point of view of the actual policy. You could say the same about the others. East Timor is timely. Today is November 16, and two or three days ago there was another massacre there in which journalist Allan Nairn was beaten up badly. There was a little flurry of interest. But East Timor has been the scene of a virtually genocidal takeover by the Indonesian army. It didn't just happen. It happened because of direct and critical and decisive U.S. support running through every administration since the Ford administration and particularly the Carter administration, which poured in aid, barred U.N. intervention, did everything to ensure that the Indonesians would be able to take the place over and in the course of it kill nobody knows how many people, 100,000, 200,000 people out of a population of 700,000. So it continues. The fighting and the atrocities continue, the repression continues, the American aid continues. We're not alone. British Aerospace is one of the contractors for Indonesia. The Dutch have helped, as have the Swedes. Canada is a major supporter because it's a big investor in Indonesia. The U.S. is way on top because of its size. We can outlend Canada. But essentially anybody who can make a buck was in there.

One of the most grotesque cases is Australia. Australia has a special relation to Timor. There were Australian guerrillas fighting the Japanese in Timor, a couple hundred of them during the Second World War. The Timorese lost maybe 40,000 lives helping defend a couple hundred Australian commandos who were cut off there. In return for this favor the Australians have supported the invasion from the outset. They have now, right in the middle of the Gulf War, been bringing to conclusion a treaty with Indonesia to exploit Timorese oil in the Timor Gap between Timor and Australia. It was a little rough to put forth while we were screaming about Iraq and Kuwait, like Libya making a deal with Iraq to exploit Kuwaiti oil. When this question was raised, the foreign minister, who is dying to get a Nobel Peace Prize for helping broker the Cambodia thing, a very pompous and foolish guy, made some speeches in Parliament about how there's no legal requirement not to accept acquisition by force. He said the world is an unfair place littered with examples of acquisition by force. That's when it's Timor and Indonesia. Of course, if it's Iraq and Kuwait we have to stand up and make sure that small countries etc. All of this in the same breath, practically. So it is around the world. That's Timor. It's a monstrous disaster. There's going to be a little flurry of rhetorical concern after the latest massacre, but it'll go nowhere. Indonesia is a rich powerful country that opened itself up to Western exploitation after Suharto came into power, killing maybe half a million people. Therefore he's a moderate and at heart benign, as the *Economist* put it, basically a good guy, and if he wants to conquer another country and wipe out a quarter of the population, it's none of our business.

What about Grenada? Grenada was going to be liberated. It's actually one thing that's been successful in Grenada. It's now one of the leading places for offshore banking, like laundering drug money. There are no legal constraints and everything is wide open. So it's a major center of criminal activities carried out by the major banks. They may not have any facility there other than a fax machine, but that's the location, and it's part of the whole international drug trade and criminal syndicate trade. Unemployment's going up. Nothing's developing. There's a little bit of tourism. They can shine shoes for whitey like they're supposed to be doing, but that's about it.

Panama is back in the hands of the roughly 10 percent wealthy European elite that used to run it before the Torrijos populist military dictatorship, which is what the U.S. wanted. The banks are back in. Money laundering is up. Drug peddling is up by a lot. Unemployment is up.

Nicaragua is a basket case. It's so horrible, probably the poorest country, poorer than Honduras now. Probably the poorest country in the hemisphere next to maybe Haiti. We can run down the list. Every foreign policy triumph is a total catastrophe from the point of view of the people there. But that doesn't matter, because it only has to be a triumph on the front pages of the U.S. newspapers in order to serve its function. That function is actually dual. First, to make sure that the world is under control. Second, to make sure that the American population is not paying attention to what you pointed out at the beginning, the fact that the society is collapsing around them. They don't want people to pay attention to that, so therefore you need triumphs. You obviously can't have domestic triumphs. That's even beyond the imagination of the commissars. So you have foreign policy triumphs. That's what you need a press corps for, an intelligentsia to turn these catastrophes into foreign policy triumphs. First you terrify the population about a foreign enemy and then you stand in awe of the magnificence of your leader, who saved you in the nick of time. We do this every two years or so. We're doing it again right now, with Libya.

DB: *What do you know about the situation in West Papau (Irian Jaya)?*

That's a real horror story as well. There's not much material on it. It was more or less given to Indonesia. It was part of the Dutch Empire, but unlike East Timor, which wasn't, the people of Irian Jaya wanted independence, of course. There are only about a million people, they're called tribal, meaning indigenous people. It's West Papua. There was a sort of a deal during the Kennedy years with Sukarno, before Suharto took over. By 1969 there was a transfer, authorized by the international community. They were transferring this area that's now Irian Jaya over to a real genocidal regime who was going to destroy it. But the West wanted that, because there are resources there. There would be a way to develop them if Indonesia takes over, because they just want to rob the place and help the West rob the place. So they moved in and there was a fair amount of killing and repression and transmigration schemes, which countries like Canada are involved in. They describe them as great humanitarian efforts. Java's overpopulated, so Canada, out of its benevolence, will develop new areas in Papau and help bring the Javanese peasants over there.

Meanwhile, you eliminate the natives and you can guess what happens. Exactly what's gone on in there nobody knows for sure. There are estimates of dead running from thousands to maybe 300,000. There apparently was use of chemical warfare. The London Anti-Slavery Society has just come out with a pamphlet about it, and there have been a couple of studies, mostly by the Australians. There is one anthropologist, George Monbiot, who traveled through there a while ago and wrote an interesting book.

But it's just the destruction of an indigenous society by a Third World semi-fascist state strongly supported by the West because Indonesia is oriented toward allowing us to exploit resources. So it's another atrocity story, one that nobody talks about.

DB: *You've talked about the internal crisis in the U.S. playing itself out in very destructive ways and the widespread random violence: a postal worker who runs amok in Michigan; yesterday a student goes berserk in Iowa; and two weeks ago it was a massacre in Texas. Is there any connection between official U.S. violence internationally and what's going on domestically?*

There have been some studies of that, and I have not seen details, so I hesitate to talk about it. But the studies claim to show a correlation between international violence and domestic violence. Whether that's true or not I'm not certain. There is also so much imaginary violence, just turn on a television set at random and chances are you'll watch a murder or some woman getting her throat slit. There are some people like George Gerbner, who's dean of the Annenberg School who's done studies on violence in children's TV. It's just mind boggling. Kids are watching the most atrocious, sadistic murders constantly. A kid will see dozens of murders a week, or maybe in a day. International violence just adds to the sense that you kill. And so does ordinary life. What is there around? In downtown Boston, for example, it's become a badge of honor for a teenaged kid to have a bullet wound, kind of like a dueling scar in aristocratic German circles. If you don't have a bullet wound you're not a real man. Twelve year olds are coming into school with guns. That's mind boggling.

DB: *I was interested to note that you actually talked about government involvement in drugs in the ghetto. That's usually something you stay away from.*

I said that I wouldn't be surprised. I don't know of any evidence for it. Certainly there are plenty of people in the black community who believe it. There are some things that certainly do raise suspicions. The drug epidemic in the 1960s did play a big role in wiping out communities that were beginning to get organized, mobilized and contribute to this crisis of democracy that the elite was worried about. Maybe it's unrelated and maybe it's not. I don't know.

DB: *You often quip that you've been giving public talks for years with the same title: The Current Crisis in the Middle East. Other than U.S. interests in oil and support for Israel, and those are reasons enough, is there anything under the surface that we're not seeing?*

I think those are the main things we're not seeing. Support for Israel you can't miss, but the way in which this is tied in with control over resources, the kinds of alliances that exist between Israel and the Gulf monarchies or the way in which all of this fits into general American policy, I don't think anybody's seeing much of that. There are other things, of course, but I think that's the core of it. It's not a big secret. Back in the 1940s Saudi Arabia in particular was recognized as strategically the most important area in the world, as Eisenhower called it. It wasn't because they liked the sand.

DB: *In an answer to a question in a prior interview (October 15, 1991), you attributed the lack of interest in and lack of affinity for the Palestinians in the U.S. to "anti-Arab and anti-Muslim racism." Your answer, quite frankly, left me a bit unsatisfied. There's a preponderance or a good number of American Jews in the progressive movement. Do you think that contributes to ambivalence or confusion about the Middle East?*

Oh, yes. I would not be satisfied with that reason either, and you can show that it can't be the whole story, because anti-Arab racism doesn't prevent us from loving the Emir of Kuwait, or the Saudi Arabian royal family. They're just fine. What I should have said is that the endemic anti-Arab racism in the country, which is extraordinary, contributes, makes it easy to carry out the policies of denying rights to the Palestinians, which are pursued for other reasons. For example, the support for Saddam Hussein in his destruction of the Kurds was not anti-Arab racism. Kurds are not Arabs. But it had its motives.

In the case of the Palestinians, at the heart of it, if the Palestinians were sitting on oil or had money and were playing the game the way the U.S. wanted, if they were a powerful military force, or they had high level military technology or oil wealth and were run by a bunch of gangsters who were willing to do whatever the West wants, then anti-Arab racism wouldn't influence our atti-

tude toward the Palestinians. But the Palestinians have
none of those attributes. They don't have wealth, at least
by the standards anybody cares about. They don't have
power. They're a nuisance. They have an unresolved nationalism which stirs up other nationalist sentiments in
the Arab world. They have been displaced in recent history by what from the Arab point of view looks like just
another European invasion. All of that makes them not
only zero in value, but negative in value. They're zero in
value because they contribute nothing to U.S. power or
wealth. They're negative in value because their unsatisfied nationalism is a force for arousing what from the U.S.
point of view are disruptive forces, meaning nationalist or
independence forces throughout the Arab world. Conse-
quently, they are valueless. At that point the anti-Arab
racism moves in and makes it easy to treat them as
valueless.

Anti-Arab racism is no joke. For example, suppose a
correspondent in the *New York Times* said that his advice
to Syria was that they should run Israel the way they run
the Bekaa Valley in Lebanon. That is, take over Israel,
run it the way you run the Bekaa in Lebanon, but give
Hymie a seat in the bus, don't take everything away from
him, maybe he'll lessen his demands. If that happened,
that person would not be elevated to chief diplomatic
correspondent of the *New York Times*. I'm talking about
Thomas Friedman. I've just paraphrased word by word,
except it wasn't give Hymie a seat in the bus, it was give
Ahmed a seat in the bus, and it wasn't Syria taking over
Israel, it was Israel taking over the West Bank and run it
like you run south Lebanon. But the parallel is exact.
Nobody cares here, because if you're a dove you say we
ought to give Ahmed a seat in the bus, like some Arab Nazi
might say maybe we ought to give Hymie a seat in the bus.
But here it's a nice liberal attitude.

DB: *Is it the Nicaragua story all over again? The threat of a* *good example.*

With the Palestinians? I don't think quite.

DB: *Objectively speaking, what threat could a truncated, tiny Palestinian state pose to U.S. power?*

The threat is that Israel would have to withdraw. There are some problems with Israeli withdrawal. Israel's a central component in the U.S. power system there. If Israel withdraws, it can be integrated into the region as undoubtedly its technologically most advanced sector, but it's not going to be an Israeli Sparta. It's going to have to enter into compromises in order to obtain even things like water to drink. Take the water alone. It's all secret, classified material, so nobody really knows the details. But probably Israel uses something on the order of eighty percent of West Bank water. It relies on it. Its own water resources are very limited. There are conceivable alternatives, maybe a deal with Turkey or nuclear desalinization, maybe steal the water from the Litani River in Lebanon. You can imagine other possibilities, but they're limited. Control over West Bank water is very significant.

The same is true of the Golan Heights. The Golan Heights, among other things, is primarily a water source, the headwaters of the Jordan. A substantial part, maybe a quarter of Israel's water comes from that part of the occupied territories alone. That's what the fuss has been about with regard to the Golan Heights, way back to 1948-49. On top of that, what's called Jerusalem, which is now a vastly expanded area, takes over a substantial part of the West Bank, and the suburbs. The areas around it are pleasant suburbs for Tel Aviv and Jerusalem. You live up in the hills, it's cool, you can see the ocean on a nice day, you commute to Tel Aviv. They're not going to give that up unless they're forced to.

The United States doesn't want them to give those

things up because Israel does play a role in U.S. planning. Therefore they have human rights, because they have guns and technology and know how to fight and can help with intelligence matters. They do the kinds of things that are valuable, and therefore they have rights. The U.S. doesn't want them to lose that power. So it's not that a Palestinian state would harm U.S. interests. It's not like Nicaragua. It's not the danger that it might succeed and stir up other nationalist forces in the region who would want to model themselves on its success. I don't think that's the threat. The threat simply is that it would entail Israeli withdrawal.

DB: *So you're still subscribing to the strategic asset theory, that the U.S.'s local cop on the beat is still Israel?*

One of them, as it always has been, or certainly back to the early 1960s. It was thought about in those terms ten or fifteen years earlier. But since the early 1960s at least, Israel has functioned as a basis for U.S. power. Probably the most important period was the 1960s, when Nasserite Egypt was considered, and rightly so, a potentially independent nationalist force in the Arab world and in fact throughout the Third World. This was the period when nonalignment and Bandung meant something and Nasser was a leader. He was stirring up what they called "radical Arab nationalism," anti-Western Arab nationalism, anti-feudal Arab nationalism. There was a proxy war going on between Saudi Arabia, which is the core of U.S. interests, and Nasserite Egypt and the Yemen in those years. Israel was considered a barrier to Nasserite pressures against Saudi Arabia. It's recently been reported by Andrew and Leslie Cockburn in their recent book, *Dangerous Liaison,* that Israel actually even provided troops, probably Yemenite troops to Saudi Arabia. That I can't verify. But U.S. intelligence wrote about the recognition of Israel as a barrier against Nasserite pressures. If you look at the map and the strategic relationships you know that this has got to have been the case. My own assumption is that Saudi Arabia and Israel probably had a kind of tacit alliance which maybe we'll never find out about.

DB: *There was that triangle, Iran-Saudi Arabia-Israel.*

In American scholarship it's called a "two-pillar policy," Iran and Saudi Arabia. But that's because Israel's a holy cow, you are not allowed to talk about it. The fact of the matter is that it was a three pillar policy, with Iran, Israel and Saudi Arabia. Technically, Saudi Arabia was at war with both Iran and Israel. Iran had taken over some islands in the Gulf and there was a big hassle about that. But the fact is that the Iranian military under the Shah was one of the protectors of the Saudi Arabian elite, so there was trouble in Dhofar, down in the southern part of the Arabian peninsula and Iranian counterinsurgency troops would go in there along with Jordanian and British and so on. This system is pretty well understood. It's not a big secret. Israel has been a big part of it and doubtless still is.

DB: *I know about what happened in the 1960s and 1970s. I'm thinking more about the post-Soviet collapse and the Iraq war.*

The Soviet Union had nothing to do with it, it's a red herring. Don't forget, for seventy years, every time you wanted to invade somebody you'd yell about the Soviet Union. That was almost never true. It's true that targets of U.S. attack tended to get Soviet support, but that's about the limit of the truth of that story. Apart from that, appeal to the Soviet threat was just a device to mobilize support for Third World intervention. You can see that very clearly. After the Berlin Wall fell, you can't even pretend there's a Soviet threat any more. When the U.S. invades Panama, where's the Soviet Union? It's interesting that the White House annually puts out a glossy booklet directed to Congress explaining why we need a bigger military than ever in the past, bigger weapons, etc. The one that came out in March 1990, right after the Berlin Wall fell which indicated there's no longer any possible pretense that the Soviet Union is around, was interesting. It differed from the ones in earlier years, because this time the reason we need a bigger military with more missiles—the bottom line is always the same, it's just the reasons that can change—is because of the growing technological sophistication of Third World countries, in particular in the Middle East. This was before the invasion of Kuwait, where they said something like the threat to our interests could not be laid at the Kremlin's door.

Now we can concede it, since it's not useful any more to lay the threat at the Kremlin door, we can concede it's never been there. In fact, the threat has always been exactly the same everywhere, what they call radical nationalism, independence, in other words, which would tend to get supported by the Russians for reasons of state, basically, if nothing else, if they were a target of U.S. attack.

DB: *You've been calling this the "problem of the vanishing pretext."*

I've been talking about this for many years. In my view, the Cold War was basically a North-South confrontation, with a big, strong piece of the South now returning back to its proper status as a Brazil.

DB: *Let me understand something further about Israel in terms of the local cop of the beat. Why didn't police headquarters in Washington call up and say, get in on the attack on Iraq?*

It couldn't possibly work. There was a very tricky thing going on there. You had to bring the Arab dictators into the alliance. The Arab dictatorships, especially the

Gulf tyrannies, which are the only ones that anyone really cares about, they could not possibly maintain control of their own populations if they were in overt alliance with Israel attacking a neighboring Arab country. Most of the Arab world was very strongly opposed to the attack on Iraq, and the tyrannies were having a hard time controlling their own populations. There were huge demonstrations from Morocco all the way to—even Indonesia, way out there. Because of its Muslim population, it was never able to take a public stand in favor of the war. Same in Pakistan. Throughout the whole Third World this was true, but particularly in the Arab world. In the Arab world, if Israel, the arch example of Western colonialism, was taking part in the attack against Iraq, helping destroy the Iraqi people, it would have been extremely hard, even for the best run tyranny, to control its own population. So it was an absolute necessity to keep Israel on the sidelines.

Furthermore, there was nothing they could contribute. The U.S. had such overwhelming power. Israel's a powerful state by regional standards, but when you get the U.S. in there, the major industrial power, the major superpower, with no constraints, no deterrent, no limits on what it can do, to add Israel would just be getting more planes in the way.

DB: *One of your favorite papers in Boston, the Globe, says the Middle East is "littered with American peace plans." Camp David is the one that's always heralded and presented and referred to as the model and paradigm for the Middle East peace process. Anthony Lewis writes about it ad nauseam. Sol Linowitz, the Carter negotiator for Camp David, is quoted about it. You've outlined the process whereby Egypt became a U.S. client state, removing it from the conflict, with the consequences in the occupied territories and Lebanon of undeterred Israeli force. It's been constantly repeated that the Palestinians are being offered now what they were offered at Camp David. It's my understanding that they weren't even present at Camp David.*

They're not present now, either. That's not incorrect. Let me go back to the statement in the *Globe* editorial about being littered with American peace plans. That's true, but it's true by definition. It's not a fact, just a point of logic. The reason is peace plans that aren't American don't count. In fact, the Middle East is littered with all sorts of peace plans, all blocked by the United States, but they're not even part of the record, because a peace plan is something that the U.S. puts forth. There have been a series of U.S. peace plans, that is, efforts to institute the preferred U.S. arrangement for the region. It's not a secret what that is. That means nothing for the Palestinians, no international involvement, just the Monroe Doctrine extending to the Middle East, Israeli power secured, arrangements between the various states of the region, crucially the U.S. allies, the Gulf monarchies, Israel, Turkey. If you could take the tacit arrangement and make it formal, that would be called "peace" in the United States. Anything else isn't peace.

DB: *Sabra Chatrand had a piece in the* New York Times.

She doesn't understand. She's picking up propaganda. This is about the autonomy. If you want to know these things, you read people like Avner Yaniv, Israel's main strategic analyst, or William Quandt, the American from the NSC who was involved in the negotiations. They all recognized the consequences. The consequences were obvious at the time. I haven't yet talked about the Palestinians. The Palestinians were offered autonomy, and people who say that's the same autonomy they're being offered now are correct. You said they weren't represented; that's correct. But they're also not represented now. There are some people whom the U.S. and Israel will allow in, and if they want to sign the capitulation, that will be okay with us. That's what representation means. The autonomy is approximately the same. It's exactly what the U.S. and Israel have always wanted. That's why Begin accepted it. Autonomy means pretty much what they now have and have had, namely, they run their own services. You don't put a cent in for education or welfare or anything else. You can run all that stuff yourself. And we'll take everything we want.

DB: *Pay taxes.*

They pay a lot of taxes. We'll make a lot of money out of your taxes, but we're not going to have any services for you. The Israeli press has pointed out recently that none of the superhawks who talk about taking a greater land of Israel has ever explicitly called for annexation. There are some pretty good reasons for that. If you annex the territory, you've got people there and you've got to extend Israeli law to it. Israeli law treats Palestinian Arabs, who are Israeli citizens, quite shabbily. Nevertheless you've got to recognize their existence. That means that they're going to get pensions and welfare payments if they can't work. That would probably bankrupt the Israeli treasury. So therefore you don't want to annex it. The only question is, how do you control it. One of the techniques is called "autonomy." In fact, a recent article by a good Israeli journalist, Danny Rubenstein, who's not terribly dovish, a very competent journalist, he's covered the West Bank for years and is now writing in *Ha'aretz,* just had a very good article on this. He's not in favor of a Palestinian state. But he said that autonomy means the kind of autonomy you have in a prisoner of war camp. In a prisoner of war camp the prisoners are allowed to cook their own meals, run their own cultural events, the guards leave them alone. That's autonomy. Let's not kid anybody about it. He's probably in favor of it. But he says let's not kid anyone about it.

That's what the U.S. and Israel were in favor of at Camp David and what they're in favor of today. That's essentially the same autonomy. The Sabra Chatrand article you mentioned, actually an interview with Sol Linowitz, the U.S. negotiator, claims that the Palestinians lost a great opportunity. They lost an opportunity to get this, because that's what it amounted to. Whether they should have accepted it, who knows? Maybe they could have built on it. Maybe they should accept it now. You could argue that too. But let's not have any illusions about it. As long as the United States runs the show, unilaterally, it's going to be U.S. principles that dominate. There has been for twenty years nothing for the Palestinians.

DB: *Abba Eban has been quoted as saying the Palestinians "never miss an opportunity to miss an opportunity."*

That's the Israeli racist line. They have never missed an opportunity to submit to our rule. That's about what it amounts to. You can make plenty of critical statements about the Palestinians, but to say they've never missed an opportunity to miss an opportunity is to demonstrate yourself to be a racist. Their position of power has been such that to join in with the U.S.-Israeli run initiatives would mean essentially to sign on the dotted line and say, okay, we capitulate. Which is what Abba Eban wants. He does not want Palestinian self-determination. He might accept it as a last resort if domination is too costly to Israel, but his position always has been that of the Labor Party. Israel should essentially take what it wants and not take control of the population. That's the opportunity that the Palestinians have missed.

DB: *On September 12, 1991 Bush was talking about the ten billion dollar loan guarantee to resettle Soviet Jews in Israel. He spoke about "powerful political interests" at work in Washington and then he presented himself as "one little guy against a thousand." Who is his audience for these comments?*

The American people. He's just trying to stir up a

little anti-Jewish racism.

DB: *Did he succeed?*

Yes, I think so. With a flick of the eyebrow he was able to send the lobby packing. I've always felt myself that the power of the lobby has been vastly exaggerated. That's not the way things work in the United States. The only lobbies that are really effective in the United States independent of anything else are business lobbies, but then they're just lobbying their own representatives in government. That's not the way American pluralism works. Other lobbies are effective under one of two conditions: either they're dealing with issues that don't matter much for state corporate interests, like the gun lobby. If you're interested in corporate or state power, it doesn't matter a lot if people have assault rifles and go around shooting each other. So therefore the gun lobby can be effective. Or lobbies that are involved in stirring up jingoist things can be effective, or lobbies that line up with significant sectors of real power, as the Israeli lobby has been. If AIPAC is lobbying for something that the executive or powerful elements in the executive want or favor, or major sectors of military industry want to do anyway, they will be effective. Apart from that, the chances that they'll be effective are pretty slight.

This is oversimplified. There has been a big effect of the Israeli lobby on the educated classes. Since 1967 the educated classes in the United States have had an absolute love affair with Israel. They just loved the fact that they could smash up those Third World people and put them in their place. So you had this enormous love affair going, for all kinds of complicated reasons. That meant that they got a very favorable press and there was not the kind of discussion of these issues that you have in Europe or, for that matter, in Israel itself. That's not insignificant, and you might even argue that it's been a swing factor in elite power. It's possible. But if the Israeli lobby comes up against some relatively unified state-corporate power, it's going to dissolve very fast.

Bush made some in my view quite disgusting remarks of the kind you quoted which were presumably designed by his PR agents to stir up a little bit of anti-Semitism, which is not very hard. It's pretty easy, in fact. If you wanted to really stir up anti-Semitism, he could do it very easily. If he can't figure it out I'll tell him. But they know. But it was just a little bit, a lonely little guy facing these powerful interests, rich Jews, and that was enough to send them home. Notice that the issue was an extremely narrow one: do we give them their ten billion dollar loan guarantee today or four months from now? From Bush's point of view it was not narrow. Why did Israel want the guarantees in September and not in January? Because they wanted to undermine the Madrid conference. They knew that if the U.S. came across with the loan guarantees in September, that would make it very hard for the Arab states to participate. The same reason why Israel applauded the August coup in the Soviet Union. They were hoping maybe this would kill the Madrid conference. The Israeli government didn't want that conference. But Bush very much wanted the conference, and therefore on this narrow technical issue of when do we give them the loan guarantee he was willing to send the lobby packing, which was not very difficult.

DB: *I want to talk about the media. In your view, is the myth of this adversarial relationship between the media and corporate power still intact?*

The myth is intact and will remain intact. It's just too valuable to lose.

DB: *Even though there's been a slew of books, including—*

These books don't exist. If you want to look at what

actually exists, I just got a study put out by the Kennedy School on the media in foreign policy. The only questions that are allowed focus on: are the media too adversarial? So did Peter Arnett [who stayed in Iraq at the beginning of the bombing] cross the line? That's the issue that you raise. Sure, there's a critical literature, but it's not supportive of power, therefore it doesn't exist. You could prove with the certainty of quantum physics that the media are an agency of propaganda for state-corporate interests, and it wouldn't make the slightest bit of difference. It's the wrong proof. That's all.

DB: *You told me that this literature is useful in terms of arming—*

It helps organize people. It's not going to penetrate the Kennedy School. How could it? But it's like Witness for Peace. If they come back with information about Central America, it's not going to affect the academic world or the newspapers, but it will affect solidarity groups.

DB: *What would be an effective media strategy? Would you suggest trying to get articles and information into the mainstream media or create genuine independent alternatives, or both?*

Both. No institution is independent of what's happening in the greater society. As there is more ferment in the larger society, there will be more ferment in the media and openness will develop that wasn't there before. There will be limits. If it goes to the point of really threatening power, there will be a limit. But you can push those limits pretty hard, and there are people who do it. It's very fine to do. More pressure on the media would give them more opportunities to do it.

At the same time, alternative media is a demeaning term, but independent media, as Jeff Cohen and others call it, I think it's the right term, which are not part of the state-corporate nexus, can offer lots of opportunities.

Their very existence has an effect on opening the media. If you can't ignore them they become competitive. Also, they just offer options, they democratize the country, which is always a good thing.

DB: *There is an undercurrent of conspiracy theories about in the land, and I know that you are asked about them, ranging from who killed JFK to the October Surprise to BCCI-CIA, S&L, banking scandals, etc. The purveyors of some of these theories are people like Craig Hulet, Bo Gritz, Fletcher Prouty, Dave Emery, the Christic Institute and others. Chip Berlet and Sara Diamond have both documented cases where progressive groups and radio stations have actually promoted some of this information. What's your take on these conspiracy theories? It's a little cottage industry now.*

It's not a little one. It's been a big one for a long time, and it drains tons of money from left movements. There are a lot of things to say about it. Talking about the mood of the country is a pretty dangerous thing. My impression from traveling around is that it's a very frightened country. This is true of the most reactionary and the most liberal areas. Everywhere I go, and I go to all kinds of places, everybody's scared. Everybody thinks somebody is doing something to them, and they don't exactly know who. They don't understand why they're badly off. We're good, we're rich, so why are we poor? Somebody's got to be doing something to us. They keep being frightened by foreign enemies. Just as you're frightened by aliens from outer space or Indians attacking covered wagons. There's a sense that somebody's taking something from us that we deserve. Enemies all about.

There's very little in the way of serious political analysis, like analysis of the obvious institutional sources of policy and decisions. That's off the agenda. People are very cynical. They don't believe anything. If I gave a talk somewhere and said that George Bush is from outer space and drinks children's blood or something, people would probably say, why not? Sounds plausible. In this kind of state people are open to anything: religious fundamentalism, conspiracy theory. You can't see what's really happening, because that's off the agenda. Unpleasant things are happening. You don't understand why they're happening. You don't deserve that kind of treatment. So in that circumstance it's extremely easy to say there's some secret team out there who stole our nice country from us.

Index

About the Contributors

David Barsamian is the Director of Alternative Radio, an independent production service, which is broadcast on public radio stations throughout the United States, Canada, Europe, Australia, and on shortwave on Radio for Peace International. He is a regular contributor to *Z*, and other periodicals. His previous book of interviews is *Stenographers to Power: Media and Propaganda*. For a free cassette catalogue of Alternative Radio programs write to 2129 Mapleton, Boulder, CO 80304, U.S.A.

Noam Chomsky is a long-time political activist, writer, and Institute Professor of Linguistics at the Massachusetts Institute of Technology. He is the author of numerous books and articles on U.S. foreign policy, international affairs, and the media. His most recent books include *Deterring Democracy, Year 501: The Conquest Continues, Rethinking Camelot* and *Letters From Lexington: Reflections on Propaganda*.

Alexander Cockburn is a columnist for *The Nation*. He is the author of *Corruptions of Empire* and *The Fate of the Forest* (with Susanna Hecht). His most recent book is *Encounters with the Sphinx: Journeys of a Radical in Changing Times*.

About Common Courage Press

Books for an Informed Democracy

Noam Chomsky notes in *Chronicles of Dissent* that "No institution is independent of what's happening in the greater society. As there is more ferment in the larger society, there will be more ferment in the media and openness will develop that wasn't there before. If it goes to the point of really threatening power, there will be a limit. But you can push those limits pretty hard, and there are people who do it. Independent media, which are not part of the state-corporate nexus, can offer lots of opportunities. Their very existence has an effect on opening the media. If you can't ignore them they become competitive. Also, they offer options, they democratize the country, which is always a good thing."

Founded in 1991, the mission of Common Courage Press is to push those limits by publishing books for social justice on race, gender, feminism, economics, ecology, labor, and U.S. domestic and foreign policy. The Press seeks to provide analysis of problems from a range of perspectives and to aid activists and others in developing strategies for action.

You can reach us at:

Common Courage Press
P.O. Box 702
Monroe, ME 04951
207-525-0900

Send for a free catalog!